Policy Implications of Re[illegible] Advances in Evolutionar[illegible] Institutional Economics

This collection is inspired by the coming retirement of Professor Wolfram Elsner. It presents cutting-edge economic research relevant to economic policies and policy-making, placing a strong focus on innovative perspectives.

In a changing world that has been shaken by economic, social, financial, and ecological crises, it becomes increasingly clear that new approaches to economics are needed for both theoretical and empirical research – for applied economics as well as policy advice. At this point, it seems necessary to develop new methods, to reconsider theoretical foundations, and especially to take into account the theoretical alternatives that have been advocated within the field of economics for many years. This collection seeks to accomplish this by including institutionalist, evolutionary, complexity, and other innovative perspectives. It thereby creates a unique selection of methodological and empirical approaches ranging from game theory to economic dynamics to empirical and historical-theoretical analyses.

The interested reader will find careful reconsiderations of the historical development of institutional and evolutionary theories, enlightening theoretical contributions, interdisciplinary ideas, as well as insightful applications. The collection serves to highlight the common ground and the synergies between the various approaches and thereby to contribute to an emerging coherent framework of alternative theories in economics. This book is of interest to those who study political economy, economic theory, and philosophy, as well as economic policy.

Claudius Gräbner is a Research Associate and PhD candidate at the Institute of Institutional and Innovation Economics at the University of Bremen, Germany

Torsten Heinrich holds a post-doctoral position and teaches at the University of Bremen, Germany

Henning Schwardt received his PhD from the University of Bremen in 2012. He has authored and co-authored books on economic development and microeconomics, as well as peer-reviewed articles in many well-known economic journals.

Routledge Advances in Heterodox Economics

Edited by Peter Kriesler
University of New South Wales

Over the past two decades, the intellectual agendas of heterodox economists have taken a decidedly pluralist turn. Leading thinkers have begun to move beyond the established paradigms of Austrian, feminist, institutional-evolutionary, Marxian, post-Keynesian, radical, social, and Sraffian economics – opening up new lines of analysis, criticism, and dialogue among dissenting schools of thought. This cross-fertilization of ideas is creating a new generation of scholarship in which novel combinations of heterodox ideas are being brought to bear on important contemporary and historical problems.

Routledge Advances in Heterodox Economics aims to promote this new scholarship by publishing innovative books in heterodox economic theory, policy, philosophy, intellectual history, institutional history, and pedagogy. Syntheses or critical engagement of two or more heterodox traditions are especially encouraged.

27 The Problem of Production
A new theory of the firm
Per L. Bylund

28 A New Economic Theory of Public Support for the Arts
Evolution, Veblen and the Predatory Arts
Arnaldo Barone

29 Economic History and Thought
An unresolved relationship
Edited by Monika Poettinger and Gianfranco Tusset

30 Varieties of Economic Inequality
Edited by Sebastiano Fadda and Pasquale Tridico

31 Reclaiming Pluralism in Economics
Edited by Jerry Courvisanos, Jamie Doughney and Alex Millmow

32 Policy Implications of Recent Advances in Evolutionary and Institutional Economics
Essays in Honor of Wolfram Elsner
Edited by Claudius Gräbner, Torsten Heinrich and Henning Schwardt

Policy Implications of Recent Advances in Evolutionary and Institutional Economics

Essays in honor of Wolfram Elsner

Edited by

Claudius Gräbner, Torsten Heinrich and Henning Schwardt

Routledge
Taylor & Francis Group
LONDON AND NEW YORK

First published 2016
by Routledge
2 Park Square, Milton Park, Abingdon, Oxon OX14 4RN

and by Routledge
711 Third Avenue, New York, NY 10017

First issued in paperback 2018

Routledge is an imprint of the Taylor &Francis Group, an informa business

British Library Cataloguing in Publication Data
A catalogue record for this book is available from the British Library

Library of Congress Cataloging in Publication Data
Names: Gräbner, Claudius, editor. | Heinrich, Torsten, editor. |
Schwardt, Henning, editor. | Elsner, Wolfram, honoree.
Title: Policy implications of evolutionary and institutional economics /
edited by Claudius Gräbner, Torsten Heinrich and Henning Schwardt.
Description: Abingdon, Oxon ; New York, NY : Routledge, 2016.
Identifiers: LCCN 2015048237| ISBN 9781138887268 (hardback) |
ISBN 9781315714257 (ebook)
Subjects: LCSH: Institutional economics. | Evolutionary economics. |
Economic policy.
Classification: LCC HB99.5 .P645 2016 | DDC 330.15/52–dc23
LC record available at http://lccn.loc.gov/2015048237

ISBN 13: 978-1-138-61143-6 (pbk)
ISBN 13: 978-1-138-88726-8 (hbk)

Typeset in Times New Roman
by Cenveo Publisher Services

Wolfram Elsner

Contents

Figures

Tables

Notes on contributors

Sebastian Berger is a Senior Lecturer of Economics at the University of the West of England, winner of the 2009 Helen Potter Award (Association for Social Economics), and trustee of the Kapp Foundation.

Ping Chen is a Research Fellow at the China Institute at Fudan University, Shanghai, and Professor at the National School of Development in Peking University, Beijing, China. He received his PhD in physics at the University of Texas at Austin in 1987. His field is economic chaos and economic complexity.

Christian Cordes graduated in economics at Hanover University in 1998. He then joined the Evolutionary Economics Group at the Max Planck Institute of Economics in Jena. He earned his PhD in Economics at the Friedrich Schiller University Jena in 2003. Afterwards, he was a guest researcher at the Centre for Research on Innovation and Competition (CRIC) at the University of Manchester (2004) and a visiting scholar at the University of California (2005–6). After his habilitation, he became a research group leader at the Max Planck Institute of Economics in Jena and a faculty member of the DFG Research Training Group 1411: Economics of Innovative Change. Since 2011, he has been Professor of Economics at the University of Bremen. His fields of research are the biological and psychological foundations of economic behavior, the evolution of business cultures and multinational enterprises, and the determinants of human behavior in an organizational context.

Shuanping Dai is Junior Professor of Economics at the IN-EAST School of Advanced Studies and Mercator School of Management, University of Duisburg-Essen, Germany. His research interests lie in institutional economics, network games, innovation, and the Chinese economy.

Claudius Gräbner is a Research Associate and PhD candidate at the Institute of Institutional and Innovation Economics at the University of Bremen. He holds an undergraduate degree in social sciences, economics and law from the University of Erfurt, Germany. His research interests include computational economics, development economics, game theory, and econometrics. One focus is the evolutionary analysis of social institutions and the methodology of social sciences. His recent research on this topic has been published in the

Journal of Institutional Economics, *Journal of Economic Issues*, and the *Forum for Social Economics*.

F. Gregory Hayden is Professor of Economics at the University of Nebraska-Lincoln, and recipient of the Veblen-Commons Award. In addition to his university position, he has served in numerous government positions and on public boards, councils, and commissions. His research has been devoted mainly to three areas since receiving his PhD in Economics at the University of Texas-Austin. They are: (1) the development and application of the social fabric matrix, (2) the development of a meta-policy-making paradigm; and (3) the application of pragmatic philosophy to policy analysis. The three areas have been integrated in his theory of institutional economics research and his public policy analysis. Consequently, his publications are extensive and diverse.

Torsten Heinrich studied economics at the Dresden University of Technology, Germany, and the Universidad Autónoma de Madrid, Spain, and received his PhD from the University of Bremen in 2011 with a thesis on technological change and growth patterns under conditions of network effects. He works on complexity systems, agent-based modeling, simulation, and strategic games in economics on which he edited special issues in scientific journals and authored both journal articles and monographs. He holds a post-doctoral position and teaches at the University of Bremen.

Jakob Kapeller is an economist who accidentally became a philosopher. He is currently engaged as the head of the Institute for Comprehensive Analysis of the Economy (ICAE) and is also affiliated with the Department of Philosophy and Theory of Science at Johannes Kepler University Linz. Jakob serves as an editor for the *Heterodox Economics Newsletter* (www.heterodoxnews.com). His research interests include the epistemology of the social sciences, the history of political and economic thought, heterodox economics and economic development as well as the distribution of income and wealth.

Kalevi Kyläheiko is Professor of Economics and in particular Strategy Research at Lappeenranta University of Technology (Finland) and Honorary Professor at the University of Bremen (Germany). His research interests cover, among other subjects, economics-based strategy research, economic methodology, evolutionary economics, and the use of real options in the strategic management context. He has published about 80 articles in refereed journals and books.

Pascal Petit, economist and Emeritus CNRS Director of Research attached to the CEPN (Centre d'Economie de Paris Nord), has published books and articles on institutional economics of economic growth and structural changes. Comparative analyses of the national trajectories of modern developed economies stress the diversity of capitalist growth regimes and their crises. His recent publications include *The Hardship of Nations: Exploring the Paths of Modern Capitalism* (Edward Elgar, 2006, as editor with B. Coriat and G. Schmeder), *L'économie mondiale en 2030: ruptures et continuités* (Economica, 2013, editor with J. Mazier and D. Plihon) and *Challenges for Europe in the World, 2030* (Ashgate, 2014, editor with John Eatwell and Terry McKinley).

Andreas Pyka graduated in Economics and Management at the University of Augsburg in 1998 and afterwards spent two years as a post-doc in Grenoble, France participating in a European research project on innovation networks. Following the post-doc he worked as an assistant professor at the chair of Prof. Dr Horst Hanusch at the University of Augsburg. His fields of research are neo-Schumpeterian economics and evolutionary economics with a special emphasis on numerical techniques of analyzing dynamic processes of qualitative change and structural development. From October 2006 to March 2009 he worked at the University of Bremen as Professor in Economic Theory. He also held a visiting professorship at the TU Delft in 2007/2008. Since April 2009 Andreas Pyka has held the chair for innovation economics at the University of Hohenheim, Stuttgart.

Paolo Ramazzotti is Professor of Economic Policy at the University of Macerata. His research interests include the Italian economy, the social costs of capitalism, institutionalist thought, and the theory of economic policy. He coordinates the research area on institutional change of the European Association for Evolutionary Political Economy and is deputy managing editor of the *Forum for Social Economics*. Together with Wolfram Elsner and Pietro Frigato he has edited *Social Costs and Public Action in Modern Capitalism. Essays Inspired by Karl William Kapp's Theory of Social Costs* (2006) and *Social Costs Today: Institutional Analyses of the Present Crises* (2012).

Pier Paolo Saviotti is Visiting Fellow at the Innovation Studies Group of the cross-faculty "Institutions" program at Utrecht University and Research Professor at Kore University, Enna. He has previously taught and conducted research at INRA GAEL (Grenoble), at GREDEG CNRS (Sophia Antipolis), at the University of Manchester, at McGill University, and at the University of Zulia. He was educated at the University of Perugia, at McGill University, and at the University of Manchester. His main interests are the economics of innovation, evolutionary economics, and economic development.

Manuel Scholz-Wäckerle is a Senior Lecturer at the Department of Socioeconomics at the Vienna University of Economics and Business. He obtained his doctorate in the social and economic sciences at the Vienna University of Technology in 2010. His main research fields include evolutionary political economy, institutional and ecological economics, agent-based modeling and computational simulation. Recently Manuel has published a book on *The Foundations of Evolutionary Institutional Economics: Generic Institutionalism* (Routledge).

Henning Schwardt received his PhD from the University of Bremen in 2012. His has authored and co-authored books on economic development (*Institutions, Technology, and Circular and Cumulative Causation in Economics*, Palgrave,

2013) and microeconomics (*Microeconomics of Complex Economies*, Academic Press, 2015, with W. Elsner and T. Heinrich), as well as peer-reviewed articles, among others, in the *Journal of Economic Issues*, the *Journal of Institutional Economics*, the *Forum for Social Economics*, and *Games*.

Georg Schwesinger is a Research Fellow at the Chair of Evolutionary Economics at Bremen University. He studied biology and physics at the universities of Heidelberg and Würzburg, started his academic career at the Max Planck Institute of Economics, Jena, and obtained his PhD in economics at Bremen University in 2014. His main research fields include naturalistic approaches to economic behavior, cultural evolution, theory of the firm, and ecological economics.

James I. Sturgeon is Professor of Economics at the University of Missouri-Kansas City and an Honorary Fellow at Bremen University. He teaches institutional economics and industrial organization. He has served as president of the Association for Evolutionary Economics and the Association for Institutional Thought and was a co-founder of the latter. His research and publishing interest is in institutional economic theory.

Preface

The present volume is a Festschrift in honor of Wolfram Elsner who, as a heterodox economist, has made an impact in recent years like very few others. His path-breaking ideas continue to inspire institutional and evolutionary economists around the world. His tireless efforts as scholar, as author, as editor, as organizer of scientific events and his active involvement in scholarly organizations have helped shape the community of heterodox economists in Europe and worldwide. He worked hard to bring heterodox economists closer together over the previous decades. His contributions in service of various associations, such as AFEE, ASE, and EAEPE, among others, are a testament to his efforts in this area. At the same time, his research has played its part in defining modern heterodox approaches to policies and policy-making in directly applied work as well as in basic research.

Much of this tireless effort is inspired by the belief that a new pluralism is needed in economics; that different heterodox approaches can and should learn from each other; that education and teaching are of eminent importance; and that heterodox economists need to be vocal about alternative policy implications resulting from their work. It is this spirit that guides the present collection. The volume follows Wolfram Elsner's ideas with a pluralist heterodox framework that conjoins institutionalist theory, evolutionary economic approaches, and formal concepts from complexity theory. Depending on the questions at hand, different theoretical backgrounds are drawn on as offering the most suitable tools for addressing them. Thus a broad variety of methodological and empirical approaches is represented ranging from game theory to economic dynamics to empirical and historical-theoretical analyses. What the contributions in this volume show is the possibility of a constructive pluralism within heterodoxy and among different branches of heterodox thought. As illustrated by the work of Wolfram Elsner and his colleagues, at least in the case of institutional, evolutionary, and social economics, we already observe a convergence within heterodoxy which can serve as a true and full-fledged alternative to neoclassical economic theory.

Acknowledgements

This collection would not have been possible without the support of many heterodox economists. We are especially grateful to all the contributors to this volume. We would also like to thank Marco Lehmann-Waffenschmidt, Tara Natarajan, Agnès Labrousse, Robert Boyer and Muhamed Kudic, who contributed as reviewers and helped strengthen the quality of the book tremendously. Pascal Petit, Sebastian Berger, Jim Sturgeon, Georg Schwesinger and Paolo Ramazzotti also doubled as reviewers, commenting on other chapters and facilitating improvements, for which we owe them special thanks.

Introduction to the Festschrift for Wolfram Elsner

Claudius Gräbner, Torsten Heinrich, and Henning Schwardt

Compiling the Festschrift for Wolfram Elsner has been an honor. It allows us to express our great gratitude and respect to an important teacher, colleague, and protagonist of heterodox economics, not just in words, but, true to his approach, in action.

Wolfram has dedicated (at least) the last 40 years of his academic and non-academic life both to the advancement of heterodox theory in economics and to the institutional changes that were suggested by his extensive research. As is true for the great institutionalists before him, for Wolfram the study of economic issues was not an isolated activity for its own sake – it must come along with the commitment for the prudent and inclusive "good society" (Hayden, 2006).

So, to truly understand Wolfram's numerous contributions to heterodox economics, one must understand his unusual career, which took him outside academia for almost ten years and thus partly explains how his work, despite being of mostly theoretical nature in recent years, retained such strong connections with reality and reminds us that "the proof of knowledge is in its application in interactions, its adaptation and enhancement in practice, rather than its consumption and wastage" (Elsner *et al.*, 2015: 529).

Wolfram Elsner's unusual career in and outside economics

Wolfram started his studies of economics as one of the young idealist "68er" activists for peace and justice at the University of Cologne. Here he was introduced to the German Historical School and Social Economics by Prof. Siegfried Katterle, whose assistant he became after completing his diploma in 1974 and who served as an important inspiration for his further work.

His PhD, which he completed after three years at the University of Bielefeld in 1977, was about how the socio-economic conditions in Germany have changed due to Western European integration. He then remained in Bielefeld to pursue his *venia legendi* under Prof. Katterle, on comparative paradigms of economic institutions in the history of economic thought. The resulting book (Elsner 1986) is still an inspiring and accurate interpretation of economics as a multi-paradigmatic and contested science and an excellent epistemological justification for the study of the history of economic thought.

During his time at Bielefeld Wolfram met Prof. Paul Dale Bush who was visiting several heterodox departments in Europe at that time. This meeting had an important impact on Wolfram's further career and motivated him to apply for a research grant that would allow him to travel to the United States and to understand more directly the nature of American institutionalism that has always played a significant role in his research.

But in 1986, Wolfram officially left academia to become the director of the Office of Local Economic Development and Employment Policy in Bielefeld. It was not until 1987 that he received the grant of the DFG (German Research Association) he had applied for before to travel through the United States. He convinced his new employer to release him from his work duties for this journey which took him, *inter alia*, to the University of Nebraska – Lincoln and California State University, and was the beginning of long-standing collaborations and friendships with leading institutionalist scholars such as Paul D. Bush and Gregory Hayden (who also contributes to this Festschrift).

Wolfram was introduced to the Association for Evolutionary Economics (AFEE) and the Association for Social Economics (ASE), associations with which he was going to uphold a close connection during his entire career. After his return and besides his full-time job outside academia he remained engaged in bringing heterodox economists in Europe together, following the examples of AFEE and ASE he experienced in the USA. He became one of the founding members of the European Association of Evolutionary Political Economy (EAEPE), a place where he met long-standing colleagues including Pascal Petit and Hardy Hanapi in 1988.

In 1989, he was appointed director of the Bremen State Economic Research Institute in Bremen and head of the Economic Planning Division of the Ministry for Economic Affairs of the Senate (the state government of Bremen). His job was to foster cooperation among local firms and to foster local development. The time spent working there was going to have an important impact on his research, which was always focused on the emergence of cooperation, the evolution of institutions, and the goal of improving the living conditions of the people in the society under study.

Beside this job, Wolfram started to work as an external lecturer at the University of Bremen. This proved quite a challenge, coming on top of his full-time job in the Senate. Still, he published in renowned journals such as the *Journal of Economic Issues* (*JEI*), for example about the policies required for industrial defense cohesion (e.g. Elsner, 1993), a topic that has been important to him his whole academic and non-academic life.

His tremendous professional efforts were rewarded when he was appointed a full professor of economics six years later, in 1995. While many academics in Germany start reducing their engagements and academic productivity after they have received the security of a full professorship, Wolfram not only retained his engagement for peace and disarmament, but also worked enthusiastically on keeping Bremen as a center for heterodox economics in Germany and in building it up after a large part of the heterodox faculty left or retired in the early 2000s.

As a result of these efforts, today, the Institute of Institutional and Innovation Economics at the University of Bremen is one of the leading heterodox institutes in Germany.

He also maintained his concern for bringing heterodox economists in Europe closer together. He served as a council member for EAEPE for several years, organized the annual EAEPE conference in Bremen in 2005, and became its president in 2012, when he was elected to oversee the association's efforts to renew its relevance as a general heterodox association and to reinvigorate its fierce work for pluralism in economics. True to himself, a particular focus of his efforts is the integration of young and very young scholars into the association, trying to open doors for younger colleagues and students. He also strengthened EAEPE's ties to other associations, in particular the institutionalist associations for which he had been active since his research journey to the US almost 20 years earlier. Wolfram also contributed to the AFEE in a number of functions including member of the board of directors 2008–11.

Besides his critical engagement for EAEPE and AFEE, Wolfram took a large number of voluntary academic positions, including serving as a member of the editorial board of nine heterodox journals, editor of several heterodox book series, and speaker and discussant at a large number of EAEPE, AFEE, and ASE sessions, among others, and in particular as managing editor of the Forum for Social Economics since 2012.

But besides being an economist, Wolfram was also, following the spirit of the classical institutionalist economists, always actively engaged in public debate. He was not an academic in the ivory tower of science, but took a stance in the real world for a better socio-economic system and the "good society": his engagement as the Bremen State Official for Industrial Defense Conversion (1992–2001), his harsh criticism of European austerity policy, and his numerous interviews, public lectures and voluntary positions in various organizations and associations only show a small part of Wolfram's voluntary engagement.

Wolfram Elsner's contributions to heterodox economics

Although Wolfram's research covers a huge range of heterodox economics, he mainly worked in the area of institutional and social economics.

In particular, when working for his *venia legendi*, he focused on the foundational questions of economics as a science and fundamental issues of the philosophy of science. His later contributions were influenced by his time outside academia and have always been concerned with the solution to particular problems of public concern. Because his contributions are too numerous and diverse to discuss individually, we focus on the four main pillars of his research.

Industrial policy and regional development

In the beginning of his research career, Wolfram spent considerable effort on the discussion and development of socio-economic indicators as measures for economic development and applied them to study the structural change in Germany after the 1970s. In his work, he anticipated much of the debate about the shortcomings of the GDP as a welfare indicator today and was already arguing for multi-dimensional indicators instead. In particular, he proposed a *quality of working life* index which he evaluated for Western Germany (Elsner, 1983).

Building upon his well considered work on indicators for social well-being, he also contributed to a better understanding of how regional policy measures can be implemented effectively, e.g. in the context of industrial defense conversion (Elsner, 1993, 1995) or by mitigating the social costs associated with structural change (Elsner, 2001). As said above, he did a lot of further empirical work on the emergence and evolution of industrial clusters, in particular in northern Germany (e.g. Elsner *et al.*, 2005; Elsner, 2010). He was particularly concerned with the emergence of cooperation among different firms forming a cluster (e.g. Elsner *et al.*, 2010). This empirical work paved the way for his work on meso economics and the emergence of cooperation.

Meso economics, the emergence of cooperation and new perspectives for institutionalist modeling

Earlier than many of his fellow institutionalists, Wolfram advanced the thesis that the great institutional ideas could be effectively combined with new formal methods such as game theory and, more recently, methods of complexity science such as agent-based modeling and nonlinear dynamics. One of his first articles, published in 1989 in the *JEI* (Elsner, 1989), applied the logic of prisoner's dilemma games to the ideas of Adam Smith. Such a combination was basically unexplored at this time and was ahead of the discussions about the application of game theory in institutionalism of recent years (e.g. Field, 1994, 2001; Hargreaves-Heap and Varoufakis, 2004; Pelligra, 2011; Villena and Villena, 2004).

The article established a striking correspondence between the conflict of motives developed by Smith in his *Theory of Moral Sentiments* (1759), and the two exclusive strategies of cooperation and defection in the classical prisoner's dilemma. He further expanded this logic and provided an evolutionary and dynamic interpretation of Smith's conception of institutions that is still appealing, paving the way for his research agenda of reconciling the rich and verbal theories of classical economists with modern and formal modeling tools.

Still, Wolfram was no blind adherent to formal modeling who followed methodological trends for their own sake. One particular example in this context is his 2012 *JEI* article in which he reinterpreted P. D. Bush's theory of institutional change in a game theoretic framework. While his approach of an *evolutionary-institutional interpretation of game theory* retains the descriptive richness of insitutionalist pattern modeling, it increases the logical depth of the analysis considerably and allows important gaps to be filled in the original theory of institutional change, such as the origins of ceremonial dominance. This article still serves as an excellent example of how traditional institutionalist theory can productively be reconciled with formal modeling (Gräbner, 2016).

While in the 1990s Wolfram continuously focused on the empirical analysis of how firms and regions can establish cooperation among each other and what role public policy has to play in this context (see in particular Elsner (2001)), he then started to work on this issue on a more theoretical level, building upon his practical experience as a starting point for sound theoretical models. One theoretical topic that was of particular concern to him was the idea of meso economics: he argued convincingly against a simple micro–macro dichotomy in economic theory and proposed an additional meso layer on which clusters of cooperation may emerge and become institutionalized (see in particular Elsner (2007a), Elsner and Heinrich (2009), Elsner and Schwardt (2014)). Later, he embedded these ideas into a broader concept of the economy as a complex adaptive system that requires a particular government structure if satisfying outcomes for all members of society are to be sustained (Elsner, 2015; Elsner *et al.*, 2015).

Complexity and the need for public policy

While the concepts of direct interdependence among individuals and complexity have always played a role in Wolfram's research (see, for example, Elsner (1989)), it was not until 2004 that he explicitly introduced the concept of complexity into his work of industrial policy (Elsner, 2004). In contrast to many other scholars working in the field of complexity economics, Wolfram saw right from the beginning that if we understand the economy as a complex system, then we will also need to reconsider the role of the state. In contrast to the prominent arguments focusing on the alleged inability of governments to foresee the consequences of their interventions and on the superiority of the market as an information distribution device (e.g. von Mises, Hayek …), Wolfram showed that properties of complex systems such as path dependence, direct interdependence, and non-trivial dynamics actually make an adequate system of regulations indispensable (Elsner, 2004; Elsner and Schönig, 2005; Elsner *et al.*, 2015).

The state of economics as a discipline and a heterodox convergence

Since his habilitation thesis on economics as a multi-paradigmatic science, Wolfram spent considerable effort on studying both mainstream and heterodox economics from a meta-theoretical viewpoint. Long before the financial crisis in 2008, he criticized the allegedly value-free economic mainstream and called for reflected and pluralist economic science, that considers itself as a social science, making its value judgments explicit and working towards an improvement of the living conditions of people. His argument that the economic mainstream survives despite its stunning empirical and theoretical deficiencies simply because of its function of providing an ideology legitimizing the ruling classes (e.g. Lee and Elsner, 2008; Elsner, 2010) has recently been taken up by other well-known researchers as well (e.g. Colander and Kupers, 2014).

Working towards a change of economics as a science dominated by such an ideological mainstream, Wolfram studied the severe problems of journal rankings many heterodox economists are confronted with, but also all the other intricate institutional arrangements that help the economic mainstream sustain its dominant position in mass teaching (see below), public advising, and academic funding (Lee and Elsner, 2008, 2010; Elsner 2013). He highlighted that while many of the cutting-edge ideas in the mainstream stem from heterodox economists, at the very same time the institutional arrangements to safeguard its position as an ideological justification for the capitalist system as it is today were becoming more intense.

Against this background, Wolfram has worked towards a strong heterodox community that would be able to overcome such institutional barriers. He did so both by supporting heterodox institutions and networks, as illustrated above, and by providing essential academic contributions. One of his most interesting (and controversial) arguments is that there is something like a *heterodox convergence* (Elsner, 2014), at least among institutionalist and socio-economic schools of thought. All these schools implicitly moved towards a conception of the economy based on the concepts of complexity, the principle of evolutionary explanation (Hodgson, 1998), policy orientation, and true microfoundations. This does not mean that there is no dispute among heterodox economists. On the contrary. Advancement of heterodox theory requires the disputes among scholars of various leanings – only in this way will heterodox economists establish a proactive pluralism that may be able to survive the ideological cleansing of economics (Elsner, 2014).

Textbooks

Wolfram identified the one-sided and unreflected teaching of mainstream economics as one of the main institutional arrangements that sustain the dominance of mainstream economic thought in Western societies. He has continued working to overcome the resultant restrictions in his life as both a teacher and a researcher for quite a long time. Not only did he help build a pluralistic and heterodox curriculum at the University of Bremen, he has also published continuously on the importance of economic education for a very long time (see, for example, Elsner, 2006, 2007b).

Further, he contributed actively to a change in the textbook landscape which is still dominated by mainstream texts that are lagging far behind the cutting-edge of research both in heterodox and mainstream economics (Elsner, 2013). Together with his research associates he worked extensively on two heterodox textbooks on microeconomics (Elsner *et al.* 2012, 2015). In particular the second book, *Microeconomics of Complex Economies*, represents a huge step forward for the heterodox community. It provides an introduction to the microeconomic theory required to understand today's real-world economic issues and includes material for undergraduate, graduate, and PhD students. Young activists now have a comprehensive alternative textbook that they can offer to their economics professors when demanding the overdue change of the economics curriculum to remove the ever-present ideological bias that has been sneaked into mainstream textbooks on the backs of tacit assumptions and unspoken aspirations. They can use it to establish a proactive and viable pluralism of heterodox ideas in the future. It is this kind of effect that represents the biggest reward for Wolfram: the knowledge that his work may help others to pursue their way, towards a strengthened heterodox community and finally in their pursuit for adequate governance structures and a better society. The chapters that follow may be conceived in the same vein, and as contributions by younger and by established colleagues and long-time associates and friends to honor Wolfram's life's work.

Overview over the contributions of this volume

The book is organized into three parts. Starting from the theoretical foundations of evolutionary and institutional economics in Part I, it considers the resulting approaches to policy analysis in Part II before proceeding to applications to specific pressing issues, namely the great financial and organizational crises of our time in Part III.

In light of Wolfram Elsner's vision of an integration of a convergence of institutionalism and complexity approach and its application to policy, Part I examines the deep challenges that today's society and economy face as well as the responses that institutionalist and evolutionary theory are able to provide. Henning Schwardt, Claudius Gräbner, Torsten Heinrich, Christian Cordes, and Georg Schwesinger (Chapter 1) discuss the trade-offs that emerge in policy decisions when analyzed from an evolutionary and institutionalist perspective. They contend that constant changes to the underlying systems lead to vulnerability and economic insecurity. At the same time, questions like public regulation and support of education or health care, the transfer of social or environmental aspects into the social sphere, and public research are persistently subject to conflict. Sebastian Berger (Chapter 2) investigates the role of psychological conceptions in dominant economic theories. He finds that not only may incorrect psychological premises in economic theory lead to biased, if desirable, results, they may also have a profound and certainly undesirable impact on society. Jakob Kapeller and Manuel Scholz-Wäckerle (Chapter 3) shed light on normative questions arising from evolutionary and institutional policy approaches which they integrate into their research program of evolutionary political economy. They highlight especially the issue of evaluating novelty, social change, and development while also addressing the relation of science and political activism. Discussing the economic roles of power, knowledge, and learning as specific examples, they are able to illustrate that any reasonable science of economics is necessarily normative and outline how such a science can benefit from concepts coming from game theory, systemism, and complexity economics.

Part II of the book opens with Gregory Hayden's analysis in Chapter 4 of the social fabric matrix approach in relation to agent-based modeling, complexity economics, and original institutional economics. He holds that original institutional economics is rapidly evolving into a science of complex systems which is in need of tools to help accommodate this, something the social fabric matrix approach can provide. Paolo Ramazzotti (Chapter 5) discusses the challenges and chances of an institutionalist guidance of economic policy. He emphasizes the role of societal priorities, cognitive value judgments, and the need for progressive institutional change. Kalevi Kyläheiko (Chapter 6) uses Mäki's methodological concept of 'Models as Isolations and Surrogate Systems' to evaluate approaches to economics-based strategy research, namely Porter's sustainable competitive advantage perspective and the later resource-based view and dynamic capability view. Jim Sturgeon (Chapter 7) discusses industrial policy from the perspective of the "enduring tension" between individual and societal objectives. He contends that laissez-faire policies have failed to control this tension, thereby engendering a need for a more sustainable, less crisis-prone approach that may come from institutional economics. Andreas Pyka and Pier Paolo Saviotti (Chapter 8) develop a model of economic growth and development that is able to account not just for technological and structural change but also for the emergence of new industries. They explain the importance of this in the context of an evolutionary complex systems perspective for modeling long-run economic development.

The final chapters of the collection in Part III apply evolutionary and institutionalist approaches to the triple crisis in economic (and also financial), social, and ecological systems. Ping Chen (Chapter 9) analyzes the financial crisis of 2008 in the context of the theoretical background of the policies that arguably brought it about. He proceeds to suggest a new theoretic framework from evolutionary and institutional economics which he exemplifies in brief sections on monetary, industrial, and technology policy. Pascal Petit (Chapter 10) discusses the triple crisis from a regulationist perspective. Emphasizing the very real and very recent dangers to democracy that are associated with developments in the lead-up to and aftermath of the financial crisis, he also addresses problems of economic growth and sustainability. Part III concludes with Shuanping Dai (Chapter 11) on national systems of innovation policies. He uses a Markov chain extension to game theory to analyze systems of innovation before extending the analysis into a discussion of policy implications.

As in many discussions of institutional and evolutionary perspectives, traces of Wolfram Elsner's work are ubiquitous in all contributions. The reason may lie in his path-breaking suggestion to bring different heterodox approaches together, so that they may enrich each other. Or it may be found in his vision of a new and comprehensive policy program rooted in evolutionary, institutional, and complexity perspectives that continues to inspire heterodox scholars. And though this volume can make but a small contribution to attaining this end, it proudly does this as a collection in Wolfram Elsner's scientific tradition and as a Festschrift in his honor.

References

Colander, David and Kupers, Roland (2014) *Complexity and the Art of Public Policy: Solving Society's Problems from the Bottom Up*. Princeton, NJ and Oxford: Princeton University Press.

Elsner, Wolfram (1983) "On constructing and implementing an extended goal variable for economic policy. the example of a quality of working life index number for West Germany (1970–1980)," *Social Indicators Research*, 13 (2): 131–70.

Elsner, Wolfram (1986) *Ökonomische Institutionenanalyse – Paradigmatische Entwicklung der ökonomischen Theorie und der Sinn eines Rückgriffs auf die ökonomische Klassik am Beispiel der Institutionenanalyse ('Property Rights')*. Berlin: Duncker & Humblot.

Elsner, Wolfram (1989) "Adam Smith's model of the origins and emergence of institutions: the modern findings of the classical approach," *Journal of Economic Issues*, 23 (1): 189–213.

Elsner, Wolfram (1993) "Industrial defense conversion: guiding the market at the regional level," *Journal of Economic Issues*, 27 (4): 1254–62.

Elsner, Wolfram (1995) "Instruments and institutions of industrial policy at the regional level in Germany: the example of industrial defense conversion," *Journal of Economic Issues*, 29 (2): 503–16.

Elsner, Wolfram (2001) "An interactive economic policy approach to manage structural change: the case of industry conversion in the German state of Bremen," *International Review of Applied Economics*, 15 (4): 411–28.

Elsner, Wolfram (2004) "The 'new' economy: complexity, coordination and a hybrid governance approach," *International Journal of Social Economics*, 31 (11/12): 1029–49.

Elsner, Wolfram (2006) "Heterodoxe Ökonomik und ihre Einbeziehung in eine pluralistische Lehre," Thomas Dürmeier, Tanja v. Egan-Krieger, and Helge Peukert (eds), *Die Scheuklappen der Wirtschaftswissenschaft. Postautistische Ökonomik für eine pluralistische Wirtschaftslehre.* Marburg: Metropolis, pp. 145–60.

Elsner, Wolfram (2007a) "Why meso? On 'aggregation' and 'emergence,' and why and how the meso level is essential in social economics," *Forum for Social Economics*, 36 (1): 1–16.

Elsner, Wolfram (2007b) "Heterodox economics and its integration in pluralist teaching: a German case," in John Groenewegen (ed.), *Teaching Pluralism in Economics*. Cheltenham, UK and Northhampton, MA: Edward Elgar, pp. 189–99.

Elsner, Wolfram (2010) "Regional service clusters and networks. Two approaches to empirical identification and development: the case of logistics in the German port city-states Hamburg and Bremen," *International Review of Applied Economics*, 24 (1): 1–33.

Elsner, Wolfram (2013) "State and future of the 'citadel' and of the heterodoxies in economics: challenges and dangers, convergences and cooperation, in: *Intervention European Journal of Economics and Economic Policies*, 10 (3): 286–98.

Elsner, Wolfram (2014) "Social economics and evolutionary institutionalism today. theoretical components and "heterodox" convergence in a socio-economic perspective," *Forum for Social Economics*. Online at DOI: 10.1080/07360932.2014.964744.

Elsner, Wolfram (2015) *Policy Implications of Economic Complexity and Complexity Economics. Towards a Systemic, Long-Run, Adaptive, and Interactive Policy Conception*, MPRA Working Paper 3252.

Elsner, Wolfram and Heinrich, Torsten (2009) "On the co-evolution of institutions and platform size – with an application to varieties of capitalism and 'medium-sized' countries," *Journal of Socio-Economics*, 38 (5): 843–58.

Elsner, Wolfram and Lee, Fred (2010) "Assessing economic research and the future of heterodox economics. Failures and alternatives of journals, departments, and scholars rankings," *Intervention: European Journal of Economics and Economic Policies*, 7 (1): 31–42.

Elsner, Wolfram and Schönig, Werner (2005) "Economic and corporate governance," *Corporate Ownership and Control*, 3 (1): 71–80.

Elsner, Wolfram and Schwardt, Henning (2014) "Trust and arena size: expectations, institutions, and general trust, and critical population and group sizes," *Journal of Institutional Economics*, 10 (1): 107–34.

Elsner, Wolfram, Heinrich, Torsten, and Schwardt, Henning (2015) *The Microeconomics of Complex Economies. Evolutionary, Institutional, Neoclassical, and Complexity Perspectives*. Amsterdam: Academic Press/Elsevier.

Elsner, Wolfram, Hocker, Gero, and Schwardt, Henning (2010) "Simplistic vs. complex organization: markets, hierarchies, and networks in an organizational triangle – a simple heuristic to analyze real-world organizational forms," *Journal of Economic Issues*, 44 (1): 1–29.

Elsner, Wolfram, Hübscher, Andreas, and Zachcial, Manfred (2005) *Regionale Logistik-Cluster. Statistische Erfassung, Stärken und Schwächen, Handlungspotentiale. An den Beispielen Bremen, Hamburg und Rotterdam*. Frankfurt: Peter Lang Verlag.

Field, Alexander J. (1994) "Game theory and institutions," in Geoffrey M. Hodgson, W. J. Samuels, and Marc R. Tool (eds), *The Elgar Companion to Institutional and Evolutionary Economics*, Vol. 1 Aldershot: Edward Elgar, pp. 271–6.

Field, Alexander J. (2001) *Altruistically Inclined? The Behavioral Sciences, Evolutionary Theory, and the Origins of Reciprocity*. Ann Arbor, MI: University of Michigan Press.

Gräbner, Claudius (2016) "Agent-based computational models – a useful heuristic of institutionalist pattern modeling?," *Journal of Institutional Economics*, 12 (1): 241–61.

Hargreaves-Heap, Shaun and Varoufakis, Yanis (2004) *Game Theory: A Critical Introduction*. London and New York: Routledge.

Hayden, F. Gregory (2006) "Policymaking for a good society," *The Social Fabric Matrix Approach to Policy Analysis and Program Evaluation*. New York: Springer.

Hodgson, Geoffrey M. (1998) "The approach of institutional economics," *Journal of Economic Literature*, 36 (1): 166–92.

Lee, Frederic S. and Elsner, Wolfram (2008) "Publishing, ranking, and the future of heterodox economics," *On the Horizon*, 16 (4): 176–84.

Pelligra, Vittorio (2011) "Intentions, trust and frames: a note on sociality and the theory of games," *Review of Social Economy*, 69 (2): 163–88.

Villena, Mauricio C. and Villena, Marcelo J. (2004) "Evolutionary game theory and Thorstein Veblen's evolutionary economics: is EGT Veblenian?," *Journal of Economic Issues*, 38 (3): 585–610.

Part I

Foundations of institutional and evolutionary policy perspectives

1 Economic complexity and trade-offs in policy decisions

Henning Schwardt, Claudius Gräbner, Torsten Heinrich, Christian Cordes and Georg Schwesinger

Introduction

Policies are measures societies put in place in order to foster the achievement of certain objectives. In order to be able to influence outcomes in a way that is desirable, an understanding of the system to be shaped is required. You need to know what can be done, and you need to know how that may be achieved. Without a conception of the relation of factors in a system, policies cannot be systematically successful. Some have argued that such an understanding would be impossible and have therefore objected to any policy interventions into the economy (e.g. von Mises, Hayek). It was the important contribution of Wolfram Elsner (Elsner, 2005, 2015; Elsner *et al.* 2015) to show that using institutionalist theory and complexity economic methods, a sufficient understanding can in principle be achieved. Even more, such a perspective shows the necessity of an active role for public policy. Evolutionary institutional perspectives on policies are based on an understanding of economic and social systems that may constantly be changing. They are not aiming at the identification of economic laws derived in a static environment; rather, a general understanding of a system's behavior and motion is sought. Based on this understanding, what can be achieved by implementing policies can be delineated more clearly. So can what degree of freedom there is in the system for attempts to redirect its dynamic onto a path that appears more desirable to the group. Trade-offs, not only between different aspects of economic objectives, but also between economic and non-economic outcomes, may become easier to grasp. What a society desires to achieve is a part of the process of determining policy measures (Martins, 2015). Illustrative examples are abundant in every sphere of economics and society. They include property rights legislation with the purpose of temporally cross-financing innovations, public investment in infrastructure, healthcare, research, and education, or disinvestment in such fields, the expansion of the economic sphere into culture or the conservation of nature, and many others. We will return to these examples below.

Policy formulations have to be understood as part of a continuous process, not only as exogenous measures limiting agents' possibilities for action. The system itself is changing, and thereby, possibly, the way it functions can change as well. This may refer to a constant shift, or a dynamic with a certain degree of regularity and repetitiveness, say financial market stability over time, as a function of the risk build-up from individual decisions under different circumstances and expectations. Policies have to be reassessed against this changing background, then, and possibly adapted to fit the changes in the functioning of the system. A static set of rules cannot hope to succeed in achieving objectives in a changing system. A concise value-base is a necessary component of such assessments (see also Ramazzotti in this volume).

The institutional perspective adds connections of the economic sphere to other societal spheres. Against this background, policies have to take into account that they affect the different interests and values in a society. Such effects will involve trade-offs between different objectives in terms of time-horizon, distribution, and the impact on other societal interaction spheres, among others. These trade-offs will be the focus of this chapter. As such, we build on Elsner's various contributions to this topic (Elsner, 2001, 2012).

The overall structure of this chapter is as follows. We will start with a brief rehash of the core pillars of an evolutionary institutional system for economic analyses, and the principal challenges for the formulation of policies in an environment for which this analytical system is adequate. The next section will discuss more specifically the role and position of public agents in such a system. A principal factor for policies to acknowledge and take into account is that it is unlikely for provisions not to have to accept trade-offs between different groups. These will be discussed in the fourth section of this chapter. The final section concludes.

An evolutionary institutional perspective on economic systems

The term evolutionary economics is employed to cover analytical frameworks that integrate notions of change in economic systems into their analytical structure. An evolutionary framework analyzes systems that do not simply move from equilibrium to equilibrium in the wake of "shocks", but systems in which factors can produce dynamics of change endogenously. Dynamics may affect the system itself, and its shape and functioning, just as it may concern systems' components, such as agents. An evolutionary framework allows economic issues to be analyzed without being tied to a static foundation, but rather acknowledging change as an integral aspect of modern economies.

An institutional perspective integrates social rules and norms – institutions – as a critical aspect of an analytical framework. These institutions provide the foundation for interdependent actions, by constraining the space of acceptable individual actions. Such constraints reduce the complexity that agents have to confront in a way that enables them to actually interact.

The original institutionalists built an analytical framework that integrates an evolutionary and institutional perspective. Here, institutions have emerged from individual interactions, and become habituated as "correlated patterns of thought" (Veblen, 2010; Waller, 1982; Bush, 1987; Elsner, 2012). Institutions do not determine behavior, of course, and individuals may always decide to act differently than is proscribed. Still, for coherence and continuity, as the foundation for stability, a sufficient (whatever that may mean in a specific situation) adherence to an institutional framework is required. The habituation that follows from stability shapes individual action as well as individual expectations about others' actions. Instrumental motivations, of human curiosity and sociality, offer the potential of changes to be introduced to such patterns. Still, social control mechanisms help stabilize the institutional sphere in a group. Beyond the individual level, we therefore also find a dimension to them that is detached from any specific individual. Defining this combination of individual and group level and its effects, Commons (1931) describes the institutional sphere as embodying "collective action in control, liberation, and expansion of individual action." Institutions shape the ability of individuals in groups to coordinate and cooperate in their activities (Elsner, 2012). A crucial aspect of institutions is that they both depend upon individual behavior, but at the same time affect individual decision-making. Wolfram Elsner therefore rightfully argues for the use of a meso-level, where institutional emergence takes place. This meso-level is connected to the micro-level both via upward and downward effects. This fact constitutes the need for a systemist perspective on the economy (Wilber and Harrison, 1978; Gräbner, 2016).

The different provisions for adequate behavior within a group are linked by the values motivating individual agents. That means that certain behavior patterns may stay in place, but the motivation behind them may change over time. Values underlie and connect behavior patterns (Bush, 1987). The general direction that a change of values is assumed to have is from group-focused instrumental, where problems at the group level are addressed suitably for the group, to individualistic, or ceremonial, behaviors, where invidious distinction is the main motivator for following certain provisions. Put differently, social problem-solving abilities of diverse groups are shaped by their institutional framework. Such institutional frameworks develop over time, typically in path-dependent dynamics. Differences in institutional frameworks are equivalent to differences in the problem-solving abilities of respective groups. In stable environments, over time, the relative problem-solving ability of groups declines as individualistic motives take over (Ayres, 1996; Elsner 2012).

The social problem-solving abilities in a group also shape the level of technology that is in reach for that group. Technology is a combination of skill and equipment; skill is exercised using equipment, matter becomes material if utilized in acts of skill (Ayres, 1996). The ability to employ potential effectively is related to the rules, norms, and values that guide individual behavior. The ability to extend our technological potential derives from our openness to learning and experimenting. In turn, this openness is again a function of the acceptable behavior in place, and that behavior's direction in activities. Individuals thus are the drivers behind the process, while the system they move in shapes the space for the next steps they may take. As technological change builds on itself – new capacities emerge from the combination of existing abilities – given structures can have long-run ramifications. Changing the path, for instance to accelerate the speed of technological change, will tend to require actively involved measures to supersede the potential limitations of a given situation (Chang, 2008; Schwardt, 2013).

A constantly changing system

This institutional perspective includes the potential for ongoing changes, making it a natural part of evolutionary approaches to economics (Ayres, 1996; Veblen, 1898; Lee, 2011; Elsner, 2012). In parallel to shaping technological potential, motivations of individuals act as drivers of changes in the institutional framework. Inquisitiveness opens the doors to the possibilities for new technology. Learning and social dynamics influence the set of rules and norms in place. An increasing motivation of finding status within a given structure, on the other hand, exerts a push toward ceremonial motivations, especially in a long-running stable environment. Finally, technological potential and institutional provisions influence each other, in dynamics of circular and cumulative causation. Approaches focusing on more detailed aspects of the larger process have shown that there is no reason to suspect any particularly good results in such processes, even before we factor in a possible trend towards a ceremonialization of structures (David, 1985; Arthur, 1989; Foley, 1998). Even if selection processes are at work, there is no guarantee that the best (or even a good) solution is selected spontaneously. A path emerges in the process, not the selection of one solution for the system over others.

Changes thus manifest in different dimensions of social environments. They are the outcome of endogenous developments driven by individual agents responding to the structures they face, while maintaining their capacity for experimentation. Into which direction these energies are turned depends on the values that prevail at a given point in time. Opposed to the belief that some characteristics of the larger system ("economic laws") remain unaltered during those changes, an evolutionary institutional perspective recognizes that the system itself may take on different characteristics over the course of its path. We can distinguish between changes that recur over time, such as in the level of economic activity and risk exposure of individuals in financial markets (Minsky, 2008), or it may refer to fundamental alterations in the system's functioning (for instance, as described in Nell (1998) with reference to the impact of changes in production technology on stabilizing or destabilizing dynamics at the macroeconomic level).

In such a system, there is scope for strategic action by individual agents. They are not totally constrained by the characteristics of their interaction system. Their actions and reactions, anticipations and expectations, introduce a further impetus for the dynamics of change, though some constraints arising from Veblenian instincts, fixed modes of learning, habituation, or inclination to act fair if the environment permits do exist. They can shape their environment to some degree, and shape that of their surroundings as well. This scope for strategic action, for instance allowing the restructuring of others' decision-situations to one's own advantage, introduces possibilities for developments that are not particularly desirable from the perspective of the group as a whole. Power is an aspect of human relations and can be exercised in the framework we have adopted here.

Furthermore, the system itself, we have said, can change with the outcome of cumulative individual actions. There are influences and systemic characteristics that lie outside the scope of individual agents' reach as well as grasp but that changes in response to the sum of individual actions, nevertheless. Individuals can be affected by developments that are neither a consequence of their action nor within the realm of their control. That means agents in the systems we consider here are vulnerable to developments outside their scope of influence. In common understanding, that means that they are not seen as responsible for the effects they may face. Vulnerability refers to a susceptibility to adverse developments in the economic system. It is translated into economic insecurity, describing the impact on the material basis of individuals' living and circumstances. A distinction between the vulnerability of agents that is the result of systemic characteristics, and the insecurity of agents that is shaped by the measures possibly taken to address the effects of their vulnerability, helps designate areas of policy focus more clearly.

Challenges for policy formulation in constantly changing systems

If the principal characteristics of the system under observation are captured by these aspects, then policies cannot be static. There will be no rules that can hope to continue to produce the same outcome over time as the underlying relations between factors and causes and their effects in the system are developing.

As a consequence, policy frameworks have to be formulated to take into account this changing nature of the environment they are dealing with. Objectives will more reasonably be defined in terms of ranges for indicators, and these, in turn, have to be woven into a set of indicators to describe desirable markers to touch along the path of the system development. While a separation of different fields of interest is still necessary to handle any given issue, the openness of the system we are dealing with will require more frequent assessments of spillovers between different arenas (see also Ramazzotti in this volume).

A system that continues in existence has to be somewhat stable. Modern societies – and economies as parts of them – have developed over time. Experience and knowledge have been gained over time, therefore, on the various aspects of these systems, and have accompanied the changes undergone. Policy-making capacities have developed over time, and have required a continuous process of involvement, exchange, and learning in order to be able to accomplish the objectives set for policy-makers. Discarding these capabilities by reducing policy-making to the execution of narrow rules may result in a reduction of the long-run ability to steer the process of technological and economic change in an instrumental fashion.

As already stated in the introduction, the objectives of policies should be clear, and clearly stated. There will be different paths in pursuit of the eventual objectives. Which of these appear more promising overall will then have to be evaluated. Beyond specific objectives, this will involve the overall approach to the economic system. Risks from the economic sphere emerge from social structure and construct. They are man-made insofar as they are the outcome of the interactions of people that have an impact on the economic sphere. The great advance of industrialization was the reduction of risks and adverse effects emerging from nature. How to deal with man-made risks in social relations is a question that has to be answered in order to define the scope of policies and the abstract framework that those policies are set in.

One example of a question that is close linked to the issues concerning the understanding of the system is whether, in the face of vulnerability and insecurity, one tries to influence the system by putting rules in place that reduce its volatility and the resulting economic vulnerability of agents, or does one accept the said volatility and focus on reducing the impact it has, limiting the level of economic insecurity? The question is one of emphasis rather than exclusiveness – that is if one wants to address these issues at all, of course. What your options may be and how different approaches influence the resilience of the overall system, and its capability to function in service of the objectives formulated for its utilization will depend on the nature of the system, and the understanding of that nature that has been reached (Elsner, 2015).

The role of public agents and policies

Looking at the role of public agents in the economic systems of modern societies, we find that the reasons for involvement are defined by the necessity for structures to shelter individual agents from the fall-out of systemic developments, on the one hand, and the necessity to structure and stabilize the possibilities for interactions of these agents, on the other (Hayden, 2006).

Reasons for involvement

The possibilities that damage may done by individual actions (be they consciously done or not), either accepting a severe reduction in other agents' results as a consequence of exercising power affecting these or because of systemic effects that are emerging on a higher level of aggregation, makes considerations of a possible counterweight or corrective reasonable (see also Sturgeon in this volume). So does the possibility of general systemic effects and characteristics of the system itself that remove certain areas from the influence of each individual agent.

The negative impact of developments outside individuals' influence introduces the question whether such impacts may be mitigated. The answer given to this question, and the more detailed approaches adopted for addressing resulting issues, have shaped the role that public agents have been playing, and continue to increasingly have to play, in modern economies.

Involvement in mitigating the effects of individual vulnerability has commonly been viewed as desirable. It tends to coincide with a reduction in insecurity. From the definition of the normal and an average, and deviations from the normal, the path of people's interpretation of their environment has led to a conception of generic risk, and a recognition of occurrences that are not planned by any given individual but still cannot be avoided in large groups (say, accidents at the workplace). From here, a number of societies decided to treat certain aspects of work lives as at least somewhat outside the control and thus responsibility of any single individual, and rather cover them as risks that are faced in certain circumstances. Also introduced have been measures to shelter individuals from systemic effects and their fall-out, such as unemployment. A specific view on how far individuals' responsibilities stretch has shaped the detailed provisions included under more general categories. Devising these protective structures has been the purview of public agents, either setting them up directly or creating the legal space for them. In many instances, a continuation of communal structures aimed at mitigating environmental risks has been a convenient route to pursue.

Systemic effects are one part of the reason for involving public agents, and involving them more and more. The other area to cover is enabling, structuring, and stabilizing the economic sphere itself, as the platform for exchanges between agents. As this economic sphere has grown more complicated and more complex over time, the demands towards public agents have increased in lock-step.

Just as the uncodified social rules and norms fulfill a function in societies by reducing the intricacy of decision situations and thus enabling behavior, so do codified rules and norms. They provide structure for private activities. This not only creates a much reduced space for potential courses of action, and thereby makes decision-situations more accessible, it also makes the formulation of expectations more reliable (Elsner, 2012) and enables individuals to pursue certain actions that would otherwise be impossible, e.g. safely navigate car traffic. As already stated above, an additional factor is the value system out of which these rules and norms have been born. While private parties can find agreements, if there is no framework to work in this will be cumbersome, and as there is no enforcement independent of the parties involved, will fail more often than not (on informal structures, see Greif (1993) for an example).

Setting up a formal framework helps overcome related issues; guaranteeing it is a core part of that structure. By codifying rules and structures, space for interaction is created that would not otherwise exist. How provisions are set up in detail shapes how responsibilities and obligations are distributed among the parties to an exchange. They also shape the degree of negotiating power of the parties involved, thus affecting the distribution of wealth in and sustainability of the system. For issues that are concerned with exchanges and transactions, decisions have to be made about the distribution of responsibilities and risks. There are always different choices that can be made which allow the exchanges and transactions entered into to expand and the economic sphere to thereby grow. As this involves decisions about the rights of some and the obligations of others, and vice versa, there is no neutral point or framework against which these could be readily assessed. In turn, the space for interactions that is thereby created shapes the interactions themselves, the view taken on them, and openings for changes that take up the given situation and lead to the emergence of the dynamics of development rooted in it.

Public agents as part of economic systems

The public sector is a part of societies, not a separate entity within those societies (Polanyi, 2001). Furthermore, public agents are part of the economic sphere and not separated from it. To conceive of public and private in terms of an antagonism leaves important aspects of their respective roles and requirements out of the equation. Where policy matters are concerned, this may result in a serious distortion of analyses and thus suggestions derived from them. This goes beyond the fact that interests of agents in the private sector diverge, possibly widely, with public agents acting as mediators or backers of some interests over others, among other roles. Even those who may perceive more constraints from public sector activity than others will find that their operations rely on actions taken in the public sector to a substantial degree, and may even find that their future activities are enabled more than constrained by the fact that their scope for action is limited at a given point in time. For example, selling goods one has produced requires markets, and markets themselves cannot be conceived without a certain institutional structure and a functional state supplying the legal system required for effective exchange (e.g. Hodgson, 2014).

Of course, the public sector is utilized for setting up the codified rules that establish the structures for exchanges and transactions. Socially sanctioned informal rules then complement and supplement these formal rules. However, beyond simply constraining private agents by a set of rules those formal provisions fulfill a more varied role. A number of the provisions, as extensions of social rules and norms, are necessary to enable private activity, to supplement private activity, or to support the provision of inputs for private activity. Without a functioning public sector, there would not be an extended space for economic activities.

There is also therefore no neutral reference point that could serve as the single measure of undisturbed and undistorted exchanges. There are numerous detailed provisions that can change and leave the general exchange arena intact, albeit with potential alterations to prices, quantities, and quality of goods exchanged. There is no way to determine which is the proper combination of rules and structures (if we allow ourselves to indulge in the thought that such a point might at least theoretically actually exist). As we will discuss in more depth in the following section, decisions about the structure to set up or permit to continue will entail the weighing of costs and benefits and their accrual in different parts of the system and for different members of society.

Furthermore, public agents operate within this set of rules and partake in economic activities. As a basic, and widely agreed upon first notion, this includes the provision of goods and structures which private agents cannot be expected to provide themselves. These are generally areas where the amortization of investments is difficult or impossible for private agents, but that enhance the functioning of the social provisioning process. Some gray areas are included in which it is societal values that are drawn on to decide whether or not goods should be offered by private agents on a for-profit basis. A for-profit provision, in education or healthcare, for instance, may be found to exclude many beneficiaries from those areas of societal activity and, narrowly evaluated, reduce the size of positive external effects tremendously. Other societies may prefer the exclusion of some individuals and the long-run potential costs (in terms of forgone education and reduced health) that a full integration of these areas into the economic sphere may lead to in exchange for the realization of more immediate profit options for some members of society (Schwardt, 2015). We will return to this aspect in more detail below.

Beyond the provision of goods by the public agent, a partnership, for instance in research (Mazzucato, 2013), is a possibility for fruitful engagement of public structures, as is the role of coordinator of private activities, where, again, research and development partnerships, for instance in local clusters, come to mind as an example. Also, of course, non-negligible is the role of the public sector as a major source of demand in an economy. The direction of public sector involvement then shapes current production structures, and thus also the potential paths for their further evolution.

Overall, public agents shape the system, are part of the system, and are accompanying the process of social provisioning and the shape its changes take over time. This involvement requires a planning process, just as in any private company, to integrate short-term goals, medium-term markers for continuous corrections, as well as overarching and long-term objectives in more abstract terms (as presented, for instance, in Sen's "Development as Freedom" perspective (1999)). An integration of all agents involved through suitably framed participatory structures may slow parts of the process down for a while, but can on the other hand be expected to contribute to its acceptability and thus stability over the longer run, especially as a weighing of the different interests involved will have to entail compromises and trade-offs.

Trade-offs between different objectives

A result of the aforementioned characteristics of the modern economic system under investigation and the options open for influencing its unfolding path is that there will be a strong likelihood of trade-offs between different objectives. The main categories for grouping these trade-offs in our subsequent discussion will be temporal and distributional, referring to opportunities in the future bought at the cost of constraining options in the near term, and decisions regarding shorter-term costs and benefits and the groups to bear these. Trade-offs will also have to consider the distribution of impacts between different arenas of society. For a longer-term assessment of measures, an interesting aspect to include in their evaluation will be how far you allow the mode of thinking applied in one societal sphere rule in others. For instance, how far can an economic or business evaluation carry the organization of areas of society that had before been excluded from it, such as education or health in social democratic Europe during the postwar decades, and what longer-run developments might follow that entail a shift in the development path of societies.

Temporal trade-offs

The aspects of planning that involve temporal trade-offs are more or less strongly connected to objectives formulated with a view on the path an economy may take.

Constraints are in place that relate to the sustainability of the path in question, and may, depending on the values observed, include aspects such as the maintenance, or even at least slight but continuous improvement, of standards of living, as a necessary aspect for questions of political and systemic stability (Friedman, 2005). Other aspects include the vulnerability that modern economic systems lead to, and how to lessen the insecurity this results in (in different terms, see Polanyi, 2001). How heavily such constraints weigh in the process will depend on the overall value system in place, i.e. how much individuals are committed to increasing the well-being of future individuals as measured by what they may be willing to give up in terms of short-term gains, or reductions of insecurity, that accrue to them but that are not expected to increase future potential.

Increased living standards are the result of an enhanced problem-solving capacity, embodied in technological progress. The growth that enables material betterment is the result of structural changes in an economy. These changes bring upheaval at the microeconomic and sectoral levels. On the macroeconomic level, they may result in turbulence as a consequence. In the early stages of development processes, this turbulence is not necessarily very pronounced, especially with the possibilities that current understandings of macroeconomic relations permit (Wray, 2012). The changes still involve noticeable demands on the way of living and giving up customary social structures as a part of the process.

Things do get more involved when more complicated structures have had time to evolve. On the macroeconomic level, counter-measures can still be put in place. However, the upheaval that is threatened as part of the processes of change, may become more pronounced, and the transition from obsolete structures to current ones may prove to be more involved. Examples may include issues such as resource utilization and changes, for instance, in energy sources, but may also refer to locked-in structures in general. Dampening such effects is one area where public sector structures play a crucial role. Striking the balance between fostering change and maintaining stability can be an involved process here. The paths open for technological changes are defined by existing standards and overcoming these may be rather difficult.

No (short-term) profit-oriented company can be expected to lay the foundation for changes without support from the public sector in such situations (Mazzucato, 2013). Established standards may have received continuous attention upgrading them, so that a cost advantage in production and habit on the customer side additionally stand in the way. Establishing a new standard as a viable alternative is difficult in such circumstances and will be very costly. The additional advantage that user numbers in network bring will have to be countered as well. At the same time, existing interests tied into current structures cannot be expected to respond too positively to such efforts.

Another area that plays a part for the ability to upgrade technologies is their diffusion. As said, technology is the combination of skill and equipment. New technologies combine existing skill and equipment in new ways, in a learning process suggesting new solutions to existing problems or solutions to new or unsolved problems. Existing capacities therefore influence the potential for technological advances. A spread of knowledge is a prerequisite for a continuous development process, then. However, the spread of knowledge is closely linked to its utilization. In modern economies, an integration of knowledge, skill, and equipment in production processes is a major route for achieving this spread. In fact, the upgrading of technologies in production processes in response to competitive challenges is generally held to be one of the principal positive attributes of the system (Schumpeter, 1997). In an uncertain environment, the increased profit potential that an innovation may lead to is thus one of the main motivators for accepting the risk that accompanies the introduction of novelty in a capitalist environment. Competitors' easy access to novelties would reduce that profit potential. For policies, therefore, a protection of the advantage of an innovation – exclusive user rights – and the societal need for access to new technologies have to be balanced. There is no ready-made formula for handling such situations, and the same issue may be treated differently over the lifecycle of a technology.

Aspects of current distribution

Regarding aspects of distribution, a shorter time horizon is more likely, as of course temporal trade-offs respond to distributional considerations as well. However, thinking of distribution, we focus on aspects of current patterns of allocating revenue and costs of economic activity. Typically, different groups in society are affected differently.

There is no market mechanism in the neoclassical sense that would lead to a certain distribution of capital and labor income, defined by their respective marginal products. Negotiating power, itself a product of both state and non-state rules and institutions, shapes the distribution of income in economies. Besides conditions that reflect employment conditions in a region, rules and norms governing labor market relations, alternative income schemes, and labor conditions in general, among others, may influence income generation and income distribution. The higher the relative negotiating power for one group involved, the higher we can expect their take of overall revenue to be. That relative power depends on current economic circumstances as well as rules and norms governing labor relations. Still, there are some bounds within which shares can be expected to remain. Workers generally have to be able to sustain a living with their earnings.

Owners have been granted rights to using material from the social knowledge fund for private gain. As machinery has gotten more involved over time, granting private rights of use to those who could finance this machinery – even though the knowledge behind it is part of the social knowledge fund – has been a way to integrate better endowed interest groups into modernizing societies and help them maintain their influence. Owners hold, and have held, a position of influence that cannot be neglected. They may also always decide to allocate their funds elsewhere, so that a certain share of revenue will have to be afforded to them for maintaining stability. From some vantage point, introducing a temporal element, it is feared that a reduction of the profit share of income below a certain threshold would have negative consequences for the level of technology development in a group, so that a certain share of revenue has to be permitted to owners as it is assumed that investment was financed from profits.

On the other hand, a larger share of revenue for workers means that purchasing power is more broadly spread. For investment spending, and thereby an opportunity to introduce novelties, for instance, this is a positive aspect, as expectations about potential future revenue should be positively related to developments of purchasing power. Investments are valued by the stream of revenue they are supposed to generate. The physical character of investment goods does not change, but their projected revenue streams do and influence investment behavior as well as the utilization of existing structures. However, for each individual recipient of capital income, a reduced labor share of income may appear advantageous. Influencing the perception of a situation is therefore also an interesting aspect of managing economic – and broader – relations in societies. In any given situation, a zero-sum game is given. However, over the longer run, a more even distribution may permit larger increases in value-added, as a more stable situation, with significant purchasing power broadly accessible, may provide a much more fruitful ground for technological advances and for longer-run healthier profits based on an ongoing investment activity. Trying to influence considerations of proper returns to physical investments, and notions of societal developments instead of individualistic orientations, can then contribute to a more stable and more even development path. Current distribution patterns lay the groundwork for such potential developments. Decisions that concern distributions of revenue directly and measures that may influence what is perceived as an acceptable distribution may thus have a noticeable influence on the potential paths for economies to follow.

In terms of costs of activities, their distribution is likewise subject to rules and norms, where our focus here is on codified rules. How we conceive of costs influences how we view their distribution and what potential problems we may identify. As we will address issues of the effects of economic activity on non-economic societal arenas, our focus here will be rather narrow. Under this rather narrow focus, aspects of policies that focus on the availability of public goods, payments of subsidies and taxation, as well as adverse effects and externalities, make up the bulk of measures. The shape and direction of activity and change under economic constraints will respond to the specific provisions in those measures.

The impact of the economic sphere on other societal arenas

Finally, a major area of concern involves the impact that measures designed to address issues of coordinating activities in the economic sphere may have on other societal interaction spheres. Arenas that come to mind that are closely aligned with and easily affected by economic activities are, for instance, the environment and the cultural sphere, the social sphere, or, more narrowly in terms of sectors, education and health. Aspects of all of these arenas are part of the economic sphere, as well, and part of the impact economic activity has derives from this overlap. Other influences are only indirect but nonetheless noticeable.

Costs in those areas are often not accounted for from a narrow economic perspective. Trade-offs occur in a different manner than in the areas discussed above. Short-term monetary gain can be realized by pulling aspects of life previously left out into the economic sphere. Its expansion is reflected in growth rates. However, these shifts can lead to costs, in economic terms, such as reduced output or quality of output, as well as in non-economic terms such as reductions in the freedom to move and decide, or a failure to generate increased possibilities for an individual to do so. Therefore, a number of factors are difficult to account for and estimate. This does not mean that they do not exist, however. The trade-offs faced have more to do with temptation, then, and a narrow perspective or short-term focus. In general, in the areas referred to, a short-term cost reduction or monetary gain comes at the cost of longer-term negative effects of some kind or another which may be more difficult to pin down as they are not evaluated in terms of monetary units but rather involve value judgments concerning a situation and how we perceive it. A negative influence of the export of myopic economic rationality to other spheres, or at least the potential for such a negative influence, can be discerned. How far such influence can reach depends on rules in place that limit the degree of this influence, in concrete terms or indirectly (see below). Having said this, the general extension of the economic sphere has certainly contributed to increasing individual freedom, as the wider integration of people into formal economic exchanges permits more autonomous decisions about life choices, such as getting or staying married, for instance.

The conversion of nature, the environment, into resources, or land, on a property-based foundation, as well as the use of free inputs, from water and air or as a disposal site, lies at the heart of economic activities. Damage to the environment, even if not accounted for, is noticeable and detrimental to others around. Still, it accompanies the economic process and its extension is generally seen as acceptable as a trade-off for the reduction in vulnerability and insecurity that an embeddedness into a modern economic system can signify. The damage, or rather the activity resulting in damage, can be limited, of course, or banned outright at times. In the face of the reality of needing to earning a living and feeding people, too severe restrictions may, however, be counterproductive. Still, the conversion of nature into a resource can also reduce the quality of life of others, even as some generate profits. Examples include the loss of nature reserves, the loss, on a smaller scale, of recreational areas, or simply the loss of the tranquility and view that some undeveloped stretches of land may have enjoyed before a strip mall was put in its place. Moving areas of life from a "one person one vote" arena to a "one dollar one vote" arena can be expected to facilitate activities that benefit fewer people and harm larger numbers, even if that harm is not readily expressed in monetary units.

A trade-off between a short-term monetary cost reduction or even monetary gain and an effect on the cultural sphere can be identified as well. Receptiveness and appreciation for cultural offers has to be learned, and many things are acquired tastes. Providing opportunities for doing so requires efforts that signify a short-term economic cost. On the side of the artists, a long learning process to master the means necessary for an expressiveness that is technically sophisticated and artistically deep precedes the ability to contribute to a meaningful cultural sphere. As economic necessities for individuals and institutes do not cease to exist over that time period, some support can enhance the availability of cultural expressiveness. If we believe that such expressiveness and variability within it can contribute to a fuller life then evaluations of cultural matters under an economic mindset appears likely to reduce such potential in a society.

In the education sector, also eventually opened up to broader access with increased economic freedom and its shift to a public sector responsibility, a shift towards a more economically minded approach can be expected to result in noticeable changes in the dynamics of the sector. The same is true for the health sector (Schwardt, 2015). A first effect is that a shift in the cost of education to individuals will exclude some from the benefits it can bestow and thus reduce societal potential. Individual payments also increase the necessity to acquire marketable skills, over genuine and general education, or at least may easily foster that perception. The approach to educational structures can therefore be expected to change in line with such shifted perception and expectation. At the same time, financing education from tuition more than as a public structure increases the possibility of demands concerning the curriculum being formulated by the, by now, customer. As the pressure to earn an adequate income increases, this may be expected to enhance demands that marketable skills be taught. On the other hand, a shift in education structures towards easily perceivable market-oriented content on the side of education institutes will increase the chances of raising sufficient income through tuition. An enhanced service offer, outside the scope of education itself, towards networks and job placement may be another factor to enhance the attractiveness of an education provider. Reshaping an education sector along those lines means that aspects that defined the sector in the past will be lost. Where these aspects have contributed to people growing into the capacity to lead fuller lives, this may be seen as a loss. Insofar as different perspectives on problems and different ways to go about solving them can help offer more stable solutions, the restriction of abilities that is the result of narrower structures may result in a reduction of economic potential and technological dynamics as well over time.

As far as people's health is concerned, similar points apply. Restricting access to healthcare based on an ability to pay, even if that ability may only be reduced temporarily, may well have negative impacts on a person's future life. Accepting an economic perspective, this may well reduce future earnings capacity below its otherwise potential.

None of these points relies on an ethical or moral component for their argument. The constraints that bring a reduction in the collective provisioning of capacities to increase freedom in these areas of life can easily go counter to the objective of increased individual autonomy.

Conclusion

An evolutionary institutional perspective on economic systems is built on the notion of continuous change along various dimensions. The institutional framework of rules, norms, and values is an integral part of this system. Institutions enable interactions and individual activities by constraining the overall space that is accessible for agents. Formal rules – the purview of policy – define a part of the system, in a way that often intends to change calculations of costs and benefits related to specific activities. What unit is chosen for expressing these costs and benefits depends on the evaluation criteria selected for specific areas of interest. For instance, for economic policies, a unit of measure that may be fruitfully employed is monetary. What kind of approach policies take for supporting specific behaviors and dynamics can in and of itself already influence behaviors and their changes.

Processes of change are assumed to be open-ended. There is no corrective within the system that would guarantee any particular advantageousness to them from a perspective focusing on current problems, nor a perspective focusing on the emergence of future improved problem-solving capacities. The openness of processes and their outcome require active management so that decent results in the near term and stepping stones in the intermediate term for reaching more abstract goals in the long run have to be set, supported, coordinated, and continuously updated.

As societies are not homogeneous, this policy process has to integrate different interests. Public agents are part of the overall system and process, but they also serve as intermediaries and instances of the control of private power and ambition. The process of policy formulation is therefore not easy, but has to straddle the divide between these different aspects of changing societies, including different interests as well as different values.

In any case, different interests can at times be opposing interests, way beyond just distinct focuses in different areas of life. Balancing these different interests, different perspectives, and different values in a manner that enables the continuation of an instrumental development path is the task policy-makers face, and by the nature of the problem structures faced trade-offs between different interests become necessary.

As this brief chapter has shown, these trade-offs may be rather more involved. A part of the difficulties presented by them is that the policies embodying trade-offs set the system onto a specific range of paths, and thereby have a noticeable influence on near- as well as long-term conditions. Trade-offs are unavoidable and decisions on trade-offs influence the future path of a system. Issues involved here include the direction that a value system may be taking, the interpretation of adequate and acceptable behavior in social situations, and the consequences that result from decisions about the organization of communities of people and the articulation of interests and granting of concessions in those communities.

Formulaic and static policy rules cannot hope to successfully meet the challenge that is presented to policy-makers under these conditions. Policies have to be formulated, evaluated, and reformulated in a continuous process to match the changes in economic and general social matters. An awareness that decisions concerning the trade-offs between different aspects of the process and interests in the process do not only have an impact on the immediate future, but contribute to shaping the development path of a system makes the decision-making process more difficult, to be sure. An awareness of these issues can also contribute to making it better, though. This awareness has to be grounded in an instrumental set of values, and embedded in participatory structures that permit a voice to all who are concerned.

References

Arthur, W. Brian (1989) "Competing technologies, increasing returns, and lock-in by historical events," *Economic Journal*, 99: 116–31.

Ayres, Clarence E. (1996) *The Theory of Economic Progress*. UMKC Internet edition at http://cas.umkc.edu/econ/Institutional/Readings/Ayres/tep/TEP.html.

Bush, Paul D. (1987) "Theory of institutional change," *Journal of Economic Issues*, 21 (3): 1075–116.

Chang, Ha-Joon (2008) *Bad Samaritans: The Myth of Free Trade and Secret History of Capitalism*. New York: Bloomsbury Press.

Commons, John (1931) "Institutional economics," *American Economic Review*, 21: 648–57.

David, Paul A. (1985) "Clio and the economics of QWERTY," *American Economic Review*, 75 (2): 332–7.

Elsner, Wolfram (2001) "Interactive economic policy: toward a cooperative policy approach for a negotiated economy," *Journal of Economic Issues*, 35 (1): 61–83.

Elsner, Wolfram (2005) "Real-world economics today: the new complexity, co-ordination, and policy," *Review of Social Economy*, 63 (1): 19–53.

Elsner, Wolfram (2012) "The theory of institutional change revisited. the institutional dichotomy, its dynamic, and its policy implications in a more formal analysis," *Journal of Economic Issues*, 46 (1): 1–44.

Elsner, Wolfram (2015) *Policy Implications of Economic Complexity and Complexity Economics: Towards a Systemic, Long-Run, Adaptive, and Interactive Policy Conception*, MPRA Working Paper No. 63272.

Elsner, Wolfram *et al.* (2015) [To follow]

Foley, Duncan K. (1998) "Introduction," in D. K. Foley and P. S. Albin (eds), *Barriers and Bounds to Rationality: Essays on Economic Complexity and Dynamics in Interactive Systems*. Princeton, NJ: Princeton University Press, pp. 3–72.

Friedman, Benjamin M. (2005) *The Moral Consequences of Economic Growth*. New York: Alfred A. Knopf.

Gräbner, Claudius (2016) "Agent-based computational models – a useful heuristic of institutionalist pattern modeling?," *Journal of Institutional Economics*, 12 (1): 241–61.

Greif, Avner (1993) "Contract enforceability and economic institutions in early trade: the Maghribi traders' coalition," *American Economic Review*, 83 (3): 525–48.

Hayden, F. Gregory (2006) *Policymaking for a Good Society. The Social Fabric Matrix Approach to Policy Analysis and Program Evaluation*. New York: Springer.

Hodgson, Geoffrey M. (2014) *Conceptualizing Capitalism*. Chicago: Chicago University Press.

Lee, Frederic S. (2011) "Modeling the economy as a whole: an integrative approach," *American Journal of Economics and Sociology*, 70 (5): 1282–314.

Martins, Nuno O. (2015) "Advancing heterodox economics in the tradition of the surplus approach," in Tae-Hee Jo and Zdravka Todorova (eds), *Advancing the Frontiers of*

Heterodox Economics – Essays in Honor of Frederic S. Lee. London and New York: Routledge, pp. 213–29.

Mazzucato, Mariana (2013) *The Entrepreneurial State*. London and New York: Anthem Press.

Minsky, Hyman P. (2008) *Stabilizing an Unstable Economy*. New York: McGraw-Hill.

Nell, Edward (1998) *The General Theory of Transformational Growth – Keynes After Sraffa*. Cambridge: Cambridge University Press.

Polanyi, Karl (2001) *The Great Transformation: The Political and Economic Origins of Our Time*. Boston: Beacon Press.

Schumpeter, Joseph A. (1997) *Theorie der wirtschaftlichen Entwicklung, Eine Untersuchung über Unternehmergewinn, Kapital, Kredit, Zins und den Konjunkturzyklus*. München und Leipzig: Verlag von Dunckel & Humblot.

Schwardt, Henning (2013) *Institutions, Technology, and Circular and Cumulative Causation in Economics*. Basingstoke: Palgrave Macmillan.

Schwardt, Henning (2015) "Technological-institutional foundations of the social economy: a framework for the analysis of change in the social provisioning process," in Tae-Hee Jo and Zdravka Todorova (eds), *Advancing the Frontiers of Heterodox Economics – Essays in Honor of Frederic S. Lee*. London and New York: Routledge, pp. 296–312.

Sen, Amartya (1999) *Development as Freedom*. Oxford: Oxford University Press.

Veblen, Thorstein (1898) "Why is economics not an evolutionary science?," *Quarterly Journal of Economics*, 12: 373–97.

Veblen, Thorstein (2010) *The Theory of the Leisure Class*. Bremen: Europäischer Hochschulverlag.

Waller Jr, William (1982) "The evolution of the Veblenian dichotomy: Veblen, Hamilton, Ayres, and Foster," *Journal of Economic Issues*, 16 (3): 757–71.

Wilber, Charles K. and Harrison, Robert S. (1978) "The methodological basis of institutional economics: pattern model, storytelling, and holism," *Journal of Economic Issues*, 12 (1): 61–89.

Wray, L. Randall (2012) *Modern Monetary Theory – A Primer on Macroeconomics of Sovereign Monetary Systems*. Basingstoke and New York: Palgrave Macmillan.

2 Social costs and the psychology of neoclassical economists

Sebastian Berger

Introduction

Institutional economists since Veblen have explored the circular cumulative causation[1] between material and institutional factors, including the modes of thought of neoclassical economists that lead to socio-ecological damages (Veblen, 1919, 1925; Georgescu-Roegen, 1979; Kapp, 2011). The goal of the present article is to trace the less tangible losses that occur within the psychology of neoclassical economists that give rise to more tangible losses (damages/costs) as these economists shape the world according to their habits of thought. This is an initial step towards a more elaborate psychograph of neoclassical economists, that is persons who feel attracted by, believe in, defend, and promulgate neoclassical habits of thought as the one and only "capital T truth" in economic matters. Neoclassical economics is here understood as an umbrella term for modes of thought that are mechanical and arithmomorphic, and are associated with the image of the economy as a cyborg (Mirowski, 2002). In the first part, the article honors Wolfram Elsner's contribution to the philosophy of economics, that is his treatise on "incommensurable losses" in the development of economic paradigms that serves as a rationale for recourses and reconstructions of older ideas. A brief recourse to Kapp's economics shows that an inquiry into the lacunae of modes of thought raises psychological questions. Consequently, the second part explores psychological questions that have been posed but thus far left largely unanswered by philosophical, historical, and cultural investigations of neoclassical economics. While the inquiry assesses characteristics of neoclassical modes of thought, it cannot be emphasized enough that it is not intended to be a character assassination of the neoclassical economist. This article is not about demonstrating revulsion, revealing a dirty secret, or a wholesale vilification of neoclassical economics – after all, even Veblen had something positive to say, albeit on a very basic level, about Marshall's neoclassical cause-effect analysis (Veblen, 1919). Rather, the aim is to raise awareness of psychological factors that dovetail with cultural, historical, and philosophical factors to form the mindset of neoclassical economics. The author recognizes the contextual and interested character of this investigation that results from nearly a decade of working as an academic economist.

Elsner's philosophy of economics, or: recovering what's "lost in calculation"

The notion and meaning of "losses" in the development of economic science is the subject matter of Wolfram Elsner's magnum opus *Economic Institutions Analysis* (1986). According to its main thesis, "losses" exist due to discontinuities in the development of economic paradigms, which contradicts the linear "progress" narrative told typically by neoclassical economists and their textbooks. The treatise demonstrates the unexhausted "evolutionary potential" of institutional economics, summoning the support of Joseph Schumpeter's dictum of the "inspirative function" of the history of economics that can influence contemporary developments in economics. The context of his contribution is the "post-empiricist" debate in the philosophy of science (for a summary of this debate see Bernstein (1983)) as Elsner applies one of the main insights of this debate, namely that hermeneutic recourses to and reconstructions of past economic ideas are a way to improve today's understanding. Elsner argues that in economics, however, these recourses occur primarily due to the competitive attitudes of rival economic paradigms. He refers to the notion of "incommensurable losses" that are not objective but relative to each of the competing and incommensurable paradigms. That is, an idea constitutes a loss only when a given paradigm views it as a loss that can provide a competitive advantage. This analysis implies that the underlying purpose of paradigms is to attain a position of power, and that the recovery of losses is thus purely power-driven, lacking a hermeneutic attitude that involves a genuine interest in understanding "the other." This leaves open the question as to what happens to a paradigm's losses that its proponents do not recognize either because they are unwilling or because they lack the capacity for it? In trying to answer this question, this article explores the losses of neoclassical modes of thought to which its adherents turn a blind eye.

Elsner's insights have been applied by the present author to reconstruct Kapp's open system approach (Berger and Elsner, 2009) and heterodox theory of social costs (Berger, 2015a). One of the insights is that Kapp conceptualizes social costs as losses that arise due to the market calculus that has a built-in tendency to shift, externalize, or socialize as much of the costs of production as possible. Losses accrue in the form of damages to third parties, society at large, or future generations. Why does this happen? According to Kapp, social costs are a problem of a purely *formal* rationality that has lost touch with the *substantive* nature of the material conditions (socio-economic and ecological) under consideration, thus lacking substantive rationality. This means that the problem of social costs is here associated with knowledge that is lost in formal market calculations. Consequently, social costs can be understood as a problem of distinguishing and grounding knowledge or rationality (Kapp 1961, 1985). Social costs are thus reciprocally related to losses in the realm of modes of thought. Kapp conceptualizes these less tangible losses as a kind of systemic closure exercised by market calculation. This closure means "knowledge destruction" with regard to aspects of life that do not possess monetary exchange value per se and cannot be adequately brought under the purview of the market calculus. This means that markets lose sight of states of balance of the natural and social environment, which are a prerequisite for the fulfillment of human needs. That is, markets ignore the open system character of the economy (for a similar conception of the limitations of markets see Luhman's systems theory in Valentinov (2013)). The formal rationality of markets is, according to Kapp, mirrored in the habits of thought of neoclassical economists, which causes them to lose sight of the humanitarian notion upheld since antiquity that the human being is the measure of all things. Thus the formalism of neoclassical economics is viewed as contributing to the disintegration and dehumanization of social reality (Berger, 2015b).

Earlier calls for a psychology of neoclassical economists

But what stands in the way of recovering the losses of neoclassical habits of thought? Indeed, Kapp raises the question why neoclassical economists refuse to understand the open system character of the economy and why they remain in an "intellectual freeze" (Kapp, 1976). Already his major and most influential work *The Social Costs of Private Enterprise* (1950) criticizes neoclassical economics by quoting Alfred N. Whitehead's philosophy of science:

> Systems, scientific and philosophic, come and go. Each method of limited understanding is at length exhausted. In its prime each system is a triumphant success; in its decay it is an obstructive nuisance. [...] No science can be more secure than the unconscious metaphysics which tacitly it presupposes [...] Without adventure civilization is in full decay.
>
> (Ibid.: xxxi)

And Kapp agrees with Whitehead that

> '[t]he transitions to new fruitfulness of understanding are achieved by recurrence to the utmost depth of intuition for the refreshment of imagination' [...] [and that] 'if science is not to degenerate into a medley of *ad hoc* hypotheses, it must become philosophical and must enter upon a thorough criticism of its own foundations' applies with equal force to economics.
>
> (Ibid.: 243–4)

Moreover, he refers to Thomas Kuhn and John Dewey in his belief that the new paradigm needed to effectively deal with the environmental crisis required "destructive innovations" that would be "forthcoming if at all only from the outside of the discipline – from men and ideas who possess a wider range of reference and possible range of application" (Kapp, 2015: 290). Yet, a full explanation for the "intellectual freeze" required, according to Kapp, an investigation of the social-psychological determinants of neoclassical economics:

> [T]he majority of people seem to require a justification of the social and economic systems in which they participate, quite apart from the fact that the

> beneficiaries of such systems have a self-regarding interests in such normative rationalizations [...] we do maintain that a demand exists for biased explanations, which in turn account at least partially for the survival and popularity of particular modes of thought. [...] [the] prevailing orthodoxy [i.e. neoclassical economics] [...] tends to defend itself against its critics by introducing new assumptions, simplifications, and refinements whenever one of its conclusions is challenged. The relative lack of "success" of [institutionalism is due to] its challenge to the alleged superiority and rationality of the system of business enterprise, as compared with previous and alternative forms of economic organization. Certainly the "failure" of institutionalism has not been due to the superior relevance and generality of conventional theory – although again it must be admitted that the latter's precision and superficial plausibility, though spurious in actuality, have given it an advantage. This is particularly true among a fraternity of social scientists who share the popular quest for certainty and determinate solutions, and who have equated quantitative conclusions and mathematical symbols with science, even if those symbols and conclusions have no definable counterpart in reality.
>
> (Kapp, 2011: 18)

This quote echoes the insights of notable economists and philosophers: John Maynard Keynes (1936: 32–3) (on factors lending "intellectual prestige," "virtue," "beauty," "authority"), John Dewey (1960) ("quest for certainty"), Nicholas Georgescu-Roegen (1979) ("arithmomania"), Thorstein Veblen (1925) ("business-friendly ideas"), and the Duhem-Quin thesis ("auxiliary hypotheses preclude falsification") (Mirowski, 2014). Furthermore, Kapp's handwritten comments reveal his central conviction that "no culture can be adequately analyzed if one leaves its idols intact – its sacred cows" (Kapp, 2011: 276 n1). The reference to "sacred cows" means that Kapp perceived the calling into question of neoclassical modes of thought as a calling into question of society's core religious precepts, which relates to the psychology of myths and religion. The task of the remainder of the article is to continue Kapp's forays by exploring the psychology of neoclassical economists in more detail. Thereby, this article showcases the fruitfulness of the "Elsnerian recourse" to Kapp's economics that has stimulated this new inquiry.

Open psychological questions

The more recent discourse in the philosophy of economics leaves several questions unanswered that all point towards the need for a psychological inquiry into the habits of thought of neoclassical economists. Consider, for example, how Deidre McCloskey's proposal for "storytelling" in economics is sustained by the hope that such a turn helps to foster a community of sophisticated readers willing to try other ways of reading, to persuade economists that they are not so different from poets and novelists, and to raise self-consciousness, which has the advantage for culture at large of contributing to the peace of toleration, and bringing economists back into the conversation of mankind (McCloskey and Donald, 2014: 73). McCloskey argues that if "economists [...] [learn] an adult's way of being a scientist [by opening up once again to the metaphorical nature of reality], [they] could reunify the cultures of science and literature" (ibid.: 122). She also calls for an economics that admits that we cannot know the truth, but affirm that we can come to agree on some truth. All past groundings of transcendental truths since Plato are deemed fake. McCloskey urges adults to be able to recognize that their standards are not God's own, not transcendent and not a-historical, while affirming that standards are still worth discussing. Yet, this becoming an "adult" is not a purely rational affair, as McCloskey herself argues when she identifies fear as the main cause behind the adoption and persistence of the religion of modernism by neoclassical economists, and she notes the discrepancies between its coercive and dogmatic practice and its self-image of truth-seeking (a kind of double truth) (McCloskey, 2001).

At this point of the narrative psychological questions seem to step into the foreground: why does somebody shy away from becoming an adult, what is she afraid of, and why does somebody operate based on double truths? It is not difficult to derive further questions of such a psychological nature from the contemporary discourse in the philosophy of economics:

- What is the (psychological) function of assumptions? (Mäki, 1994)
- What desires and wishes are projected into the discipline and why does it remove itself from the realm of the human individual, eliminating its idiosyncrasies? (Mirowski, 1994)
- How is it possible to emphasize the virtues of competition while insisting on the monopoly of neoclassical economics? (Hands, 1994)
- What gets shunted by neoclassical economists, that is what is "the other" that gets denied an opportunity to speak as the voice of unreason? What are the internal (psychological) elements that give a theory discursive force and create agreement among its self-selected followers? What makes for the self-congratulatory attitude of neoclassical economists and its attempt to insulate its practice from the scrutiny of its rules, their discursive formation, their implicit epistemological norms, and their situatedness in society and culture? (Cullenberg *et al.*, 2001)
- Why is there such a low standard of self-criticism in neoclassical economics? What elements of fantasy, desire, affect are invested in the system of neoclassical knowledge? How does the human subject experience this expert system of knowledge? How is the discipline-specific habitus inculcated via a largely unconscious process of identification with hero ideals? (Steinmetz, 2005)
- What makes for the willingness of neoclassical economists merely "to compete within a given set of rules and institutional structures" without questioning them? (Colander, in Mearman 2012: 417)

The present article follows Steinmetz's proposal (2005) to investigate such questions as a case of the "unconscious of science" on the grounds of Sigmund Freud's notion of "epistemophilia" (desire for knowledge), Pierre Bourdieu's "unconscious scientific habitus," Alfred N. Whitehead's epochal "unconscious assumptions" and Slavoj Žižek's "hero ideals." The unconscious is here understood as knowledge that is not accessible to conscious awareness but can pattern conscious thought and practice. This psychology of a social group is also supported by organizational research that evidences the existence of aspirational Selfs based on inculcated hero images (Thornborrow and Brown, 2009). The main claim is that fundamental intellectual alignments are generated and reproduced to some extent without the conscious agreement of participants (Steinmetz, 2005). Moreover, Mearman's work on the self-identity of economists finds psychological treatments valuable because they allow "factors typically excluded, such as emotion, or values to be reintroduced as factors affecting the way the economist approaches questions. Fundamentally, psychological approaches capture attitude, which could shape and be shaped by their decision whether to join a group [...]" (Mearman, 2012: 417). Psychology has been assigned a prominent place also by Mirowski who assesses the "psychological equipment" that allows neoclassical economists to remain in error and not change their theory with a "steely self-confidence" (Mirowski, 2013).

Lost in fear: rationalization, repression, compensation, isolation, and projection

The first systematic psychology of neoclassical economists was developed by Walter Weisskopf (1949). As chairman of the economics department at Roosevelt College he had thanked Kapp for his "extremely interesting article on 'Economics and the Behavioral Sciences'" and stated "there is hardly anything in your paper with which I do not agree wholeheartedly" (Weisskopf to Kapp, 2 June 1954, unpublished manuscript). The article referred to emphasizes the need for an integrated approach to social knowledge based on cultural and philosophic anthropology as well as social-psychology. Exploring the reasons why neoclassical economists reject the changes proposed by Kapp, Weisskopf looked towards Sigmund Freud's theory and identified the fear of social exclusion as the root problem. This fear causes the psyche to isolate and repress thoughts and ideas that go against powerful real-world social institutions and interests. That is, the neoclassical concept of "perfect rationality" plays a key role in repressing the possibility of "irrational" behavior. Reducing fear by repressing troubling thoughts is here interpreted as a defense mechanism of the ego in order to obtain a well ordered picture of economic reality. The neoclassical method of formal abstraction is viewed as a result of the psychic function of isolation, which favors elegance just as much as harmony, and abstracts from conflicting aspects of reality. Furthermore, the conflict between the ego and superego is resolved by projections. The (formal and perfect) demand of rationality of the superego is simply accepted as universal truth and projected onto reality where it assumes a moral-ethical system. The goals of society are viewed as natural and identical with the goals of the individual. The perfectly rational and informed economic agent

Homo Oeconomicus is projected into a world of fundamental uncertainty and irrationality. Weisskopf also sees the psychic function of compensation as working hand in hand with repression. Impulses are being repressed and the lack of need satisfaction is compensated by wishful intellectual constructs. Therefore, neoclassical economics is deemed primarily a defense mechanism used by the ego to deny facts and substitute pleasant illusions and wish dreams for an unbearable reality. Weisskopf concludes that all the above mentioned psychological functions are operational in the neoclassical complex of ideas consisting of harmony, equilibrium, perfect information, and perfect rationality. All this happens on the unconscious level and Weisskopf cautions his readers to view this process with humility and awe rather than conceit. For him, it is no coincidence that the complex of ideas parallels Western ideals (for this section compare Weisskopf (1949)).

The subsequent magnum opus *The Psychology of Economics* (Weisskopf, 1955) goes beyond the author's earlier purely Freudian interpretation of neoclassical economics by drawing on Max Weber's work and the post-Freudian social-psychology of Erich Fromm. The spirit of capitalism is viewed as a "value complex" of largely unconscious habits of thought. The latter emerged with Protestantism and were slowly secularized and pushed into the unconscious. In this context neoclassical economics fulfills a significant social-psychological function as the bastion of rationalism in modernity. Weisskopf argues that rationalizing and repressing non-rational and unconscious impulses is necessary to endure life in an industrial society. Neoclassical economists are therefore likened to "high priests" who induce students to believe that there are irrefutable economic laws that prove that humans are rational:

> You are as industrial society wants you to be. You are a completely rational, conscious being, whose main purpose in life is [...] to maximize utility by equalizing expenditures at the margin. The mode of life which industrial society imposes on you is what you really want.
>
> (Weisskopf, 1955: 248)

According to this perspective, neoclassical economics appears as "valium," which is prescribed to calm down the human being who is torn between the ideal of rationality and her other potentialities. Importantly, Weisskopf points out the paradoxical situation that this calming function seems not to be affected by the admission of neoclassical economists that the Homo Oeconomicus model is only a hypothetical construct that has been empirically disproven and that there are several developments even within neoclassical economics that contradict it (Weisskopf, 1955). The psychology of this paradox as a kind of conceptual schizophrenia will be discussed below.

Algorithm as myth and knowledge culture, or: losing experiential authority, the "feminine," and community

Weisskopf's psychology of neoclassical economists as priests with an unconscious Protestant value complex is positioned in the context of capitalism and Western industrial society. This emphasizes the importance of cultural myths and religion that influence the psychology of neoclassical economists. In the cultural perspective neoclassical economics is a "cultural artifact" that contributes to constructing the world in its own image, which is confirmed by surveys showing that the study of economics leads to less cooperative, less other-regarding behavior by celebrating the self-interested calculating (rational) individual (see Marglin (2008) for this entire section). Marglin points to the emotional exhilaration felt by students of economics when they hear that, according to the "invisible hand" theory, acting on self-interest is morally justified and even a social virtue. Neoclassical economics is viewed as encapsulating the myth of modernity because it appeals to the consciousness of a people by embodying its cultural ideals and by giving expression to deep commonly felt emotions. That is, it is a "fiction" that forms part of the ideology of society. Marglin argues that a myth should not per se be seen as a disease but should rather be rendered conscious, differentiated and integrated:

> The first precondition of transcending the limits of our myths [...] is to recognize them for what they are [...] the foundational assumptions of [neoclassical] economics are cultural myths rather than universal truths [...].
> (Ibid.: 38–9)

The neoclassical approach to knowledge is, according to Marglin, at the core of the myth and has the following psychological characteristics. First and foremost knowledge is abstracted from its context and ontologically reduced to algorithms. Referring to Oliver Sacks's clinical histories, Marglin notes that an exclusive focus on algorithmic knowledge is associated with "tragic distortions of human beings" (ibid.: 129). Consequently, self-development as the process of becoming oneself is excluded because it is incommensurable with the algorithmic knowledge that Homo Oeconomicus and his given preferences demand. This mode of thought is deemed incapable of thinking about the human relationships that form a community because it focuses on depersonalized knowledge. The latter economizes on the higher human faculties, such as affection, community, reciprocity, personal obligation, and love. Holism as the "feminine" map to navigate social interactions goes "underground" because algorithmic knowledge and its exaggerated quest for certainty denies what is learned from intuition and authority, from "touch and feel," that is experiential knowledge.

According to Marglin, experiential knowledge is transmitted from master to student, from parents to children valuing the reinterpretation rather than the defeat of the authority of the fathers. The rejection and acceptance of certain types of knowledge as disorderly has been entangled with conceptions of social order since ancient Greek times. According to Marglin, the rise of insecurity and social disorder is due to "the erosion of the authority of the father." Personal authority is central to experiential knowledge and the attraction of algorithmic knowledge is the challenge it poses to non-algorithmic authority. Algorithmic knowledge has the effect of strengthening precocious individualism and has been adopted as a Western ideal largely unconsciously since Descartes. Algorithmic knowledge imitates the form of a mathematical theorem to remedy the emerging disunity and uncertainty of modernity. Yet, the exclusive focus on algorithmic knowledge is, according to Marglin, to blame for the failure of neoclassical economics to provide workable explanations of economic phenomena. Thus, economists face the task of explaining the economy "with one hand tied behind the collective back" (ibid.: 147) and experiential knowledge and community do not receive the nurturing and attention they require. Personal authority and convention are rooted in community, such that experiential knowledge is rooted in community. Marglin concludes that our economic knowledge and understanding are distorted by the myth of neoclassical economics, i.e. an ideology that subordinates experiential knowledge to algorithmic knowledge.

In sum, knowledge losses are located in the realm of experiential and intuitive knowledge, the higher human faculties (affection, community, reciprocity, personal obligation, and love), and knowledge of "vices and weaknesses of markets" (ibid.: 67). This incompatibility between neoclassical economics as a knowledge culture and the rest of culture is a common theme in cultural economics (Marglin, 2009; Jackson, 2009; Davis, 2010; Throsby, 2001; Klamer, 1996; Hartman, 1977; Boulding, 2013). The remedy prescribed by Marglin is to raise the level of consciousness regarding the living neoclassical myth as the main task of a psychology of knowledge. One way to pursue this task is to explore the archetypal dynamics of knowledge cultures. This means categorizing the latter based on how they relate to the archetypal experiences. Evidencing the emotional matrix regarding experiential authority, nature, the feminine, and novelty, Marglin's account provides valuable leads for an archetypal psychology of neoclassical economics as knowledge culture.

Archetypes and complex formation, or: the lost shadows

The project of understanding economics through archetypes has been embarked upon by Integral Economics (Gerber and Steppacher, 2014, 2012; Arnsperger, 2010; Lietaer, 2005). The goal is to integrate the psychology and "inner life" of economists into economic analysis. Archetypes are, according to the psychologist Carl Gustav Jung, the primary source of psychic energy and the psychic symbols that bind and structure this energy (Stein, 2010). Archetypes are the symbolic representations of biological instincts and belong to the spiritual rather than the biological realm. An understanding of archetypical dynamics can yield important insights into religion (including cultural myths, such as neoclassical economics) and prevent destructive consequences for human beings whose consciousness is under the control of an archetype.

> [An archetype] mobilizes philosophical and religious convictions in the very people who deemed themselves miles above any such fits of weakness. Often it drives with unexampled passion and remorseless logic towards its goal and draws the subject under its spell from which despite the most desperate resistance he is unable, and finally no longer even willing, to break free,

> because the experience brings with it a depth and fullness of meaning that was unthinkable before.
>
> (Jung, in Stein, 2010: 99–100)

Pictures, symbols and ideas can through archetypes give human beings the feeling of a sense of life and the importance of their actions, thereby generating motivations and values. When in the grip of an archetype human conscience can be virtually possessed by an idea. Jung therefore describes archetypes as *spiritus rector* of the intellect, which is then being used to justify and rationalize the archetypical idea. In this case it is not the intellect but the archetype that provides the motivation for the justification of the idea. Archetypes give form and meaning to instincts and help human beings to achieve spiritual aims. They manifest themselves in ideas and dreams and it is the duty of human beings to deal with this material ethically (Stein, 2010).

In his account of the 2008 financial crisis, Peukert outlines how a Jungian archetypical psychology of neoclassical economics' ideas can become a research program for the analysis of the emotional meaning and the long-term spiritual transcendence of its "political-financial-scientific complex" (Peukert, 2013; Berger, 2011). According to this view, the latter fails to integrate the archetypes of the ruler, the warrior, and the magician. This failure shows in the actualization of a complex taking the form of the tyrant, the sadist, and the hyper-rational. For example, on a linguistic level neoclassical economics is associated with terminology, such as "rigorous," "hard," "parsimonious," and "discipline" that has been deemed sadistic (McCloskey, 2001), considering that the synonyms for "rigorous" are "austere, strict, stringent, inflexible, severe, stern, harsh, hard, rigid, heavy-handed, ramrod, tough" (Merriam-Webster Dictionary, 2015). The human beings subjected to the power of this complex exhibit the largely unconscious behavior (shadows) of the weakling and the masochist, and arbitrary behavior. This shadow is then projected onto others, such as heterodox economists, to avoid cognitive dissonance. Archetypal psychology views the failure to effectively deal with cognitive dissonance as the root cause of the development of the ego's shadow complex (Stein, 2010: 106). As evidenced by Marglin's and Weisskopf's accounts above, neoclassical economists exhibit the seemingly contradictory combination of normality ("you are rational and well-behaved the way the economics profession and society want you to be") and exceptionalism (the algorithmic hero fighting experiential authority, the feminine, etc.). Drewermann detected this contradiction in his psychograph of catholic priests and interpreted it as a turbulence that emerges when the Self is experienced as a void. The feeling of worth is derived from the "specialness" of the hero while the right to existence is derived from one's "normality" (Drewermann, 1989).

According to Peukert, the archetypes of the Great Mother and the lover are being completely suppressed by the neoclassical complex, so that its shadows become widely spread, namely addiction (work, drugs, sex) and insatiability, as, for example, the main behavioral assumption of Homo Oeconomicus confirms. The Great Mother is a dominant theme in the Jungian literature (see, for example,

Neumann, 1989; Hauke, 2000; Walker, 2002; Hillman, 2005). It views the suppression of this archetype as creating a collective shadow that is rooted in the prohibition against the maternal body and repressed femininity, both of which lead to an impaired ability to promote life. The reasons are seen to be a feeling of inferiority vis-à-vis the creative feminine and the separation from the mother, similar to Freud's Oedipal incest prohibition (Hauke, 2000). Hillman argues that notable Western hero archetypes, such as Faust, are responsible for this development. It is primarily the problematic relationship with their mothers that leads them into the disintegration of good and evil, and antagonism towards their fathers, that is the disintegrated *senex-puer* archetype (Hillmann, 2005). In this interpretation the Faustian bargain with the devil represents archetypally the disintegrated shadow complex (Binswanger, 2011; Stein, 2010: 108–10). The latter contributes to the killing of Philemon and Baucis, representing the elimination of a way of life in harmony with nature, which Faust's industrial and paper money-driven economy cannot replace (Binswanger, 1994). Peukert argues that heterodox economics with its sensitive-hermeneutic method and open system approach is the needed reintegration of the suppressed archetypes of the lover and the Great Mother (Peukert, 2013). This conforms with archetypal psychology, which views Sophia (wisdom) as feminine maternal wisdom that is not abstract disintegrated knowledge, but wisdom of loving participation (Walker, 2002).

"Max U.": a phallocentric hero without soul and full natural body

Archetypal analysis assigns a key role to hero archetypes (Hillman, 2005). Similarly, Otto Rank's work *Beyond Psychology* (Rank, 1941) develops a psychology of unconsciously introjected hero imagos that drive theory formation via a soul that is conceived of as a "creative double" (Rank 1962). Rank refers to Marx's proletariat as a hero imago while Klamer's "Max U." aka Homo Oeconomicus can be considered as the hero imago of neoclassical economists (Klamer, 2001). Amariglio and Ruccio (2001) point out the importance of Homo Oeconomicus which is the last bastion of defense that neoclassical economists resort to when they are pushed to defend the integrity and unity of their work. Neoclassical economists take on the attributes of this hero imago, which Klamer simply describes as their "favorite character" or a "metaphor." That is, the problem-solving and soulless Max U. empties the economic subject (including economists themselves) of any and every form or moral character. According to Klamer, Max U. is a silent character, not preoccupied with his ends, which are given to him. He knows everything and only assesses the constraints and benefits of the best alternative. In other words, he is reducible to a constrained maximization problem. Life is turned away from natural forms and becomes more abstract as Max U. operates in an abstract system of stylized forms. In fact, Max U. is without qualities that would make a subject human. He has no history, is devoid of moral sentiment, knows no tradition, is oblivious of the uncertainties and insecurities that plague everybody who has to make a real choice. Max U. is an absent subject in a formal structure that has meanings only because of its formal properties and he cannot tell humans how to get through life or how to live. He is a dead subject because he is left without real choices and without meaningful subjectivity.

Klamer is convinced that the resilience of Max U. rests on the conviction of the community of its creators who find meaning in the exercises that Max U. makes possible. Part of this meaning is derived from the fact that Max U. allows the meta-narrative of enlightenment to be sustained and gives its manipulators a sense of control. Furthermore, it enables the application of analytical skills, that is to set up problems, work out the algorithm, and find a solution (Klamer, 2001: 93). According to Klamer, Max U. turns economists into a new breed of technocrats who are intrigued by the intricacies of a fully articulated system in the same manner as a computer analyst is intrigued by the possibilities of a new computer (compare also Mirowski (2002) on neoclassical economics as a cyborg science). Led by their hero imago neoclassical economists desire to speak in purely technical language which requires only precision and mathematical operations (ibid.: 98). Indeed, it is possible to view Max U. as the younger brother of Robinson Crusoe, who has been the hero archetype of liberal political economy since its beginning. Already Karl Marx had critiqued the "Robbinsonites" for misconstruing Defoe's protagonist as a-historic and a-social (Whyte, 2014). It seems that Klamer's prediction is correct that the impressive mathematical apparatus of neoclassical economics will be rendered meaningless the day that the hero archetype of Max U. no longer captures the neoclassical psyche and imagination. However, Klamer does not address the possibility that Max U. might be outlived by his older and more resilient brother Robinson Crusoe. Klamer's remedy is a return to a prudent hero archetype, which he traces back to the work of Adam Smith. The prudent hero is frank and open, capable of friendship, humble modesty, and equitable justice, while being correct and exquisitely beautiful in its outline.

Feminist economists have argued for some time that there is a kind of phallocentrism at work in the predominantly male neoclassical economics profession (Nelson, 2001). In fact, Homo Oeconomicus is disembodied and possesses no sexed identity (Hewitson, 2001: 228). Neoclassical economists redefine the womb as capital, such that the mother as a sexed body disappears in a one-sex model. This is a phallocentric construction, in which fetus and mother are awarded male subject positions as self-possessive individuals who enter womb contracts. The uterus as rental space mitigates the threat of integrating mothers and the specificity of the female body into economic knowledge culture. This allows the idea of purely male procreation and eliminates the mother, which has been the myth of many phallocentric cultures of the past. This myth disavows the problem of sexual difference and maintains the myth of Homo Oeconomicus as a "universal individual." This permits the extension of neoclassical discourse into the realm of nature (Hewitson, 2001). It has further been noticed (Amariglio and Ruccio 2001: 147) that it is the absence of a full natural body that makes bodily reproduction and the laboring body disappear from economic inquiry. In this view, neoclassical economics is based on a flat body without depth. Everything that is done resides on the surface, in the form of corporeal images that are functions of bodily orders, such as consumption and investment. In this sense there are multiple Selfs that are fragmented into different orders, yielding a dispersed and fragmented map of the body.

Cognitive dissonance, cognitive capture, and double truth, or: losing history, wisdom, and the care for the self

As we have seen above, it is the inability to deal with cognitive dissonance that causes the disintegration and suppression of archetypes, the rationalization of contradictory behavior, the ingestion of cultural myths via hero images, and the formation of unconscious shadow complexes that accumulate the "lost" psychic content. Mirowski applies cognitive dissonance theory to understand neoclassical economists as a community of religious believers in Homo Oeconomicus (Mirowski, 2010, 2013). Cognitive dissonance theory was developed in the context of research into the behavior of a sect called "The Seekers." When faced with proof that their predictions failed to come to pass, Seekers maintained their belief by formulating ad hoc supporting hypotheses that are not individually falsifiable. The main reaction of economists to the challenge of their post-2008 critics was to defend the Homo Oeconomicus model while at the same time proposing behavioral economics as an improvement. The problem is that behavioral economics explicitly does not aim at changing the Homo Oeconomicus model, thus declaring the incommensurable A and non-A to be true at the same time, a kind of "conceptual schizophrenia." This approach provides the superficial feeling of change without a true change of model or mind. It avoids dealing with cognitive dissonance, maintaining Homo Oeconomicus as a kind of icon at all costs and against all odds. Another problem is that behavioral economics boils down to the sadism of blaming the losers for their own plight (Mirowski, 2013: 18).

According to Mirowski the model of Homo Oeconomicus is also at the core of the neoclassical theory of scientific knowledge, which treats knowledge as a commodity for the sake of market governance (Mirowski, 2011). This makes for a "treacherous quicksand" of reflexivity full of "double truths" that lead to "near Freudian slips" (Mirowski, 2011: 43–4). The double truth is that an economist assumes "God-like abilities" in that

> she arrogates to herself a constitutional capacity that she denies to her little agent offspring: the ability to survey the rules and institutions of the model, to critically engage in self-reflexivity [...] [Economists] pretend to glare down on the world from Mount Olympus [...].
>
> (Mirowski 2011: 335)

Yet, neoclassical economics derived its own scientific model selectively from nineteenth-century energetics (Mirowski, 2011, 1989) while ignoring other models of science. Thus the neoclassical self-image of a superior and independent system of knowledge clearly constitutes a double truth. The double truth seems to rear its ugly head also in the fact that its physics envy did not make neoclassical economics more scientific as is evidenced by the fact that it does not practice falsification and does not have the courage to revise its knowledge like physicists. Avoiding cognitive dissonance and adopting double truths work in tandem with cognitive capture via private sector liaisons with the "bankster-regulator-industry complex," which itself practices a ritual of denial, secrecy and non-democracy (Mirowski, 2013).

Homo Oeconomicus is at the root of this self-image that loses sight of the less glorious truth concerning the historical development of its own model. As a consequence of double truth, the teaching of neoclassical economics is a kind of "brainwashing" and attack by the "walking dead" (Zombie ideas) who hold culture in thrall (Mirowski, 2013: 18). An archetypal interpretation based on ancient Greek mythology provides the image of students who are unaware that their fate is the same as that of Metis (wisdom) who was devoured by Zeus (Mirowski, 2013: 28). Due to their alignment with neoliberal epistemology neoclassical economists have lost sight of the fact that science serves higher purposes than money, that knowledge is about care for the Self, that it is possible to speak truth to power, and that false consciousness is real in the sense that people can be and are being manipulated against their best interest (Mirowski, 2013: 76). The moral quest to discover one's own and only "true Self" is, according to Mirowski, not part of the fragmented Homo Oeconomicus. The latter lives in the double truth of having such a plastic Self that it is never an obstacle to transforming itself into whatever the market wants while at the same time professing the belief that the market gives them what they want. The fragmented personality and vanishing Self has difficulty saying who is at the helm of the agency in a culture that is obsessed with reconfiguration and dismemberment of the soul. Mirowski identifies the gambler as the new hero image in neoclassical economics contributing to a Self image of the daredevil. Mirowski argues that neoclassical economics primarily functions as a facade (in particular its principle texts project a face of the discipline to the world) for the vacuum at the core of a fragmented economic science, which is made up of a "pointless succession of fashions" (Mirowski, 2013: 25). His remedy is to expose double truths and to muster the courage to expose oneself to cognitive dissonance, which is a kind of (Nietzschean) strong methodology (Mirowski, 1994).

Psychology of neoclassical economists as priests

All of the above authors highlight the psychological issues involved in neoclassical economics understood as myth or religion. Hans-Christoph Binswanger interprets in greater detail this aspect of neoclassical economists as a religious community, emphasizing the role of the "psychological weight" of the belief in Homo Oeconomicus and Smith's invisible hand. Binswanger traces these concepts back to the habits of thought of the Stoa, which had quasi-religious status and was the main ideological rival of Christianity for hundreds of years during the Roman Empire. The key idea is that the Good arrives unintentionally by the pursuit of vices. According to Binswanger, it is this quasi-religious character of neoclassical economics' habits of thought that allowed it to become a substitute for the

Christian religion of the feudal era (Binswanger, 2011). In this context it is noteworthy that Giorgio Agamben's archeology of "oikonomia" – while recognizing Smith's own account of its Stoic sources – traces the concept of the invisible hand to its biblical origin and the "mystery of the economy" in Christian theology (Agamben, 2011: 283).

McCloskey (2001) identifies another religion with which neoclassical economists made a pact, that is the "religion of modernism" that represses traditions such as rhetoric and hermeneutics, inspired by the fear of ambiguity, polysemy, obscurity, mythopoeic allusion, and primitivism. The modernist elements of neoclassical economics are responsible for the self-image of a triumphant avant-guard that has defeated tradition, shook off history, transcended time and space, believes in the future more than in the past or present, destroys the past, arrives at the abstract, divorces form from content, believes that form will do the job as if by machinery, and that ornament, culture, and history are mere error terms. Modernism aspires to transcendent and ineffable truth and believes in the tyranny of the lonely genius who seeks a system to impose upon us all. Modernism seeks "crushing proof," "compelling demonstration," that which cannot be doubted, by putting nature to the rack. It seeks conviction which serves to defeat others. Modernism is elitist, exclusive, regulated by lordly experts rather than common sense, distrustful of sense perception with a preference for technicality. Obscurity keeps it in the hands of trained elites. At the same time, the above characteristics of modernist neoclassical economics are, according to McCloskey, just another version of Platonism that seeks to get to the bedrock of certainty. Plato's separation of belief (mere things heard, common opinion) from transcendent truth is here viewed as responsible for the coercive religion of modernism, the worship of experts, and the coercion to obey the guardians and experts. Transcendent truth diverts effort from the search for terrestrial truth. As modernists, neoclassical economists have problems seeing that their view is a view, as well as knowing other truly contending views, and evaluating the differences to generate wisdom (for this paragraph see McCloskey, 2001).

Considering that several of the above accounts liken neoclassical economists to priests or believers it seems fitting to refer to the relevant insights of Eugen Drewermann's psychograph of catholic priests (1989). The latter is deemed a "phenomenology of extreme ontological uncertainty" as catholic priests do not live from within the person but predominantly from the predetermined organizational structure of the institution. Drewermann asks the question how somebody can get to the point to not want to live from within one's true Self but according to some generally prescribed ideal, "willing to play the game" of somebody else? How does the wish emerge to delegate one's existence fully into an officially mandated character mask instead of becoming oneself? How is it possible that the internalized forms of coercion and external guidance are declared the essential truths of one's own life? The answer, according to Drewermann, is that the confirmation by others eliminates the experience of a permanent feeling of doubt towards one's own being. Office and power are absolutely needed in order to be able to live and institutionalized power justifies their existence. The fear of social exclusion leads to the identification with the expectation of others which promises great rewards. The over-fulfillment of group norms out of fear of rejection becomes a way of conspicuous behavior to intimidate others. This resembles a kind of flight into generalities that represses entire regions of the psyche, the abyss of which creates anxiety and disgust with oneself. Generalities are declared as personal such that the personal becomes general, which results in a kind of non-existence of one's identity, that is a dishonesty or lie. Those who have lost touch with their true Self take control of the Self of others in order to hide their own loss of Self. The corset of borrowed importance saves them from falling apart. Personal risks of inner faces and dreams are avoided and instead official confirmation is sought as the truth of the Self, its guarantor for the entire value of the Self. This reflects a flight from being a person. If society produces people who sense insecurity in the deep roots of their existence, then the corset of an office is the last remaining support. The path to becoming a fully accepted member of the group becomes meaningful because it avoids the pain and the fear of the Self, and the fear of others. Everything that seemed small, unimpressive, repressed and shy in one's undeveloped person now proves to be a higher calling, an expectation of love, recognition, respect, esteem. All ridicule, fears, longings, and never acknowledged expectations now receive a goal in becoming a darling of the group. Those who reject them are now the hoi polloi, disbelievers, and enemies of the cognoscenti. But, a belief as a means to repress fear begins to produce fear itself due to ontological uncertainty, such that regimentation, supervision, and control become necessary. The destructiveness of religious institutions furthers the depersonalization of its recruits who try to obtain official status to escape the dilemma of personal non-existence. This results in a governance of a suppressed and fragmented Self (for this entire section compare Drewermann, 1989).

Persecuting blasphemers and losing openness

The religious character of economics is indeed viewed as the leading cause of the suppression of all the dissenting schools of thought in economics in the twentieth century. Lee (2009) draws an analogy between the elimination of heterodox economists and the death penalty imposed on blasphemers. This view is supported by anecdotal evidence from young heterodox economists on the tenure track. If they want to question neoclassical truths in the classroom by assigning appropriate teaching materials they are told that getting tenure means they need to "lay low" for five years and that only thereafter can they perhaps start to speak their mind. They are also admonished that what they want to teach "is not of concern to the students." They are instructed that now it is their "turn to suffer" and "to do as they are being told" because their senior colleagues also had to suffer through teaching this material. Perversely, those who insist most religiously on the teaching of neoclassical economics do not want to teach this material themselves, so that courses in the principles of neoclassical microeconomics get shoved around like rotten eggs to the person with the least power. Lists of approved neoclassical economics textbooks are circulated and heterodox economics texts censored in obscure "approval" processes without any kind of coherent, substantive, or convincing rationale. To their dismay young heterodox economists are told that the content of their favored heterodox economics textbook "is not economics." They are even temporarily prohibited from teaching by their academic dean until their syllabus mirrors exactly the tables of content of leading neoclassical economics textbooks. Purely neoclassical entry and exit tests are instituted to assess student "progress," but in reality serve to control content and to make sure that students get thoroughly brainwashed.

Dow specifies Lee's "blasphemy thesis" in the sense that she views heterodox thoughts as those that are being suppressed by neoclassical economists. Dow describes various communication strategies but views the potential for genuine dialogue pessimistically due to the extreme intolerance exercises by neoclassical economists. Her conclusion is that the development of heterodox economics will take place outside of economics departments (Dow, 2011). She also considers it alarming how unaware and unreflective neoclassical economists are (Dow, 1997). Some authors view the religious war of neoclassical economists against their "other" as simply pragmatic in the sense that mainstream views are those represented at the leading universities and journals that receive most funding and are willing to "play the game" (Colander, 2009). Yet, Lee and Dow identify differences in ontology, methodology, and theory. They share Lawson's thesis that the ontology of the open system, which is non-dualist (order and chaos, fuzzy mathematics) is also the core of pluralist heterodox economics as opposed to the closed system view of neoclassical economics (Dow, 2011: 71). This resonates with Peukert's view that suggests that heterodox economics' sensitive hermeneutic method is the essence of the open system approach, which is the archetype of the lover that helps to integrate disintegrated archetypes. In this sense, an open system approach that still awaits full actualization in economics is the suppressed "other" of neoclassical economics. This suppression may be the reason for Mearman's psychological findings that heterodox economists adopt a contrarian and controversialist position (forced to by neoclassical economists?), while considering themselves to be more open and tolerant than the mainstream (Mearman, 2012: 418).

Conclusion

The preceding investigation demonstrates the fruitfulness of a psychological understanding of neoclassical modes of thought. A number of psychological phenomena were identified, such as double truths, inability to deal with cognitive dissonance, cognitive capture, fear of social exclusion, rationalization, projection, repression, introjection of hero imagos, disintegrated archetypes, complexes and shadows, fragmentation of Self and bodily functions. The diagnosis is that neoclassical habits of thought are induced by the fear of ontological uncertainty and social exclusion from the economics profession, as well as the subjugation to cognitive capture and the inability to deal with cognitive dissonance. What is "lost" from these habits of thought is externalized or socialized and shows up in the form of social damages emanating from the economic system designed by neoclassical economists.

The lost content is also repressed and creates a shadow complex that is personified by heterodox economists. This latter group exhibits more "openness" towards experiential knowledge and a greater range of ways of interpreting and communicating this knowledge. This is why heterodox economists claim to be integrating the archetypes of the Great Mother and the lover, which are suppressed by neoclassical economics' modes of thought. These characteristics turn heterodox economists into a "hook" for a mix of psychological projections that result in scapegoating, bullying, and visceral persecution: (1) an object of fear due to the feared content in the unconscious shadow complex; (2) a cause of cognitive dissonance and ontological uncertainty that is avoided at all costs; (3) a threat to cultural norms and powerful institutions that are considered sacrosanct; and (4) the evocation of emotions related to experiences of father and mother figures that are too painful to face. Due to the entangled relationship between heterodox and neoclassical economists this inquiry also points out the need for a more detailed psychology of the modes of thought of heterodox economics that should address among others its "contrarian attitude" (introjected hero archetypes: Spartacus, proletariat?), potentially disintegrated or suppressed archetypes (lover, Great Mother, *senex-puer*), the limits to openness and its relation with closure, its integration of experiential and algorithmic knowledge, its failure at creative imagination that has locked it into the losing shadow position, and what Amariglio and Ruccio (2001) have identified as its narrative of the "expulsion from the Garden Eden." One of the benefits of psychological treatments is that here, as Mearman rightly observes, it can highlight contradictions (why are some self-classified heterodox economists less open than even neoclassical economists?) and avoids static or dualist categorizations (Mearman, 2012).

Thus the inquiry demonstrates the fruitfulness of a hermeneutic approach to understanding modes of thought, that is archetypal psychology. Its roots in neoplatonism allow archetypal psychology to adopt the therapeutic methods of fictionalizing, mythologizing, and pathologizing experienced images (Moore 1989; Hillmann, 1994, 2005). This brand of archetypal psychology is also referred to as "post-Jungian" so that it is not surprising to find parallels with "postmodern" Jungian psychotherapy (see Hauke, 2000, for the following goals of therapy). The psychological inquiry is therapeutic because it deflates the artificially inflated neoclassical habits of thought. The latter are understood as part of a complex that needs to be better integrated with other parts of the psyche. Exploring and understanding the neoclassical complex is like caring for a wound that is at the same time the eye, that is the precondition for understanding anything at all about life and to affirm it in its infliction. This is an opportunity for consciousness to celebrate itself and to free especially young economists from being absorbed into the "mass-economist" of unconscious collective projections. As such it is also a revolt against a false religion and the dictatorship of faith that is not backed experientially. Raising consciousness through therapy retrieves lost elements of humanity through lost and abandoned experiential knowledge. Because ideas are corporeal, staying safely in a fixed established position would be equivalent to psychosomatic emphysema and thus undesirable (for the material basis of mind see also Hermann-Pillath, 2013).

Archetypal psychology views the mind as having a poetic basis and therefore finds itself in agreement with the hermeneutics of Charles S. Peirce, that is the philosophical foundations of institutional economics (Mirowski, 2014). It also provides a basis for a "poetic economics" that is truly therapeutic (Berger, 2015b). The goal of such a therapeutic poetic economics is "soul making" via reinstating experiential knowledge, openness towards "the other," the fostering of creativity, aesthetics, and ethics, the care for the Self, and the nurturing of human wisdom. The goal is not relativism or nihilism. It shares some of the aspirations of "story-telling" in economics, that is the attainment of higher levels of self-awareness, peace and toleration via "deliteralizing" (McCloskey, 2014). It is also capable of incorporating the psychological phenomena of double truths, cognitive dissonance, conceptual schizophrenia, and cognitive capture (Mirowski, 2013) by looking at disintegrated and suppressed archetypes, complexes and shadow formation. And, it permits an understanding of neoclassical economists as protagonists of a drama, in which the economic system of their making produces increasing levels of social damages (see Binswanger, 2011, for this interpretation based on Goethe's Faust and Mirowski, 2013, for the interpretation of the current economic crisis as "a set of avoidable tragedies"). The main insight for economic policy is that increasing levels of social damages can only be prevented if economists engage in therapeutic self-reflection.

Acknowledgements

This article has grown out of a research project conducted during a postdoc at the department of economics at Harvard University in 2013. I would like to thank Professor Stephen Marglin for institutionally supporting this research project and for taking the time to further my thought process with insightful comments during several in-depth conversations. I would also like to thank Alan Dyer and Rolf Steppacher for their thoughtful remarks. The usual disclaimers apply.

Note

1 For the various meanings and applications of this concept see Berger (2009).

References

Agamben, Giorgio (2011) *The Kingdom and the Glory – For a Theological Genealogy of Economy and Government*. Stanford, CA: Stanford University Press.

Amariglio, Jack and Ruccio, David (2001) "From unity to dispersion: the body in modern economic discourse," in Stephen Cullenberg, Jack Amariglio, and David F. Ruccio (eds), *Postmodernism, Economics and Knowledge*. London and New York: Routledge.

Arnsperger, Christian (2010) *Full Spectrum Economics: Towards an Inclusive and Emancipatory Social Science*. London and New York: Routledge.

Berger, Sebastian (ed.) (2009) *The Foundations of Non-Equilibrium Economics: The Principle of Circular and Cumulative Causation*. London: Routledge.

Berger, Sebastian (2011) "Bookreview – Die große Finanzmarktkrise," *Journal of Economic Issues*, 45 (4): 1027–9.

Berger, Sebastian (ed.) (2015a) "Introduction," in *The Heterodox Theory of Social Costs – by K. William Kapp*. London and New York: Routledge.

Berger, Sebastian (2015b) "Poetic economics and experiential knowledge: how the economist K. William Kapp was inspired by the poet Ernst Wiechert," in *Journal of Economic Issues*, 49 (3): 730–48.

Berger, Sebastian and Elsner, Wolfram (2009) "European contributions to evolutionary institutional economics: the cases 'open systems approach' (OSA) and 'cumulative circular causation' (CCC)," in Wolfram Elsner and Hardi Hanappi (eds), *Advances in Evolutionary Economics: Evolutionary Models, Non-Knowledge, and Strategy*. Cheltenham: Edward Elgar.

Bernstein, Richard (1983) *Beyond Objectivism and Relativism – Science, Hermeneutics, and Praxis*. Philadelphia: University of Pennsylvania Press.

Binswanger, Hans Christoph (1994) *Money and Magic – A Critique of the Modern Economy in the Light of Faust*. Chicago: Chicago University Press.

Binswanger, Hans Christoph (2011) *Die Glaubensgemeinschaft der Ökonomen – Essays zur Kultur der Wirtschaft*. Hamburg: Murmann Verlag.

Boulding, Kenneth (2013) "Towards the development of a cultural economics," in *Interdisciplinary Economics – Kenneth E. Boulding's Engagement in the Sciences*. London and New York: Routledge.

Colander, David (2009) "Moving beyond the rhetoric of pluralism: suggestions for an 'inside the mainstream' heterodoxy," in Robert Garnett, Erik Olsen, and Martha Starr (eds), *Economic Pluralism*. London: Routledge, pp. 36–47.

Cullenberg, Stephen, Amariglio, Jack and Ruccio, David F. (eds) (2001) *Postmodernism, Economics and Knowledge*. London and New York: Routledge.

Davis, John B. (2010) "Bookreview," *Journal of Cultural Economics*, 34: 237–40.

Dewey, John (1960) *The Quest for Certainty*. New York: Capricorn Books.

Dow, Sheila C. (1997) "Mainstream economic methodology," *Cambridge Journal of Economics*, 21: 73–93.

Dow, Sheila C. (2011) "Heterodox economics, history and prospects [review article]," *Cambridge Journal of Economics*, 5 (6): 1151–65.

Drewermann, Eugen (1989) *Die Kleriker – Psychogramm eines Ideals*. Olten: Walter-Verlag AG.

Elsner, Wolfram (1986) *Economic Institutions Analysis – The Paradigmatic Development of Economics and the Relevance of a Recourse to the Economic Classics* [German: *Ökonomische Institutionenanalyse*]. Berlin: Duncker & Humblot.

Georgescu-Roegen, Nicholas (1979) "Methods in economic science," *Journal of Economic Issues*, 13 (2): 317–28.

Gerber, Julien-François and Steppacher, Rolf (eds) (2012) *Towards an Integrated Paradigm in Heterodox Economics – Alternative Approaches to the Current Eco-Social Crisis*. New York: Palgrave-Macmillan.

Gerber, Julien-François and Steppacher, Rolf (2014) "Some fundamentals of integral economics," *World Futures*, 70: 442–63.

Hands, Wade (1994) "The sociology of scientific knowledge: some thoughts on the possibilities," in Robert E. Backhouse (ed.), *New Directions in Economic Methodology*. London and New York: Routledge.

Hartman, L. M. (1977) "Economics as science and as culture," *American Journal of Agricultural Economics*, 59 (5): 925–30.

Hauke, Christopher (2000) *Jung and the Postmodern: The Interpretation of Realities.* London and New York: Routledge.

Hermann-Pillath, Carsten (2013) *Foundations of Economic Evolution – A Treatise on the Natural Philosophy of Economics.* Cheltenham and Northampton: Edward Elgar.

Hewitson, Gillian (2001) "The disavowal of the sexed body in neoclassical economics," in Stephen Cullenberg, Jack Amariglio, and David F. Ruccio (eds), *Postmodernism, Economics and Knowledge.* London and New York: Routledge.

Hillman, James (1994) *Healing Fiction: On Freud, Jung, Adler.* Thompson, CT: Spring Publications.

Hillman, James (2005) *Senex and Puer.* Putnam, CT: Spring Publications.

Jackson, William A. (2009) *Economics, Culture, and Social Theory.* Cheltenham: Edward Elgar.

Kapp, K. William (1950) *The Social Costs of Private Enterprise.* Cambridge, MA: Harvard University Press.

Kapp, K. William (1961) *Towards a Science of Man in Society – A Positive Approach to the Integration of Social Knowledge.* The Hague: Martinus Nijhouse.

Kapp, K. William (1976) "Economics in the future: the open system character of the economy and its implications," in Kurt Dopfer (ed.), *Economics in the Future: Towards a New Paradigm.* London: Macmillan.

Kapp, K. William (1985) "The humanization of the social sciences," eds John E. Ullmann and Roy Preiswerk. Lanham, MD, New York, and London: University of America Press.

Kapp, K. William (2011) *The Foundations of Institutional Economics*, eds Sebastian Berger and Rolf Steppacher. London and New York: Routledge.

Kapp, K. William (2015) *The Heterodox Theory of Social Costs*, ed. Sebastian Berger. London and New York: Routledge.

Keynes, John Maynard (1936) *The General Theory of Employment, Interest and Money.* London: Macmillan.

Klamer, Arjo (1996) *The Value of Culture: On the Relationship between Economics and Arts.* Amsterdam: Amsterdam University Press.

Klamer, Arjo (2001) "Late modernism and the loss of character in economics," in Jack Amariglio and Stephen E. Cullenberg (eds), *Postmodernism, Economics and Knowledge.* New York: Routledge, pp. 77–101.

Lee, Frederic S. (2009) *A History of Heterodox Economics: Challenging the Mainstream in the 20th Century.* London and New York: Routledge.

Lietaer, Bernard (2005) *An Integral View on Money and Financial Crashes.* Accessed online 2 February 2016 at: http://www.lietaer.com/images/Integral_Money.pdf.

McCloskey, Deidre (2001) "The genealogy of postmodernism: an economist's guide," in Stephen Cullenberg, Jack Amariglio, and David F. Ruccio (eds), *Postmodernism, Economics, and Knowledge.* London and New York: Routledge.

McCloskey, Donald N. (2014) "Storytelling in economics," in Don Lavoie (ed.), *Economics and Hermeneutics.* London and New York: Routledge.

Mäki, Uskali (1994) "Reorienting the assumptions issue," in Robert E. Backhouse (ed.), *New Directions in Economic Methodology.* London and New York: Routledge.

Marglin, Stephen A. (2008) *The Dismal Science – How Thinking Like an Economist Undermines Community.* Cambridge, MA: Harvard University Press.

Marglin, Stephen A. (2009) "The culture of economics," *Development*, 52 (3): 292–7.

Mearman, Andrew (2012) "Heterodox economics and the problem of classification," *Journal of Economic Methodology*, 19 (4): 407–24.

Merriam-Webster Dictionary (2015) online at: http://www.merriam-webster.com/dictionary/rigorous (accessed 15 October 2015).
Mirowski, Philip (1989) *More Heat than Light – Economics as Social Physics, Physics as Nature's Economics*. Cambridge: Cambridge University Press.
Mirowski, Philip (1994) "What are the questions?," in Roger E. Backhouse (ed.), *New Directions in Economic Methodology*. London and New York: Routledge.
Mirowski, Philip (2002) *Machine Dreams – Economics Becomes a Cyborg Science*. Cambridge: Cambridge University Press.
Mirowski, Philip (2010) "The great mortification: economists' responses to the crisis of 2007 – and counting," in *Hedgehog Review*, 12 (3).
Mirowski, Philip (2011) *Science Mart – The Privatization of American Science*. Cambridge, MA: Harvard University Press.
Mirowski, Philip (2013) *Never Let a Serious Crisis Go to Waste – How Neoliberalism Survived the Financial Meltdown*. London and New York: Verso.
Mirowski, Philip (2014) "The philosophical foundations of institutional economics," in Don Lavoie (ed.), *Economics and Hermeneutics*. Routledge: London and New York.
Moore, Thomas (1989) *The Essential James Hillmann – A Blue Fire*. London and New York: Routledge.
Nelson, Julie A. (2001) "Feminist economics: objective, activist, and postmodern?," in Stephen Cullenberg, Jack Amariglio and David F. Ruccio (eds), *Postmodernism, Economics and Knowledge*. London and New York: Routledge.
Neumann, Erich (1989) *Die Grosse Mutter – Eine Phänomenologie der Weiblichen Gestaltungen des Unbewussten*. Olten und Freiburg: Walter Verlag.
Peukert, Helge (2013) *Die große Finanzmarkt- und Staatsschuldenkrise – Eine kritisch-heterodoxe Untersuchung*, 5th edn. Marburg: Metropolis.
Rank, Otto (1941) *Beyond Psychology*. Philadelphia: E Hauser.
Rank, Otto (1962) *Art and Artist*. New York and London: W. W. Norton.
Stein, Murray (2010) *Jung's Map of the Soul – An Introduction*. Peru, IL: Open Court Publishing.
Steinmetz, George (ed.) (2005) *The Politics of Method in the Human Sciences: Positivism and Its Epistemological Others*. Durham, NC: Duke University Press.
Thornborow, Thomas and Brown, Andrew D. (2009) "'Being regimented': aspiration, discipline and identity in the British Parachute Regiment," *Organization Studies*, 30 (4): 355–76.
Throsby, David (2001) *Economics and Culture*. New York: Cambridge University Press.
Unpublished manuscript: Kapp-Weisskopf Correspondence. Kapp Archive, University of Basel, Switzerland.
Valentinov, Vladislav (2013) "K. William Kapp's theory of social costs: a Luhmannian interpretation," *Ecological Economics*, 97: 28–33.
Veblen, Thorstein (1919) *The Place of Science in Modern Civilization and other Essays by Thorstein Veblen*. New York: B. W. Huebsch.
Veblen, Thorstein (1925) "Economics in the calculable future," *American Economic Review*, 15 (1): 48–55.
Walker, Steven (2002) *Jung and the Jungian's on Myth*. London and New York: Routledge.
Weisskopf, Walter A. (1949) "Psychological aspects of economic thought," *Journal of Political Economy*, 57 (4): 304–14.

Weisskopf, Walter A. (1955) *The Psychology of Economics*. Chicago: University of Chicago Press.

Whyte, Jessica (2014) "The Fortunes of natural man: Robinson Crusoe, political economy, and the Universal Declaration of Human Rights," *Humanity: An International Journal of Human Rights, Humanitarianism, and Development*, 5 (3): 301–21.

3 Evolutionary political economy and the complexity of economic policy

Power, knowledge, and learning

Jakob Kapeller and Manuel Scholz-Wäckerle

Introduction

Evolutionary political economy is a broad frame open to several distinct perspectives. These perspectives are sometimes presented as complementary while in other instances they are considered to be contending and rival conceptions of evolutionary political economy. A closer examination of the antagonistic character of different approaches to evolutionary political economy reveals that the main tensions in the field arise out of implicit or explicit normative aspects. One main line of contention is thereby related to the question whether evolutionary political economy has something to say about the legitimacy of certain social aims, and, if not, whether it should take social aims as externally given or ignore them completely. Any answer to this general issue entails its own problems. Providing legitimacy to certain social aims necessarily entails potentially arbitrary normative considerations. Taking social aims as externally given (e.g. by consulting policy-makers or by referring to a mainstream economic conception of welfare) is equally problematic, since it simply delegates the normative responsibilities to a third party, i.e. the elected representatives. Evolutionary political economy is considered here as a still developing research program that is linked to the custom of classical political economy and its tradition of taking social aims seriously and incorporating different normative considerations when it comes to the practical application of economic theory. The basic outline of an evolutionary political economy research program is thereby closely related to an institutionalist view of the role of values in social theory, (Myrdal, 1953), rather than a neoclassical perspective, such as that given by Lionel Robbins, and its overly ambitious claims for a value-free and positive science based on a purely instrumental understanding of rationality (Robbins, 1932).

Finally, ignoring social aims drastically limits the power of science, since any political or technical application of theoretical insights always requires the specification of some set of aims (Bunge, 1967). As any scientific endeavor, evolutionary political economy hence faces the classical problem that it could possibly say something about how to reach certain aims, but, at the same time, is inept to answer which aims are worth pursuing.

Another line of tension in evolutionary political economy, which is evoked by normative aspects, relates to the evaluation of social development. At its core lies the question whether novelty and social change always lead to social betterment, i.e. whether we need to critically appraise change and novelty. A similar question is posed with respect to the relation of social change and political activism, which asks whether one should try to influence the historical course of events and whether organized political intervention was suitable for improving social development. These two questions represent a rather difficult puzzle: on the one hand, a clear-cut answer to these question would allow the identification of priorities in science (the first question) and society (the second question), while on the other hand such a clear-cut answer would afford some kind of normative judgment. Hence, these two questions represent two dilemmas, i.e. difficult puzzles, where no obvious and optimal solutions exist. The dilemma of evolutionary appraisal implies that the only alternative to a critical evaluation of novel objects and properties is to uncritically accept contradicting social developments (e.g. historical phases of increasing equality and cooperation vs. historical phases of increasing inequality and conflict) as equally beneficial. The dilemma of political participation on the other hand refers to the question whether individual agents should take history in their own hands and try to actively shape future developments, or whether such an effort is indeed futile or destructive in the face of powerful holistic mechanisms governing history and society.

Against this backdrop this article tries to address these questions by considering three topical cornerstones in evolutionary political economy, namely power, knowledge and learning. An emphasis on power highlights the contestedness as well as the path-dependency of social developments. Power is a suitable anchor for pointing to essential functions of institutions insofar as institutions can be perceived as nodes of stability and cooperation in an often rather dynamic and conflict-laden environment. Hence, institutions evolve as social interventions are sustained over time and thereby acquire social legitimacy, which may guide and coordinate the behavior of individuals. A perfect example in this respect was given by Brown (1991: 690), indicating that the mutual interplay of social intervention (e.g. mobilization politics in the form of social movements such as the feminist or the environmental movement) and institutional change. In this arrangement social interventions stem from individual agency and interest and are an integral part of institutionalization processes, as also highlighted by Castells (2009: 299). This emphasis on power serves as a guide for addressing the dilemma of political participation and argues for an understanding of history as an open process, where single outcomes are mostly temporary and the nature of social intervention is not *ex ante* determined.

Our take on knowledge in turn is more focused on the dilemma of evolutionary appraisal. Thereby we find that any sensible conceptualization of knowledge with respect to novelty cannot assume that the emergence of novel objects, properties or systems necessarily constitutes betterment or social progress. Hence, evolutionary political economists must not enshrine novelty and innovation, but rather critically examine its social and economic effects and make the underlying mechanisms transparent to a wider public. A prime and recent example for such an undertaking was given by Piketty (2014), who not only found novel characteristics and tendencies regarding the distribution of income and wealth, but extrapolated these tendencies to provide a scenario for possible social change in order to facilitate a public debate, whether the alleged transformation to a "patrimonial capitalism" really represents a desirable path of development.

Finally, our emphasis on the role of learning sheds light on the transmission of ideas from science to politics and illustrates how scientific input shapes political decisions and social outcomes. As has already been emphasized such application always entails normative considerations. Hence, it should be a main goal for evolutionary political economy to make these normative considerations in scientifically guided policy-making more transparent. This finding implies that evolutionary political economists can neither ignore nor simply import the normative aims imposed in economic consultancy. Rather, they should turn to develop a conceptual toolkit in the form of an adaptive concept of evolutionary welfare in order to make transparent and contestable statements in the realm of economic policy.

Power: accumulation, distribution, and institutions

The political economy of capitalist production

> Economics as a separate science is unrealistic, and misleading if taken as a guide in practice. It is one element – a very important element, it is true – in a study, the science of power.
>
> (Bertrand Russell, cited in Rothschild, 1971: 7)

Tracing the role of power in the history of economic thought to gain a better understanding of its impact on the development of economic theory reveals an interesting dichotomy: on the one hand there are large branches in the history of economic thought – especially in classical economics – which put questions of power center stage. On the other hand a quite different stream of works aims to prove that the explicit consideration of power in economics is a superfluous effort, since standard economic theory has already fully integrated all relevant aspects of power by subsuming the latter under general economic laws derived from an abstract analysis of highly idealized barter economies (e.g. Böhm-Bawerk, 1914). In these types of setup power is simply a function of the number and the distribution of agents within a certain environment and only relates to decisions on prices and quantities.

A prime example for the first approach – which interprets power as an important and autonomous factor of influence – is given by John Stuart Mill's distinction between the sphere of production and the sphere of distribution. For Mill, the decisive difference between these two spheres is that, while production is subject to the laws of nature, distribution is shaped by "human institution solely", since "[t]he things once there, mankind, individually or collectively, can do with them as they like" (Mill, 1848: II.1.1–2).

The consideration of power and its explicit connection to issues of distribution is a major characteristic of the first approach to power in economics, which may also be exemplified by Ricardo, Marx, or Veblen. Ricardo, for instance, invested the fortunes he obtained by means of financial speculation into agricultural land, thereby closely following the argument laid out in the "Essay on Profits" (Ricardo, 1815): since agricultural land is absolutely constrained relative to labor and capital land-owners will turn into "rentiers" – reaping rents in addition to profits – due to their prominent position in terms of economic power. For Marx, who criticizes Mill's subjugation of the sphere of production under "natural laws" as an ideological maneuver, power considerations play an even more accentuated role: power relations are not only to be seen as constitutive for capitalist development as a whole, but also determine future historical developments. Hence, it is no surprise that a series of important hypotheses in Marx's *oeuvre* – for instance, his theses on pauperization, economic concentration, or underconsumption – explicitly build on considerations of distribution and power.

More specifically, Marx argues that the production process in capitalist systems will always run through the same stages and that capital invokes a certain reproductive continuity – called accumulation. This continuity reproduces the power relations involved in every round by "separating the labor force from labor conditions" (Marx, 1867: 306) and makes the terms of labor exploitation appear as "naturally given." This aspect also underpins Marx's critique of Mill's distinction, since the production and distribution of goods are intrinsically linked, not only because the relations of production strongly influence distributional results, but also since "[e]very societal production process is at the same time a process of reproduction" (Marx, 1867: 591). It is the final step of the first period of capitalist (re)production that is on the one hand delivering surplus value for the capitalist by selling the commodity and on the other hand bonding the laborer to capital by her/his self-selling continuity, i.e. simple reproduction (Marx, 1867: 591–604). Then extended reproduction (Marx, 1867: 605–39) implies that ongoing accumulation depends strictly on materially transforming the surplus product again into capital, i.e. buying new labor or acquiring additional capital goods. The power relations in a capitalist society emerge basically from simple reproduction that is transforming money (either coming from bequest or from exploitation in terms of original accumulation (Marx, 1867: 741–91)) into capital, or in short: "labor creates capital, before capital employs labor" (E. G. Wakefield, cited in Marx, 1867: 608).

Similar to Marx Vilfredo Pareto (1955) or Thorstein Veblen (1899), who both conceived economics as one ingredient in an integrated approach to the social sciences, developed their economic approaches parallel to theories on social status and elites and thereby underscored the connections between distributional questions, social hierarchy and issues of economic, political, and cultural power.

A counterpoint to these classical approaches is provided by the idea that power relations are completely subjected to the forces of economic competition. As a consequence, this view emphasizes the role of competition as a "first-best" remedy for situations, where unequal power relations prevail and determine social outcomes. Another consequence of this view is that from a theoretical perspective a theory of competition already incorporates a sufficient theory of social power relations, since power in general is completely subjected to market forces (Böhm-Bawerk, 1914), as well as a complete theory of distribution (in the form of marginal productivity theory). Modern mainstream economics still adheres to this view and reduces issues of power and distribution to questions of economic competition (Rothschild, 2002). It remains to be seen whether the current focus on the empirics of increasing inequality of income and wealth in mainstream economic literature (e.g. Alvaredo *et al.*, 2013; Piketty and Saez, 2014) will also prompt any theoretical revisions of the standard framework of economic analysis.

While there are various ways to justify the classical stance, which incorporates power as an autonomous explanatory factor aside from the obvious impact of competition on entrepreneurial leeway, in what follows we look at just one way to do so, which has been magisterially developed in Wolfram Elsner's works (Elsner *et al.*, 2015). We deem this way highly interesting and rewarding as it provides a simple means to assessing a key idea in heterodox economics, which, although taking many presumptions of the standard approach as given, amounts to an important critique of an all too optimistic view on the social benefits of private competition as most famously advanced by Bernard Mandeville (1962 [1714]). Mandeville posits that "private vice" in the form of egocentric instrumental rationality will lead to "public benefits," that is the maximization of social welfare. While the Mandeville case is surely a possible state of affairs, the conditions required for the Mandeville case to prevail are often inapplicable. Classical examples in this context include rationality traps or references to the "tragedy of the commons," that is, the unsustainable usage of a public good in the absence of a suitable mode of social coordination. In such a setup any single agent has a strong impact on final outcomes, since isolated non-cooperators have the power to significantly affect the final results by deviating from an established rule-set or boycotting the introduction of new rules. More formally, the general structure underlying this rationale can be expressed in the form of a prisoner's dilemma, which illustrates the core property of rationality traps and tragedies of the commons, namely that myopic individually rational actions will lead to the worst possible aggregate outcome. By emphasizing the conflict between the private, short-term gains of defection and the public, long-term gains of cooperation Wolfram Elsner paves the way for an "interactive and institutional economic policy" based on a "lean policy approach" for a "complex, interactive and evolutionary economy" (Elsner *et al.*, 2015: Ch. 17.2). In doing he provides one possible answer to the dilemma of political participation as posed in our introductory section, in which the focus on the long-term gains of sustained cooperation represents a clear rationale for an ambitious approach to economic policy-making.

Institutions, coordination and frictionless exchange

The prisoner's dilemma serves as a crucial methodological device to deal with collective action situations. However, even the very basic notion of game theory has added novel content to economic theory. Coordination and cooperation between interacting agents within coordination games and social dilemmas gain theoretical priority over individual utility maximization. In consequence the methodological toolkit becomes necessarily game theory and expected utility theory as John von Neumann and Oscar Morgenstern originally emphasized. "Thus the study of the Crusoe economy and the use of the methods applicable to it, is of much more limited value to economic theory than has been assumed heretofore even by the most radical critic" (Neumann and Morgenstern, 1944: 12). Eventually this notion means that switching the methodological perspective even from one to two agents has far-reaching analytical implications for economic theory, emphasizing the need for a different core model: a "social economy" instead of a "Crusoe-economy" as von Neumann and Morgenstern (1944: 8–12) explain. Basically we distinguish between coordination games (e.g. stag-hunt or battle of the sexes), anti-coordination games (e.g. game of chicken and hawk-dove), and social dilemmas (e.g. prisoner's dilemma or tragedy of the commons). The first class of games represents preferable collective action situations, since they involve two pure strategy Nash equilibria. The second class of games implies one additional Nash equilibrium in mixed strategies besides the two equilibria in pure strategies, and the third class implies just one Nash equilibrium in pure strategies plus a social optimum equilibrium.

Obviously, from an evolutionary political economy perspective it is the anti-coordination and social dilemma games that are especially relevant, since they represent a class of situations incorporating social conflict. Hayek (1978), for instance, refers to properties of human action that are not explicitly reasonable to the carrying agent. These innate characteristics have evolved culturally; they frame human behavior and they constrain human will and choice. Hayek speaks of rules of conduct in this respect where human beings are able to establish social order along with the cultural transmission of these rules, and refers to group selection as a co-evolutionary mechanism for this transmission. However, the main problem with Hayek's evolutionary institutional analysis is his rather naive belief that the repeating social dilemma (consider the same continuity here as in Marx's case of accumulation) will be solved via rule evolution only. That is why society was never existent for Hayek, he just cared about the evolution of rules, i.e. their transmission and persistence (Boyd and Richerson, 2005: 57). It is right that this assumption renders institutional economic analysis highly dynamic and endogenous in contrast to other more equilibrium-focused approaches (Aoki, 2007). Still, the assumption that cooperation crowds out defection through a highly efficient free market-based economy in the long run can hardly be substantiated by empirical evidence. The faith that cooperative solutions will by and large prevail and deviations caused by repeated defections are generally negligible is one answer to the dilemma of political participation posed in our introduction. We would suppose that this answer leads right into a "Hayekian trap," where an optimistic stance on social development combined with a reservation against social intervention based on possibly harmful unintended consequence leaves politics without guide, since the dilemma of political participations is answered negatively: in this view, all beneficial forms of social intervention arise spontaneously out of interacting individuals. Hence, there is no need and also no advice for any kind of social planning.

The main fallacy of the Hayekian trap resides in the ignorant stance with regard to the social, economic, and cultural effects of continuously reproducing power relations. One potential reason why the Hayekian trap is still tempting for so many economists lies in the reorientation of economic discourse from problems of production to problems of exchange. Once you find yourself in a pure exchange economy, that is in an Edgeworth box, the mere theoretical existence of a contract curve is all that matters to ensure a social optimum, while the actual distribution of goods does not matter, even if it forces one participant to live under conditions of extreme deprivation. The production process becomes a neglected side problem of competition between capitalists. This assumption of frictionless exchange, where agents neither use force nor strategy, contributes to the internal consistency of concepts like the Hayekian ideal state of catallaxy or, similarly, Hodgson's (2012) moral community, but, at the same time, restricts the empirical applicability of these ideas and makes them ill-suited for providing properly nuanced and unbiased policy advice.

Knowledge: pluralism, systemism, and the meso level of political economy

In this subsection we identify three theoretical preliminaries in Wolfram Elsner's work that characterize his epistemology for a proper economics. First, a pluralist approaches facilitates the incorporation of a sufficient diversity of theories and concepts. Second, the notion of systemism provides a convincing frame for addressing basic ontological issues, related to the question of how to relate different levels of analysis in economics. One direct consequence of such a systemist approach is to employ a more nuanced conception of ontological layers. In this vein we finally discuss the 'meso' level of political economy, which proves to be of particular importance and interest in the context of an evolutionary political economy.

The role of pluralism

Introducing the core concepts of a complex social economy from a micro perspective is a rather difficult task. A central tenet in institutional economics is given by the notion of conflict (e.g. as presented in the form of social dilemmas) that Elsner *et al.* (2015) refer to in terms of economic welfare problems. The authors assume that problems of economic welfare are strongly related to social conflict, that is conflicting tensions between interdependent individual actors without obvious consensual solutions. This viewpoint eventually amounts to the argument that the traditional approach to economic welfare is largely beside the point, since it circumvents the question of social conflict by focusing solely on mutual gains as in the case of Pareto optimality. In doing so, it reduces the manifold forms of economic power and force to a question of competition and barter.

From the perspective of evolutionary political economy, welfare problems are embedded in and emerging from social processes and can be formally represented as dynamic coordination problems, which do not only mirror a central institutionalist assumption, but also reflect Adam Smith's classic interest in the constitution of social order (Smith, 1759). Elsner *et al.* (2015) follow such a dynamic institutional narrative that is more connected to the realist political economy conception by Marx, where social conflict is reproduced continuously, in contrast to a Hayekian notion of spontaneous order where rules adjust automatically to resolve all social conflict. Thereby the authors are well aware that the economy is not a purely self-sustaining phenomenon but embedded in political and cultural spheres, which come with different ideological presumptions. The resulting plurality of views and interests seems to be important for the production of economic knowledge, which inherently reflects this plurality of "preanalytic cognitive acts."

> In fact, it enters on the very ground floor, into the preanalytic cognitive act of which we have been speaking. Analytic work begins with material provided by our vision of things, and this vision is ideological almost by definition.
>
> Schumpeter (1954: 42)

Science is still part of social life and any generation of scientific knowledge is informed by the scientist's habits, practices and location in society. Heterodox economists have always argued for making these claims explicit and connected this aim for increased transparency and accessibility of economic thought with a concrete plea for pluralism in economics to officially recognize the implications the manifoldness of social and economic life carries for social research and economic investigation.

Pluralism comes into play as a rather intuitive assumption though it adds crucial challenges to scientific analysis. Ontology represents one of these highly contested territories, since assumptions about the existence of social structures, the mutually interdependent choice of individual economic agents, or the evolutionary continuity between biological and cultural reproduction carry non-trivial implications for the analysis at hand. Heterodox economists today have shown that the basic intuition behind the notion of pluralism can not only be epistemologically justified (Elsner, 1986, 2006, 2013), but also has constructive implications for research strategy and design (Dobusch and Kapeller, 2012). Additionally, a set of diverse theoretical approaches, which all make their "pre-analytical" presumptions transparent, could also provide a basic framework for addressing the dilemma of evolutionary appraisal, since the different "preanalytic acts" incorporated in these theories would provide a series of potentially interesting vantage points for the appraisal of novel objects and properties. Similarly, a pluralist approach also eases the problems associated with the dilemma of political participation as it provides a toolkit of differentiated theories suitable for formulating nuanced assessments of problems in evolutionary political economy.

Systemism: aggregation and emergence in social science

In his works on the relation of different ontological layers of reality in social research the eminent philosopher Mario Bunge (Bunge, 1996, 2004) introduces the concept of systemism – as a conceptual alternative to individualism and holism. According to Bunge the concept is anchored in the works of a series of prominent heterodox economic thinkers, like John Maynard Keynes, Wassily Leontief (Bunge, 2004: 187), Max Weber, Joseph A. Schumpeter, Thorstein B. Veblen, and K. William Kapp (Bunge, 1999: 92–3).

At the heart of a systemist perspective is an embedded understanding of individuals which put the different relationships across individual nodes center stage. The varying structure of these relationships gives rise to social systems of different kinds, size, and functionality – from small-scale families to big nation states or from corporations to traffic networks. All social systems consist of the same components, namely a specific composition of individual nodes, the structure or organization of their relationships as well as a certain environment. In this view any object is either a system or a part of one. The main feature of a social system is that it is a "complex object every part or component of which is connected with other parts of the same object in such a manner that the whole possesses some features that its components lack – that is, emergent properties" (Bunge, 1996: 20). Hence, systems are intrinsically related to ontological novelty, which comes in the form of emergent properties and may attach to aggregate aspects (global properties like a nation's culture) or individual parts (relational properties like being a firm's accountant or a politician's spokesperson). In Bunge's account these novel properties emerge due to the specific structure of a given system and do carry mechanisms whose effects lead to continuous change and the stabilization of this system. This nesting of mechanisms and novelties provides another vantage point for addressing the dilemma of evolutionary appraisal, since the effects of novelties may be evaluated with respect to the underlying system from which a specific novelty emerges, as well as with respect to its environment.

Historical experience shows that the novel effects arising from social systems, which are associated with a given relational structure of individual nodes, encompass a great variety of developments with very ambivalent normative characteristics. Figures 3.1 and 3.2 reproduce two historical examples given by Mario Bunge for France's purposes of illustration: the decline in fertility rates in the face of ongoing economic growth (Figure 3.1) as well as a theoretical description of processes in *Ancien Règime* leading to an impoverishment of the rural population (Figure 3.2). Independent of one's normative convictions it is hard to

Figure 3.1 Decline in fertility rates in the face of ongoing growth

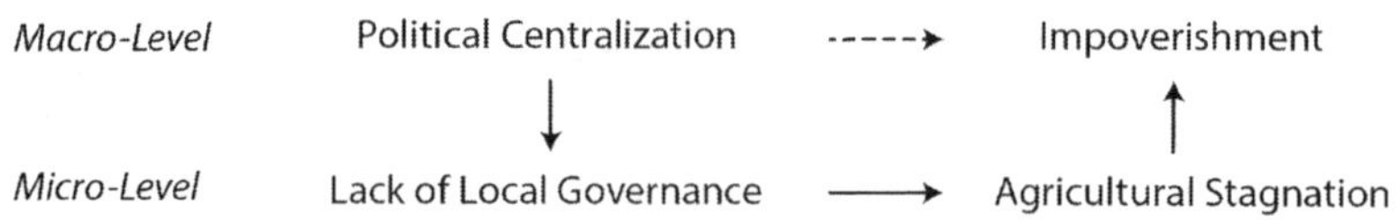

Figure 3.2 Impoverishment of the rural population in the *Ancien Régime*

understand why two such different emergent outcomes should not be ranked according to their desirability. Indeed, this illustrative example shows the necessity of engaging in some form of critical appraisal of novel developments, by looking at the effect a certain novelty exhibits on social, ecological, and economic outcomes.

Such a focus on social systems and the relationships across individuals contributes to resolving the dilemma of evolutionary appraisal as it emphasizes mutual interdependencies across different social fields and, hence, raises awareness for the potentially manifold implications triggered by a given novelty.

The meso level of political economy

A systemist understanding of political economy reveals new perspectives on the reflexive dynamics between microeconomic behavior and macroeconomic developments. These dynamics rest on social relations and contribute to the creation of emergent properties within a relational layer, which has been dubbed as the mesoeconomic level (Dopfer *et al.*, 2004; Boyer, 2008; Elsner, 2010). Institutional economists in particular are keen to highlight the systemic features of institutions, such as institutional emergence, stability, resilience, vulnerability, or lock-in, which reside on the mesoeconomic level. In contrast to the new institutional economic research program, which has given priority to a monetary evaluation of institutions in the form of transaction cost economics, Elsner and Heinrich (2011) and Elsner *et al.* (2015) emphasize the power of a realist institutional analysis, where complex problem structures are treated with a diverse set of policy measures (e.g. Ostrom, 2012). In this context Elsner *et al.* (2015) emphasize that a mesoeconomic approach closely follows the original institutional economics of Veblen, Commons, and Mitchell. From a pragmatic perspective institutions involve systemic social problem structures, where individually optimal decisions sometimes do not lead to social optima. The authors find solutions to such institutional problems highly interesting; in particular they suggest agents to transform social dilemma type payoff structures into coordination type ones via trust and signaling (compare Heinrich and Schwardt (2013) for a detailed discussion). The latter include two Nash equilibria which coincide as social optima instead of just one Nash equilibrium that is distinct from the social optimum in the former case. The coordination on the microeconomic level can thereby lead to an emergent higher-order platform size that is called meso by Elsner *et al.* (2015). The rather loose but converging dynamics on this meso level may further lead to the emergence of a macroeconomic institution that is eventually able to coordinate economic policies.

Elsewhere Elsner and Heinrich (2011) describe a concrete model featuring the properties of the previously explained dynamics. The model is based on an agent-based methodology where agents are capable of social interaction and learning from past experiences. Such aspects are essential in formalizing systemism by computational simulation (see also Wäckerle *et al.*, 2014). Mesoeconomics offers an analytical level where emergent properties in complex adaptive political economies are observable and replicable – features that can definitely contribute to resolving the dilemma of evolutionary appraisal.

Learning: methodology, economic education, and policy

In the two previous sections we have elaborated on power and knowledge in evolving political economies. Power emerges out of capitalist production along with social hierarchies, which are reproduced through the accumulation of capital. The acquisition and diffusion of knowledge is regulated by institutions of education and science, which are recursively shaped by power relations and, hence, also prone to conflict since purely internal criteria, like truth or curiosity, may collide with the requirements imposed by external interest groups. In this section we turn our attention towards economic education, the way we transmit and sustain economic knowledge within and between generations. We argue that this topic is decisive for the formation of economic policy. However, the most basic economic models taught in schools and in undergraduate programs contribute significantly to economic policy-making, and represent the common body of economic knowledge. A great deal of the success of neoclassical economics can be attributed to its very simple equation-based models that are communicated even in school and which represent stories and narratives conveying the allegedly simple mechanics of the socioeconomic world. In order to arrive at new economic policies that are able to deal with the complex problems emerging in an interconnected globalized world and thereby provide answers to the dilemma of evolutionary appraisal to empower political decision-makers to overcome the dilemma of political participation, it is suggested we turn the focus onto new modes of learning in economic education by addressing history and empirics. Computational simulation works as a novel facilitator in learning about the complexities in real-world political economies. This claim is clearly realized by Elsner *et al.* (2015) in a serious attempt to make economic education more colorful and realistic.

The historical domain: a transdisciplinary social science

The first principle that evolutionary political economy addresses in order to enhance progress in economic education is "history matters." As realists we employ the view that historical circumstances determine which economic mechanisms eventually shape production, distribution, technology, and overall economic development.

Similarly, evolution follows some general non-teleological principles or even universal laws, representing qualitative change that hosts a multitude of auxiliary theories for particular problems of change in different contexts. To this extent we understand history and evolutionary theory as complementary methods for the analysis of economic development. Until the nineteenth century, classical political economy was considered a historical transdisciplinary social science. Almost all the classics have forged political economy on behalf of historical examples, often incorporating a tremendous degree of detail. Only at the end of the nineteenth century did a transition appear in the discipline from political economy to economics. The new economic discipline was built on supposedly general, a-historical foundations with a focus on simple mathematical models. This focus on a specific variant of analytical rigor accompanied specialization in economic education and led to a significant isolation of economics within the social sciences. In contrast, the classics tried to synthesize history, sociology, philosophy, political science, economics, and psychology under the common umbrella of political economy in a transdisciplinary way. Against this backdrop we suggest the improvement of economic education by means of three historical components: evolution, economic history, and history of economic thought. The first introduces the history of biological lifeforms and highlights their thermodynamic properties as well as their potential to engage in negentropic processes, that is the ability of living organisms to keep their own entropy low by exporting (high or low) entropy (Georgescu-Roegen, 1971; Ayres, 1998). This aspect shows in a straightforward way that the economic process can never be understood as an isolated process from a closed-system perspective; rather the opposite is the case (Berger and Elsner, 2008). K. William Kapp has clearly concluded that the confrontation with ecological limits inherently demands such a transdisciplinary approach:

> The disruption of the environment and its protection raise problems of such complexity that no single academic discipline within its present boundaries can hope to make significant contributions to their solution without at least a basic familiarity with the knowledge of other relevant social and natural sciences. For this reason it is necessary that social and natural scientists concerned with environmental problems and policies engage in transdisciplinary research.
>
> (Kapp, 1977: 528)

Evolutionary theory can play a crucial role in reconnecting previously made artificial separations (Bowles and Gintis, 2011). Otherwise a clear understanding of historical developments helps to contextualize the relations between nature, technology, economy, and society. In this regard Eric Hobsbawm has always insisted on the important role of the historical method for political economy (Hobsbawm, 1975). Another excellent example is given by Braudel's (1987) history of civilizations. Both economic historians elaborate on the unfolding processes of social conflict and its political consequences for the rise and fall of nations as well as for inequality within and between countries. Economic curricula still lack this dimension, which we assess as a blind spot with regard to posing sensible answers in the face of current developments, that is when confronting the dilemma of evolutionary appraisal.

The computational domain and its contribution to social science

Over recent decades computational power has increased to such an extent that it is possible to simulate artificial worlds. Thereby computational science offers a new way of thinking about social systems by employing novel tools to study complex dynamics arising out of interpersonal interaction.

> Biology has traditionally started at the top, viewing a living organism as a complex biochemical machine, and worked analytically downwards from there – through organs, tissues, cells, organelles, membranes, and finally molecules – in its pursuit of the mechanisms of life. Artificial Life starts at the bottom, viewing an organism as a large population of simple machines, and works upwards synthetically from there, constructing large aggregates of simple, rule-governed objects which interact with one another nonlinearly in the support of life-like, global dynamics.
>
> (Langton, 1993)

The main idea behind artificial life is the simulation of interactive parts and the generation of emergent patterns. In a social science perspective the parts can make their own decisions on behalf of their local information and accessible knowledge. It is not just a single agent gaining bounded rationality in terms of Simon (1991); the complexity comes in with a multitude of boundedly rational agents interacting through different layers and social networks. One promising method for doing so is agent-based modeling, which embodies the move from "factors to actors in the social sciences" (Macy and Willer, 2002). An asset of computational social science is the possibility of formally expressing the relevant links between micro- and macroeconomic phenomena. The many advantages of this approach for teaching and learning economics are connected to its generative principle, where the focus is on the explanatory power of growing a system from the bottom up. Epstein (2006: 33) even argues that the generativist principle says that if the problem is not generated, it implies that it is not explained.

> Situate an initial population of autonomous heterogeneous agents in a relevant spatial environment; allow them to interact according to local rules, and thereby generate – or "grow" – the macroscopic regularity from the bottom up.
>
> (Epstein, 2006: 7)

In order to grow and generate a system it is necessary to change the language structure from mathematical equations to computational algorithms and programs. Although social interaction may be represented via recursive equation systems, we think that an agent-based methodology is often more suitable in this regard. It offers a flexible and appropriate choice for learning about the complexities

Table 3.1 Language structures

Level	*Prose*	*Mathematics*	*Algorithms*
0	Bits	Bits	Bits
1	Words	Variables	Objects
2	Sentences	Equations	Statements
3	Texts	Equation systems	Programs
4	Sets of texts	Sets of systems	Sets of programs

Source: Based on Hanappi (2007).

involved in real-world economies since it is analytically more accessible for students with different disciplinary backgrounds.

Hanappi (2007) explains how we can compare the different language structures and how we can make analogies on different levels of a modular (in)formal language (see Table 3.1). The algorithmic language structure is of course less precise but more open and dynamic, and therefore suitable for the analysis of evolving political economies.

More precisely, Miller and Page (2007) elaborate on the implications of using algorithmic language for bottom-up modeling in a generativist way as described before (Table 3.2). These aspects show that economic education, teaching, and learning achieves a much greater degree freedom as compared to traditional economic curricula. Elsner *et al.* (2015) make social complexity the primary object of investigation and suggest (re)integrating the historical with the analytical domain by generating comparable narratives and formalized stories of evolving complex economic systems. Still the usage of algorithmic language is not yet fully expressed in the economic realm, as noted by Epstein (2006).

The policy domain: evolutionary political economy – a theory of practice

One of the central goals in heterodox economics is to provide economic policy design with solid foundations. Evolutionary political economy is basically designed

Table 3.2 Modelling potential of the bottom-up approach

Traditional tools	*Agent-based objects*
Precise	Flexible
Little process	Process-oriented
Timeless	Timely
Optimizing	Adaptive
Static	Dynamic
1,2, or ∞ agents	1, 2, …, N agents
Vacuous	Spacey/networked
Homogeneous	Heterogeneous

Source: Based on Miller and Page (2007: 79).

as a theory of practice, it is historical, generative, and empirical. It is about multi-level governance in the learning society, the transmission and persistence of information transmission mechanisms and knowledge. We emphasize a dynamic and developmental approach to policy-making that focuses on the ability of a system to evolve and its potential to adapt to new circumstances. This approach is in line with systemic concepts such as resilience (Elsner, 2015: 23) and transformation. It follows an algorithmic idea of endogenous change and is per se experimental, meaning that policy-making necessarily involves some form of trial and error. Economic analysis has turned attention away from the production of goods and services – and its consequence for the exploitation of labor – towards a focus on exchange on markets. As we have outlined in the previous sections, the exchange-based analytical option might suit well for cases of small, closed, and local communities, but it may be too short-sighted for large-scale welfare problems of interconnected political economies. What we have rendered as the Hayekian trap can be understood as a temptation – quite similar to the temptation reward in a classic prisoner's dilemma – to refrain from taking responsibility and organizing social intervention, that is, to provide a negative response to the dilemma of political participation by opting for political abstinence. On the contrary, the evolutionary policy-maker acts in order to learn about the ubiquity of multi-level governance based on a systemic understanding of power and knowledge relations.

Here is the link between science and policy that is also followed by Elsner *et al.* (2015) who emphasize the frequent exchange between science and policy in order to reduce the complexity of problem structures. A central tenet in this respect deals with the changing role of economic forecasts, which are often more effective in influencing than in predicting economic phenomena. This constellation points to the need for a pragmatic approach to economic policy by combining risk-averse safety principles like the maxi-min rule (Wald, 1945) with greater openness for novel and even radical proposals in economic policy-making.

Concluding remarks

In this chapter we have elaborated on the role of normative aspects in evolutionary political economy. We consider social development as crucial for the evolution of political economies. We have shown that such an aim carries substantial ramifications for collective decisions that an evolutionary policy-maker faces at the end of the day. Two dilemmas immediately arise in the presence of endogenously changing microeconomic behavior and macroeconomic development. First, we emphasize the dilemma of evolutionary appraisal, which is concerned with the evaluation of emerging novelties and the comparison of different historical outcomes. The challenge of evolutionary policy-making is therefore related to a continuous critical assessment of policy choices with respect to different pathways in social development. Second, there is the dilemma of political participation where agency supposedly diminishes in light of overwhelming historical or evolutionary forces. However, evolving political economies demand energetic and active agents that are capable of coordinating and stabilizing social interventions for the greater good in order to provide a practical perspective for sustaining or creating large-scale cooperation. These dilemmas emerge around social complexity and do not allow straightforward best answers correspondingly. As a consequence we have suggested focusing on three political economic hubs catalyzing evolutionary policy-making for social development: power, knowledge, and learning. In line with Elsner *et al.* (2015), we are convinced that political economy needs to focus on these terms because they represent the central tenets for the social organization of economic activities.

Capital accumulation is the engine of innovation, but also of social stratification, because it continuously reproduces power relations between owners of capital and workers. Once entrepreneurship ceases to focus on the creation of novelties contributing to social welfare, its impact on social development might indeed become negative when innovations only increase the exploitation of social, cultural, and natural resources. We highlight that such a tendency is enforced by an overemphasis in economic analysis on the mere exchange of goods. On the contrary, it seems relevant to shift focus back to the determinants of the production of goods and services. Standard descriptions of market institutions aim to create a harmonious picture of frictionless exchange between alleged equal participants. This institutional economic conception believes in the moral good of the market and its equilibrating forces by creating moral communities, but it ignores the aforementioned evolutionary dilemmas. Other institutionalist approaches focusing on inherent power relations and a realist social development agenda are marginalized. We have argued for a (re)vitalization of a realist institutionalist approach in evolutionary political economy that takes the accumulation of capital as the core issue of any institutionalization process. For this very reason we have presented clear and concrete theoretical attempts for a road map dealing seriously with evolutionary dilemmas in political economy. Knowledge emerges as a systemic feature of economies, rather than being individually constructed or socially determined. It is shared by actors and institutions, hence relations in social problem structures matter most for the coordination of common expectations in a plural world. From an analytical perspective we emphasize the mesoeconomic level of social interaction where emerging platform sizes may lead to concrete institutionalization. Complexity science and computational simulation offer promising tools in modeling such processes where trust and power become integrated as systemic rather than atomistic concepts. In particular, the agent-based methodology creates new chances in economic education and policy-making, since simulations provoke real-utopian visions for social actors. As evolutionary political economists we nevertheless highlight the historical dimension, which points to an inherent limit to reducing social phenomena to computational models and emphasizes the need for a pluralistic stance on theories and methods. In this sense learning involves a synthesis of history and simulation, which is required to pose sensible responses to the dilemmas of evolutionary appraisal and political participation in evolutionary political economy.

References

Alvaredo, Fecundo, Atkinson, Anthony, Piketty, Thomas, and Saez, Emmanuel (2013) "The top 1 percent in international and historical perspective," *Journal of Economic Perspectives*, 27 (3): 3–20.

Aoki, Masahiko (2007) "Endogenizing institutions and institutional changes," *Journal of Institutional Economics*, 3 (1): 1–31.

Ayres, Robert U. (1998) "Eco-thermodynamics: economics and the second law," *Ecological Economics*, 26: 189–209.

Berger, Sebastian and Elsner, Wolfram (2008) "European contributions to evolutionary institutional economics: the cases 'open-systems approach' (OSA) and 'cumulative circular causation' (CCC)," in Hardy Hanappi and Wolfram Elsner (eds), *Advances in Evolutionary Institutional Economics*. Cheltenham: Edward Elgar.

Böhm-Bawerk, Eugen von (1975 [1914]) *Macht oder ökonomisches Gesetz?* Darmstadt: Wissenschaftliche Verlagsgesellschaft.

Bowles, Samuel and Gintis, Herbert (2011) *A Cooperative Species*. Princeton, NJ: Princeton University Press.

Boyd, Robert and Richerson, Peter J. (2005) *The Origin and Evolution of Cultures*. Oxford: Oxford University Press.

Boyer, Robert (2008) "Pierre Bourdieu, a theoretician of change? The view from Régulation Theory," in Alexander Ebner and Nikolaus Beck (eds), *The Institutions of the Market. Organizations, Social Systems, and Governance*. Oxford: Oxford University Press, pp. 348–98.

Braudel, Fernand (1995 [1987]) *A History of Civilizations*. London: Penguin Books.

Brown, Doug (1991) "Thorstein Veblen meets Eduard Bernstein: toward an institutionalist theory of mobilization politics," *Journal of Economic Issues*, 25 (3): 689–708.

Bunge, Mario A. (1967) *Scientific Research, Volume II*. Berlin: Springer.

Bunge, Mario A. (1996) *Finding Philosophy in Social Science*. New Haven, CT: Yale University Press.

Bunge, Mario A. (1999 [1998]) *Social Science Under Debate: A Philosophical Perspective*. Toronto: University of Toronto Press.

Bunge, Mario A. (2000) "Systemism: the alternative to individualism and holism," *Journal of Socio-Economics*, 29: 147–57.

Bunge, Mario A. (2004) "How does it work: the search for explanatory mechanisms," *Philosophy of the Social Sciences*, 34 (2): 182–210.

Castells, Manuel (2009) *Communication Power*. New York: Oxford University Press.

Dobusch, Leonhard and Kapeller, Jakob (2012) "Heterodox United vs. Mainstream City? Sketching a framework for interested pluralism in economics," *Journal of Economic Issues*, 46 (4): 1035–57.

Dopfer, Kurt, Foster, John, and Potts, Jason (2004) "Micro-meso-macro," *Journal of Evolutionary Economics*, 14 (3): 263–79.

Elsner, Wolfram (1986) *Ökonomische Institutionenanalyse – Paradigmatische Entwicklung der ökonomischen Theorie und der Sinn eines Rückgriffs auf die ökonomische Klassik am Beispiel der Institutionenanalyse ("Property Rights")*. Berlin: Duncker & Humblot.

Elsner, Wolfram (2006) "Heterodoxe Ökonomik und ihre Einbeziehung in eine pluralistische Lehre," in Thomas Dürmeier, Tanja Egan-Krieger, und Helge Peukert (eds), *Die Scheuklappen der Wirtschaftswissenschaft*. Marburg: Metropolis Verlag, pp. 145–60.

Elsner, Wolfram (2010) "The process and a simple logic of 'meso.' Emergence and the co-evolution of institutions and group size," *Journal of Evolutionary Economics*, 20: 445–77.

Elsner, Wolfram (2013) "State and the future of the 'citadel' and of the heterodoxies in economics: challenges and dangers, convergence and cooperation," *European Journal of Economics and Economic Policies: Intervention*, 10: 286–98.

Elsner, Wolfram (2015) *Policy Implications of Economic Complexity and Complexity Economics*, MPRA Working Paper No. 63252.

Elsner, Wolfram and Heinrich, Torsten (2011) "Coordination on 'meso'-levels: on the co-evolution of institutions, networks and platform size," in Stefan Mann (ed.), *Sectors Matter! Exploring Mesoeconomics*, Heidelberg: Springer, pp. 115–63.

Elsner, Wolfram, Heinrich, Torsten, and Schwardt, Henning (2015) *The Microeconomics of Complex Economies: Evolutionary, Institutional, Neoclassical, and Complexity Perspectives*. Amsterdam: Academic Press.

Epstein, Joshua (ed.) (2006) *Generative Social Science. Studies in Agent-Based Computational Modeling*. Princeton, NJ: Princeton University Press.

Georgescu-Roegen, Nicholas (1971) *The Entropy Law and the Economic Process*. Cambridge, MA: Harvard University Press.

Hanappi, Hardy (2007) *On the Nature of Knowledge*. Paper presented at the Ausschuss für Evolutorische Ökonomik (Verein für Socialpolitik), Münster (Germany), 5–7 July.

Hayek, Friedrich A. von (1978) *New Studies in Philosophy, Politics, Economics and the History of Ideas*. London: Routledge.

Heinrich, Torsten and Schwardt, Henning (2013) "Institutional inertia and institutional change in an expanding normal-form game," *Games*, 4: 398–425.

Hobsbawm, Eric (1996 [1975]) *The Age of Capital: 1848–1875*. New York: Vintage Books.

Hodgson, Geoffrey M. (2012) *From Pleasure Machines to Moral Communities. An Evolutionary Economics without Homo Economicus*. Chicago: University of Chicago Press.

Kapp, Karl W. (1977) "Environment and technology: new frontiers for the social and natural sciences," *Journal of Economic Issues*, 11: 527–40.

Langton, C. G. (1993) "Artificial life" (editor's introduction), *Artificial Life*, Vol. 1, pp. v–viii.

Macy, Michael W. and Willer, Robert (2002) "From factors to actors: computational sociology and agent-based modeling, *Annual Review of Sociology*, 28: 143–66.

Mandeville, Bernard (1962 [1714]) *The Fable of the Bees or Private Vices, Public Benefits*. New York: Capricorn Books.

Marx, Karl (2001 [1867]) *Das Kapital. Kritik der politischen Ökonomie. Band 1: Der Produktionsprozeß des Kapitals*. 20. Auflage, Marx-Engels-Werke Band 23. Berlin: Dietz Verlag.

Mill, John S. (1909 [1848]) *Principles of Political Economy with Some of Their Applications to Social Philosophy*, 7th edn. London: Longmans, Green & Co.

Miller, John H. and Page, Scott E. (2007) *Complex Adaptive Systems: An Introduction to Computational Models of Social Life*. Princeton, NJ: Princeton University Press.

Myrdal, Gunnar (2002 [1953]) *The Political Element in the Development of Economic Theory: A Collection of Essays on Methodology*. Abingdon: Routledge.

Neumann, John von and Morgenstern, Oskar (2004 [1944]) *Theory of Games and Economic Behavior*, 3rd edn. Princeton, NJ: Princeton University Press.

Ostrom, Elinor (2012) "Why do we need to protect institutional diversity?" *European Political Science*, 11: 128–47.

Pareto, Vilfredo (1955) *Allgemeine Soziologie*. Tübingen: Mohr.

Piketty, Thomas (2014) *Capital in the 21st Century*. Cambridge, MA: Harvard University Press.

Piketty, Thomas and Saez, Emmanuel (2014) "Inequality in the long run," *Science*, 344: 838–44.

Ricardo, David (2005 [1815]) "Essay on the influence of a low price of corn on the profits of stock," in Piero Sraffa and Maurice H. Dobb (eds), *The Works and Correspondence of David Ricardo*, Vol. 4, *Pamphlets and Papers 1815–1823*. Indianapolis, IN: Liberty Fund, pp. 1–42.

Robbins, Lionel (1932) *An Essay on the Nature & Significance of Economic Science*. London: Macmillan.

Rothschild, Kurt W. (1971) *Power in Economics*. London: Harmondsworth.

Rothschild, Kurt W. (2002) "The absence of power in contemporary economic theory," *Journal of Socio-Economics*, 31: 433–42.

Schumpeter, Joseph A. (1954) *History of Economic Analysis*. Oxford: Oxford University Press.

Simon, Herbert A. (1991) "Bounded rationality and organizational learning," *Organization Science*, 2 (1): 125–34.

Smith, Adam (2000 [1759]) *The Theory of Moral Sentiments*. New York: Prometheus.

Veblen, Thorstein B. (1970 [1899]) *The Theory of the Leisure Class*. London: Unwin.

Wäckerle, Manuel, Rengs, Bernhard, and Radax, Wolfgang (2014) "An agent-based model of institutional life-cycles," *Games*, 5 (3): 160–87.

Wald, Abraham (1945) "Statistical decision functions which minimize the maximum risk," *Annals of Mathematics*, 46 (2): 265–80.

Part II

Institutional and evolutionary approaches to policy analysis

4 Using the social fabric matrix to strengthen the analysis and modeling of complex systems for original institutional economics

F. Gregory Hayden

Introduction

To make for a more reasonable society requires – in addition to all the various political battles that are necessary – arduous real-world research, as called for by the social fabric matrix approach (SFM-A) to analysis, in conjunction with original institutional economics (OIE) concepts, pragmatic philosophy, and general systems principles. This is consistent with John Dewey's statement that pragmatism "introduces responsibility into the intellectual life" (1909: 312). The SFM-A requires research to find, define, explain, and integrate the detailed relationships of real-world components and happenings that specifically concern us. Karl Polanyi, from whose work the term "social fabric matrix" was taken, emphasized that such research leads to a finding that policy is paramount in structuring the real-world system that humans inhabit (1957: 249–50). So where are we with regard to the SFM-A for guiding analysis so that we can design policy for a more reasonable society? What have we learned about and from the SFM-A? To provide answers to those questions is the main purpose of this chapter.

OIE is becoming a science of systems complexity, as explained by F. Gregory Hayden (1989: 12–69, 2006, 2015); Saeed Parto (2005); Wolfram Elsner (2007, 2012); Wolfram Elsner and Torsten Heinrich (2009); Wolfram Elsner and Henning Schwardt (2015); Tara Natarajan, Wolfram Elsner, and Scott Fullwiler (2009); Vladislav Valentinov (2013, 2014); Claudius Gräbner (2016).

Consistent with complexity, the main purpose here is to extend the SFM-A and its analytical technology, the social fabric matrix (SFM), according to: (1) what has been learned about them due to their applications; and (2) what is needed from them in order to assist in modeling complex systems. This is accomplished below, with attention given directly to the SFM-A and SFM and to their relationship to particular concerns. The particular concerns include the concepts of agents and agent-based models, open systems, meso modeling, variant social criteria, rules and regulations, and the limitations of Darwinian evolution, as explained in their respective sections below. All concerns considered here are included because of their relevance to OIE's recognition of the complexity of systems. This author's conception of the meaning of complex systems is explained in Hayden (2006: 51–60 and 94–106, and 2015: 3–6). The SFM-A was developed to integrate ontological approaches and knowledge about systems principles and OIE, while the SFM was developed in order to apply such approaches and knowledge to research about working relationships in real-world settings (see http://cba.unl.edu/academic-programs/departments/economics/sfm/ for examples of the SFM).

The SFM-A approach differs from the SFM

Let us begin with the clarification made by Fullwiler *et al.* (2009: 1–3) about the difference between the SFM-A and the SFM. They explained that the SFM-A is an approach to scientific analysis that is broader than the SFM. Thus, although the SFM was designed to allow for the articulation of the SFM-A, the SFM-A can be utilized alone as a study of scientific methodology, to conduct analysis separate from the SFM and to guide applied analysis with models and techniques other than that of the SFM. "The SFM-A provides … a framework that is comprehensive and adaptable to a wide variety of socioeconomic and policy issues" (Fullwiler *et al.*, 2009: 3) while "the SFM enables a rigorous *way to go about thinking* about a particular problem or issue, from which useful information and efficient solutions can be obtained" (Fullwiler *et al.*, 2009: 9). The SFM-A is often utilized without the SFM. However, without the completion of an SFM, the application of institutionalist concepts and systems principles and the capture of the integrated detail necessary for understanding a system or making policy are hindered.

Distinction between original SFM-A digraph and the SFM application

In addition to recognition of the distinction between the SFM-A and the SFM, recognition of the distinction between the general SFM-A digraph and the application of the SFM to define and explain the system of a particular problem needs to be made. The general SFM-A digraph (presented here as Figure 4.1) found in *Policymaking for a Good Society* (Hayden, 2006: 18) contains feedback loops for every component because it was drawn to express the general idea that through indirect component deliveries, every component could, in the final accounting, contribute to an indirect impact on itself (2006: 18). The general feedback idea is correct, but its representation, as presented in Figure 4.1, could lead to the conclusion that in a specific analysis of a problem with the SFM, all particular components directly deliver to themselves.[1] They do not in reality, and, therefore, should not when completing the SFM. Because institutions function to service other institutions, social institutions directly deliver to other institutions (e.g. households deliver money to corporations) in a real-world situation, and, because ecological elements function to service other ecological elements (e.g. earthworms transform rocks and leaves to soil and deliver it to grasses), ecological system elements should be shown to deliver to each other. Thus those two sets of components in Figure 4.1 should exhibit direct feedback loops among their components. The other sets of components – cultural values, social beliefs, attitudes, and technology – should not have feedback loops in Figure 4.1. Cultural values do not make feedback deliveries to each other because they are given by the culture (not shown in Figure 4.1).

Social beliefs do not deliver directly to each other; thus, there should not be a feedback loop, as Figure 4.1 can be interpreted to indicate. Social beliefs are not what some person believes. A person may know of some beliefs, but the massive number of beliefs is not legitimized because people know about them and/or believe in them. In fact, many people may not believe in them, but they are still legitimate and enforced. Social beliefs are specified, held, and enforced by numerous institutions including legislative bodies, courts, factory operational manuals, public and private executive branches, government agencies, religious organizations, universities, and so forth. Attorneys probably know more about the specifics of social beliefs in modern society than any other group – this being one of the reasons for the explosion in the legal literature about normative law. Beyond being specified, held, and enforced by institutions, when conflicts among beliefs arise, it is within and among institutions where the struggle takes place in order to settle on the accepted beliefs. Beliefs are formulated by institutions; thus, there is no feedback among beliefs independent of institutions.

Because of the ease with which minds can confuse and manipulate attitudes, attitudes can make deliveries to attitudes; that is, one attitude in a person's mind can influence other attitudes held by the same person and, if acted on, could lead to the wrong response to social signs and symbols. An example is where a religious institution is allowed to teach that a member should not associate with people of

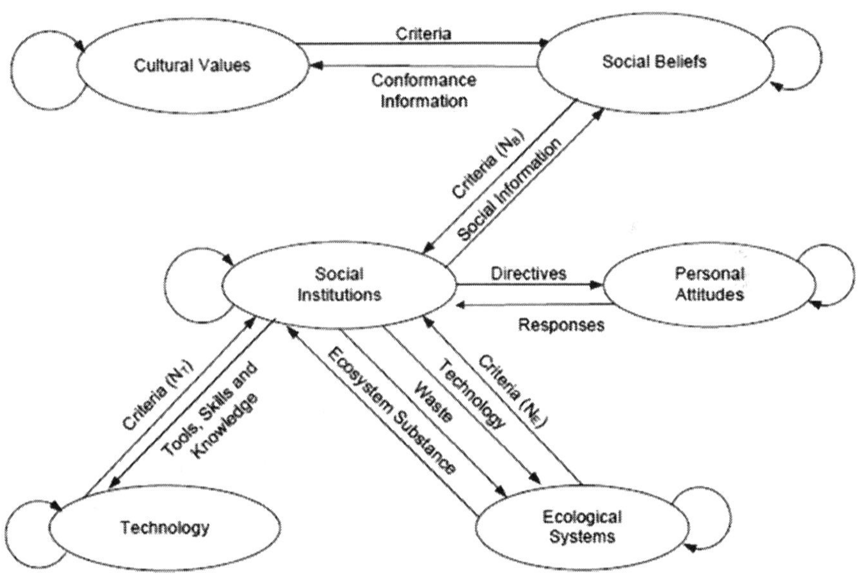

Figure 4.1 Integrated systems

Source: Hayden (2006).

another religious institution (legal in the US). That member may confuse the attitudes of the religious institution with what the attitudes are to be at the factory when that person is in charge of hiring, and may not want to hire people of the other religion (illegal in the US). In this example, the wrong attitude would lead to worker discrimination due to religion (and harm economic productivity). Persons are taught all kinds of attitudes for use on the job. For example, workers in a factory are trained to respond a certain way to what comes to them on the assembly line. Or, as another example, medical technicians who administer echocardiograms are trained to respond in a particular way to the calculus symbols on the computer screen. In both these examples, the personnel could get the idea that they should respond differently. However, in modeling social institutions, the direct delivery among attitudes becomes relevant only if the institutions allow for distorted attitudes to be expressed with the incorrect response to the signs and symbols. Persons may, in their own minds, have different ideas about how they should respond, but that does not affect the general behavior because institutions regulate, monitor, and control their actions. How appropriate the actions are depends on the institutions, not on the feedback among attitudes in the minds of different actors. Thus Figure 4.1 should not have a feedback loop for attitudes in research applications of the SFM.

Technology directly delivers criteria only to institutions, not to itself. Thus, when modeling systems with the SFM for specific problem areas, criteria are the only delivery made by technology, and the technology rows in the matrix deliver criteria only to cells in institutional columns; thus, there is no direct feedback to itself. Parts of one technology can be combined with other technology to generate a new technology – that is, a new combination of tools, skills, and knowledge – but the new combination is created by institutions (see directed edge from social institutions to technology in the illustrations above and below). For example, new apps for smart phones are not made by smart phones. After new technological combinations are made, they are used by institutions to deliver goods and/or services within and among institutions and to apply to ecological systems. The technological criteria guide many judgments made in the institutions, especially about the maintenance of the technology.

In summary, feedback loops in Figure 4.1 should be limited to the social institutions and ecological systems components. This is the case, not because the feedback loops of the other components are necessarily wrong in terms of the idea of general indirect systems feedback, but because Figure 4.1 misleads analysts to seek direct feedback loops where they do not belong in specific SFM applications that define deliveries between particular rows and columns. The changes needed in Figure 4.1, as explained here, are made in the SFM-A figure below.

Keep the SFM diagonal for institutions free of entries

Social institutions deliver to other social institutions; thus, each institution should have its own row and column in order to be able to demonstrate the deliveries among them. Thus, the diagonal cells of the SFM should not have entries. In the case where an institutional organization makes deliveries to the subunits of its own organization and the subunits make deliveries among themselves and to the parent organization, the row/column entries of the single organization should be divided into as many rows/columns as there are subunits that can make deliveries to each other, plus a row and column for the parent. This means there would be no entries in the matrix diagonal. This is not done to follow the rule in Boolean algebra to keep the diagonal empty, because seldom will Boolean manipulations be appropriate with the SFM (although there are cases where it is). Instead, it is done in order to show what is going on inside the institutional organization among its parts, and to be able to show what deliveries are being made to and from components outside the organization by and to the different organizational subunits. (See Figure 4.4 below for an example in which the SFM diagonal does not have entries.)

An agent's place in the SFM-A and SFM

Since at least the time of Aristotle, the claim has been made that the economy is humanity – that is, the economic system is the result of decisions and actions of and relations among human beings. In the process of explaining Aristotle's ethics, Irene van Staveren elucidated Aristotle's understanding of how systems are formed. For him, systems originate as a consequence of the deliberations of "rational economic actors" to form "personal relationships" (van Staveren, 2001: 153). The relationships between persons form an interdependence that leads to interaction and allocation of resources (ibid.: 47). The "economic actors combine their activities" (ibid.: 204) to form a "social contract" (ibid.: 79) and an integration of exchange relations (ibid.: 80). These claims of Aristotle are misleading; thus, they are another set of his ideas that should be retired.

The economy, as part of the social system in general, is the result of the integration of the basic SFM-A components of cultural values, social beliefs, technology, institutions, personal attitudes, and ecology – that is, economies are the result of the working of sociotechnical systems. Yes, humans are involved, but so are horses, intestinal bacteria, and trucks. Yes, humans, as directed actors in overlapping institutions, make decisions, but so do computers and dogs. When either the SFM-A or the applied SFM is utilized, it becomes clear that the economy is not humanity. Humans are part of an overall complex system into which they are integrated and are dependent on the makeup and integration of the six basic components plus the sub-elements of those components such as rules, regulations, standards, species, and so forth. It is necessary to understand such a system in order to understand a set of humans and to explain why humans prosper or suffer, why they are competent or helpless, why they are educated or ignorant. To convince humans that they are the economy means that they will not know how to approach the system or how to work in institutions to realign the economy in order to alleviate suffering and decrease helplessness. Instead, they will be looking to blame humanity for problems. The tendency in economics to make humans the determinant center of the economy has led to some confusing concepts, one of which is the definition some have given to the concept of agent.

Ambiguously defined agents and arbitrarily structured agent-based models

The concept of agent has been defined in numerous ways, but it is generally defined as an alternative word for a rational-calculating individual, as conceptualized in neoclassical economics. Such a person cannot be found in the real word. No person is born an agent. No person is born a human (Becker, 1952: 283). And, certainly, no person is born an individual, because the birthing process is very system-intensive and extensive, with broad-based social and technological involvement. After birth, extensive dependence follows. Usually what is meant by such use of the term agent is a single homo sapiens actor. The use of the term single homo sapiens actor emphasizes the helplessness of such an entity if it is not surrounded by a social matrix that furnishes protection, provisioning, and socialization. Intensive and extensive institutional social shaping is necessary before a society accepts an actor as competent to be an agent in an institutional setting.

When does agency designation follow the birth of a person? A person becomes an agent when a principal in a social institution so designates or makes an agreement with the person to act to take responsibility in a manner defined by the needs of the principal. The same is true when a corporation becomes an agent for a principal; for example, when corporations agree to contracts to serve as an agent to the government. If a principal is not involved, an entity is not an agent in a social process.

It became clear that a particular person does not fit the definition of being an individual because it became clear in modeling that people are far too dependent on the complex social matrix to be considered an isolated and indivisible separate being, which is the definition of individual. When that became clear, the term agent was slowly adopted. This has led to at least four problems.

First, although the term has changed, agent, in many cases, continues to be used and modeled as an isolated and indivisible individual with no indication about which principal in which institution generated the agency arrangement nor about the limits and boundaries of the agent's discretion and power to act.

Second, the agent is usually assumed to be an abstract decision-maker – usually a sapient one – busy from the neck up, but not active as an agent who has the responsibility to correctly perform work, for example as part of a technological function – say as a natural gas pipeline welder working under a contract.

Third, the assumption is made that social systems are agent-based, with the structure and network of systems growing out of the decisions of agents, which is contrary to what, as stated above, institutionalists have found about social systems.

Fourth, the term agent has come to mean any and every kind of entity – ranging from corporations to mosquitoes. This is especially the case in an agent-based model (ABM), and thus no kind of entity, because any concept that means everything is useless. As an example, Lin Zhu *et al.* claim to use an ABM to explain mosquito activity with regard to sugar consumption, rest, malaria parasite transmission, and biting of persons in a village (2015). They found that the more sugar and resting areas spread across a village for mosquitoes, the greater the biting activity and malaria transmission. However, mosquitoes do not determine the activities in the system. Their need for sugar and rest came from evolution; it was not bestowed by a principal (nor by the mosquitoes). In fact, in the study, various system components and social activities that contribute to the mosquitoes' activity are mentioned – to include a village (which mosquitoes did not establish), people, the distribution of sugar and resting pods provided by the social system, the lack of mosquito pesticide (that is abundantly applied in most places), the decision not to annihilate the mosquito population with the release of large numbers of sterile mosquitoes (as is done in some areas), and so forth. The system is not based on the decisions and activities of mosquitoes; thus, the system is not agent-based and neither are other complex systems.

If there are agents in socioeconomic systems, it is because of principal–agent relationships established to fulfill system activities. The principal–agent relationship is different with different kinds of institutions and among different societies. The principal–agent relationship has a long history in economic literature, but that relationship seems to be forgotten when writers turn agents into ambiguous entities that have all-powerful (but invalidly defined) connections in models. Furthermore, although the neoclassical definition of a rational-calculating individual is usually the definition of an agent in economic literature, there is no specific definition of what an agent is to be in the ABM literature.

Social systems are not agent-based

The agent-based literature often outlines a set of very different kinds of representative agents that does not indicate: (1) the complex system that defines the relationships among the agents as defined by an SFM; (2) which institution(s) laid down the responsibilities, duties, rights, prohibitions, and liabilities for each agent; (3) the deliveries that are expected from each; and (4) the theory that explains how a system might be generated from the agents to answer those questions. Different kinds of agents act according to different rules and regulations in different social situations, and each has different duties in different situations. What a corporation does in a production process is different from what a worker does, and the same corporation acts differently from country to country as laws and traditions change from country to country. A corporation in the US does not whip its workers, yet cases exist in which the same corporation in other countries does whip the workers. To make the concept of agent meaningful, it needs to be defined in a principal–agent relationship by an SFM-A, and to make it useful, the specific principal–agent positions need be included in an SFM. Socioecological systems are complex systems that are not agent-based. An analyst may wrongly designate humans or mosquitoes as agents; however, the structure and processes of socioecological systems do not emanate from a base of humans or mosquitoes. Humans and mosquitoes play roles as actors directed by the socioecological system. Socioecological systems are the result of the integration of the six component categories included in the SFM-A, with normative criteria being important for integrating the six. The key point, to paraphrase a reviewer of a draft of this chapter, is as follows. Humans cannot be individual agents as used in the ABM because humans are inherently ontologically non-individualistic because of the six vital components recognized in the SFM-A, which make for the system and which contribute to the creation of humans in the context of their social, ecological, cultural, and technological spaces.

Principal–agent relationships fulfill important duties and perform important functions, as do contractual agreements, but social-system structures and processes are not an outgrowth of agent actions. Instead, agents are created, and their duties are defined and guided by institutions. The fact that institutions are not agent-based is one of the reasons why the structures of ABMs are so arbitrarily defined. It is not possible to have a general approach or structure for completing ABMs when they are devoid of a valid conceptual base.

Principal–agent relationships in the SFM

In the SFM, the principals and agents are delivered by the different row components to the cells of the column components that represent the institutions of which the principal and agents are members. An agent does not appear as a row or column component. For example, family institutions can contract as principals with corporations as agents to perform certain functions or make decisions, which are limited by their agreement. In such cases, the institutional row of the principal delivers to the cell in the agent's column the agreement that specifies the responsibilities of the principal, and the institutional row of the agent delivers to the cell in the principal's column the agreement that specifies the duties and responsibilities of the agent. Upon reciprocal agreement, the principal institution's row in the SFM delivers monitoring and enforcement of the agent's activities to the institution of the agent (to the SFM cell in the agent institution's column) and to the columnar cells of other institutions that might be involved with the monitoring and enforcement, such as government institutions. The institution of the agent delivers instructions, regulations, contracts, monitoring, goods and/or services, and enforcement to all the cells of the columnar institutions necessary to fulfill the delivery of the goods and/or services to the principal's cell. The principal–agent arrangement does not complete its function in the social system if the institutional organization of the agent does not deliver to other institutions. The institutional organizations decide which persons in their respective institutions complete what functions in order to fulfill the agreement. There is no lone agent, as assumed in neoclassical economics. In cases when the principal is negligent in monitoring and enforcing the agent's activities and a third party is harmed (harmful deliveries made in the agent's row to the institutional column of the third party), the government often intervenes to protect the third party. This leads to additional deliveries from the government row in the SFM to cells of the various institutional columns necessary to bring about appropriate agent activity.

An occasion when an ABM would be entered in an SFM as a row/column component is if an ABM is used for a research project and there is a need to determine its effect on the research project. In such a case, the ABM would be entered as a technology to trace what criteria it delivered for institutions involved in the research project to use to make judgments. It would be entered, as Scott Fullwiler explained double-entry accounting is entered, as a technology row/column in the SFM (2009: 124–8).

Making the SFM-A consistent with open systems

Richard Adkisson extended the SFM-A to include the open systems principle and emphasized that any system analyzed should be open to its surrounding environment. Adkisson explains that the essence of the openness principle is the simultaneous connection between a system and the surrounding environment (2009: 31). Such a case is shown in Figure 4.2, where the system being analyzed, which is represented by the SFM-A digraph, is placed inside a boundary that separates the SFM-A digraph from the surrounding environment, except that the boundary is not closed. Consistent with the definition of system openness, there are deliveries (indicated with the arrows at the bottom of the figure) to the system from the environment and deliveries from the system (represented by the SFM-A digraph) to the environment. To take account of this, when constructing an SFM about the real world, a row and column need to be added to the system's matrix for the environment, or rows and columns if different components of the environment make deliveries. When constructing the matrix, the deliveries from the row(s) of the environment should be delivered to the specific column(s) that are impacted by such delivery. The delivery from the environment is not delivered generally to the system as a whole, for that would mean that there would be direct deliveries in every column (every cell in the environment row would contain a 1); instead, there should be an entry only in the SFM cells in the columns, for which there are direct deliveries from the row(s) of the environment to specific column cell(s). For example, if the system is the organ transplant unit of a hospital, the traffic environment that contains motorcycle accidents provides many organs to the hospital – more so in the summer. It is important to indicate where the organs are delivered. They are not delivered to all components in the matrix; instead, the deliveries should be indicated in the cell from the environment row to the hospital surgery column.

Generally, there is an interest in deliveries from system entities to environment entities only if the consequence of the delivery from the system influences the delivery from the environment to the system. It is only a statistical interest and not an explanatory one. Thus that connection should be presented in the matrix without an explanation of the intervening deliveries among the components in the environment that make for that connection. It is necessary to know the connection to understand how the system's own export to the environment is influencing itself, but it is not necessary to know how the connection is made. This means there should be non-system rows and columns in the SFM to record any statistical

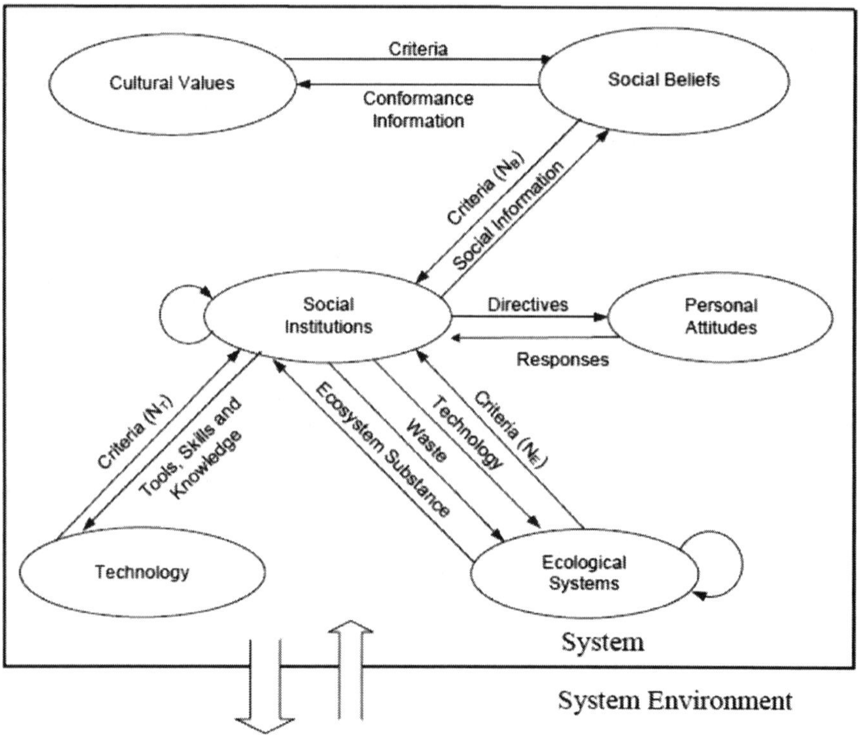

Figure 4.2 The social fabric matrix approach: relationships among values, beliefs, attitudes, institutions, technology, and the ecological system

connections between system outputs to the environment and system inputs from the environment.

Adkisson's opening of the SFM-A also increased complexity, or system "wickedness" as explained by Matthew Gray and Roderic Gill (2009: 8), for conducting real-world analysis with the SFM. Two new questions that have to be dealt with as a result of openness are: first, where are criteria from the environment delivered within the SFM; and, second, how are deliveries from the environment dealt with in the SFM when delivered directly to deliveries in the system rather than to components?

Normative belief and technological criteria from the environment outside the SFM system are delivered to social institutions – from the environment row(s) to specific institutional column(s) – because institutions are the components with the ability and responsibility to make judgments and decisions. Ecological criteria from the environment can be delivered to social institutions and/or the ecological system. They are delivered to social institutions when they are ecological criteria to which the social institutions respond by making judgments, as is the case with ecological criteria within the system. They are delivered directly to the ecological system when the ecological criteria are of a biological or physical nature that changes the working of the ecological system. In turn, such a change in the portion of the ecology in the system impacted by the environment may change one or more deliveries from the ecology to the social institutions in the SFM.

Deliveries from a system's environment may be delivered directly to deliveries in the system (to the directed edges in the SFM digraph) rather than directly to system components (in the SFM columns). This can create problems in the system for policymaking and institutional adjustment because it leads to unintended deliveries that are inconsistent with the system's normative criteria and decisions. In such cases, the components in the environment outside the system are not programmed to conform to deliveries of rows to columns as specified by the normative criteria and rules inside the system. A recent example can be seen with sheep in the French Alps where the sheep are a technology that is delivered to the ecological system by owners to harvest grass. The problem arises due to the increase in the wolf population in the region as a result of French government programs. The sheep raising and marketing system has different sequences of deliveries in the process of getting the sheep to market. The outside environment is the French government injecting more wolves into the system; thus, more of the sheep are killed by the wolves without the shepherding system making decisions for that effect. The killing is delivered directly to system deliveries – the sheep. Another example is the current problem of children acquiring asthma from walking to school because of air pollution from manufacturing industries. The pollution is delivered from the environment directly to the children that the system sends to school. This is inconsistent with the intent of either the family institution that sends them to school (family row to school column in the SFM) or the schools that send them to walk home (school row to family column in the SFM). In both of these examples, the system deliveries to the recipient columnar cells are deteriorated. Such deterioration is detected by institutional organizations in the recipient columns, and, therefore, would be entered in the SFM as a delivery in a column cell. The deteriorating activity from the system environment row is designated in the SFM as a change in the quantity and/or quality of the delivery to the system column. The system row delivery to the system column is different than intended – changed by the delivery in the environment row to the same system column. That set of deliveries will continue unless the institutional components initiate changes in the original system components when detected or establish new components to deal with the environmental impact.

The SFM-A and meso modeling

When modeling – whether principal–agent contracts, investment institutions, normative criteria, or whatever – two concerns of interest are the kinds of relationships among the parts and system boundary delineation. In conducting complex system modeling in economics, dissatisfaction grew with the simple concepts of dividing analysis between a macroeconomy and a microeconomy. Each suffered from its history, with microeconomics meaning the neoclassical concern with indivisible individual decision-makers and macroeconomics meaning concern with interactions organized among income and expenditure institutions in order to know how to stabilize the macroeconomy at points of acceptable employment and price level. Their conceptual foundations and purposes were so different that integration was not possible. Additionally, neither was based on the foundation of integrating the six components of the SFM-A. Thus, they could not be unified. This led to the meso concept for modeling complex systems – the middle way that could reach out to what was needed from what had been called microeconomics and macroeconomics, and has also led to much disagreement about how to construct meso modeling (see Dopfer *et al.*, 2004; Elsner, 2007; Elsner and Heinrich, 2009; Elsner and Schwardt, 2015). A basic necessity when constructing any complex system analysis is the necessity of constructing a boundary to know what is in and what is out of the system and how what is in and out relate to each other; that is, what small, medium, and large systems are to be fitted together. The question is about how to know what parts of a system to include in the analysis and what scientific knowledge to use. The philosophy of pragmatism provides guidance.

Basic to pragmatic philosophy is the problem orientation to scientific research. It is not possible to know what to include in the model, what theories and models to use, and what database to generate without a definition of the problem to be solved. This means there is no given meso model. For models to be useful, they must change with the problem. The relevant system components can include both extensive macro entities like a global military force and micro entities like micro-organisms, given a particular problem. The SFM-A provides guidance to find the components and flow deliveries among the components consistent with the stated problem. The rows, columns, and cell deliveries of the SFM will be different for each different problem. The problem orientation for modeling guides the search through reality to capture the socioecological components and generate empirical indicators relevant to the problem being analyzed. That capture determines the makeup of the rows and columns in the SFM, and the deliveries between the rows and columns express how they are integrated.

Real-world systems contain variant criteria

Generally, social scientists have conveyed the idea that social institutions reflect normative social belief criteria that are held to be legitimate by society. The general idea has been that a requirement – strongly stated – for the existence of social processes is that they be consistent with legitimate normative social criteria. Analysis of the real world leads to a different conclusion. Legitimacy requires that social institutions be consistent with social beliefs because without consistency institutions will not be considered fair and just, a situation that generates social instability. Instability leads to negative consequences – "turmoil and violence," to use Walter Neale's term (1980: 393). However, societies sometimes exist with ongoing turmoil and violence.

It is not always necessary that social institutions follow legitimate normative belief criteria. With an SFM analysis, the task is to define the system as it exists, and when SFMs are completed, it is clear that systems exist with illegitimate criteria being regularly enforced and utilized – often accompanied with a good deal of instability. Such criteria have been defined and designated as variant criteria.

> Given the importance of normative criteria, one should not conclude that institutions are guided only by legitimate normative criteria that are consistent with what society believes to be appropriate – the community standards, so to speak. That is not the real-world case. Many criteria, rules, regulations, requirements, and attitudes that guide institutional and organizational operations are variant criteria, rules, regulations, and requirements. Although variations from normative ones, they are enforced to guide the working of institutional processes. They deviate from legitimate community standards, but are enforced in relevant societal settings. Some are not considered moral, but are legal. Some may be common practice without being stated in legal codes or court orders. Examples are practices of corporations when corporate campaign funds and lobbyists are used to establish variant laws and court decisions through legislative actions and court cases. Or they may be cases in which variant criteria are not legal; for example, the illegal abuse of workers in a factory setting. Variant criteria and rules with long-term application can be observed in an array of very different settings and spatial extension. One is when a farmer uses illegal pesticides. Another is when illegal aliens are hired by corporations. Still another is the imposition of neoliberal Western criteria and laws onto second- and third-world economies … Variant criteria need to be included in economic and policy analysis in order to know their effects on social, economic, and technological flows.
>
> Variant criteria usually depend on power to override laws and community standards. Conflict is established in institutions between normative criteria and variant criteria – the greater the variance of variant criteria from societal norms, the greater the level of resources that must be expended to maintain them through propaganda, security personnel, workforce turnover, lobbying expenses, instruments of violence, and so forth. All modern societal institutions, whether market, Islamic, socialist, or other orientation, have conflicts between normative criteria and variant criteria. This is the case with belief, ecological, and technological criteria. Since rapidly advancing technology leads societies to become more complex, hierarchical, and in a constant state of flux, there are more opportunities for various special interests to establish niches for variant criteria sets.
>
> (Hayden, 2011: 1215–16)

Thus variant social, technological, and ecological criteria need to be included, each with their own rows and columns when completing an SFM because, without their inclusion, the analysis cannot capture how the system works and how it is delivering the problem of interest.

Rules, regulations, and requirements are created by institutions

Because of work with the SFM in real-world settings, the importance of rules, along with accompanying regulations and requirements, becomes clear. A simplified example of the relationship found among rules, regulations, and requirements in the form of directives to persons and the resulting attitudes is simply outlined in Figure 4.3. Variant criteria, as explained above, are included as $VarC_B$, $VarC_T$, and $VarC_E$ in Figure 4.3 because they function along with legitimate belief, technology, and ecological criteria. Legitimate and variant criteria influence authority institutions (I_{A1}) such as courts and legislative bodies, which formulate and deliver rules to other authority institutions (I_{A2}) such as corporations and government agencies, which use the rules to formulate and deliver regulations to processing institutions (I_P) such as factory production centers, which direct requirements to persons in order to form attitudes so that persons can respond correctly to signs and symbols in the production centers. Contrary to some conceptualizations, work with the SFM leads to the finding that rules, regulations, and directed requirements are part of a much larger set of elements within institutions. Some economists have attempted to define those elements out of institutions and narrow the definition of institutions to rules. An institution is not limited to rules or systems of rules.

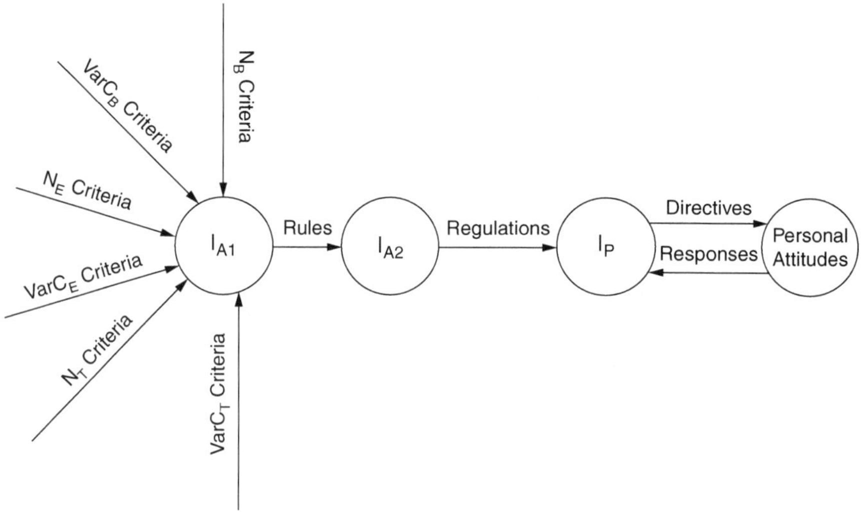

N_B – Belief Norms, N_E – Ecological Norms, N_T – Technological Norms, $VarC_B$ – Variant Belief Criteria, $VarC_E$ – Variant Ecological Criteria, $VarC_T$ – Variant Technological Criteria. I_{A1} – Authority Institution 1, I_{A2} – Authority Institution 2, I_P – Processing Institution.

Figure 4.3 From normative and variant criteria through rules, regulations, and required directives to personal action

Institutions formulate and enforce rules, and, in the case of authority institutions, deliver rules to other institutions to be made operational and enforced, but institutional organizations are much more than rules.

Institutions regularly take on new rules, which they could not do if they did not already exist to create and adopt rules. Institutions are patterns of social activity whose repetitive patterns include the organization and use of capital, technology, ecological substance, training, government monitors, knowledge, rules, and so forth – the list being dependent on the institutions involved and the problem being considered. Beyond the other functions of institutions, rule duties and responsibilities could not be carried out by institutions without all the other elements. SFM studies have clarified this in applied real-world studies. In all these SFM studies, the institutional list of non-rule components and elements is extensive. Beyond rules, the studies found that belief norms, regulations, requirements, technology, and ecological elements are involved in the institutional settings. The SFM contained in Figure 4.4, which depicts the US State of Nebraska educational finance system that delivers state money to primary and secondary public schools, illustrates that rules come from institutions that lead to deliveries made to other institutions (Hayden 2009).[2] As explained in the study, rules are delivered to the Nebraska Department of Education from the courts in cell (7,12) and from the Nebraska Legislature in cell (8,12), and, in turn, the Department of Education row delivers regulations to numerous institutional groups within state government in column 9 and columns 14 through 40. These groups perform calculations and deliver the calculations to other institutional groups as specified by requirement directives to the employees.[3] Rules cannot be implemented without respect to all the other elements of an institution, nor can an institution successfully implement rules and regulations without respect to surrounding institutions.

What researchers find when undertaking real-world analysis is that Figure 4.3 (above) is too simple. First, some of the normative and variant criteria that affect higher-level authority institutions will also directly affect lower-level authority and processing institutions. Second, alternative normative and variant criteria are likely to directly affect lower-level and processing institutions. Third, it is likely that rules delivered by higher-authority institutions will go to more than one lower-authority institution. Fourth, lower-level authority institutions are likely to make regulations for more than one kind of processing institution. Fifth, processing institutions often outsource the task of inculcating personnel with particular attitudes to other institutions – for example, for skill training. Sixth, the monitoring and enforcement of responses made by personnel are often outsourced to other institutions – for example, internal security corporations. This means that linear approaches to problems, as presented in Figure 4.3, are too simple when compared to conducting actual analysis with an SFM. All the criteria, institutions, technology, attitudes, and ecological components that deal with the rules, regulations, and requirements of a case need to be entered into an SFM so all the potential cells can be inspected to determine which contain deliveries.

Institutions that have rules, regulations, or requirements delivered to them (received in column cells) *must make further deliveries as rows*, if the process is not

Delivering Components ↓ / Receiving Components →			Social Beliefs						Authority Institutions							Processing Institutions for Regulations and Requirements																										
			Equity	Adequacy/Sufficiency	Cost/Efficiency	Comprehensive Size	Consolidation	Local Control	Courts/Legal System	Neb. Legislature/Govenor	Local K-12 Public Sch System	Property Tax Program	Property Wealth	Neb. Dept. of Education	Neb. Dept. of Revenue	Fall Membership	Formula Students	Weighted Formula Students	Limited English Proficiency	Indian Land Factor	Remoteness Factor	Proverty Factor	Adj Weighted Formula Stu	Excluded TGFOE Accts	Transportantion Allowance	Special Receipts	Adjusted GFOE	Cost Factor Growth	Aggregate Stu w/o Remoteness	Cost Group Cost/Student	Cost/Stu X Local Students	Temporary Aid Adj	Yield from Local Tax	Net Option Students	Net Option Funding	Allocated Income Tax Fund	Other Actual Receipts	Minimum Levy Adj	Lop Off	Small Sch Stabilization Adj	Stabilization Factor	Prior Year Deficiency & Correction
			1	2	3	4	5	6	7	8	9	10	11	12	13	14	15	16	17	18	19	20	21	22	23	24	25	26	27	28	29	30	31	32	33	34	35	36	37	38	39	40
Social Beliefs	Equity	1							1	1																																
	Adequacy/Sufficiency	2							1	1																																
	Cost/Efficiency	3							1	1																																
	Comprehensive Size	4							1	1																																
	Consolidation	5							1	1																																
	Local Control	6							1	1																																
Authority Institutions	Courts/Legal System	7								1	1	1	1	1	1																											
	Neb. Legislature/Govenor	8									1	1	1	1	1																											
	Local K-12 Public Sch System	9							1					1																												
	Property Tax Program	10									1		1																				1									
	Property Wealth	11																																								
	Neb. Dept. of Education	12									1					1	1	1	1	1	1	1	1	1	1	1	1	1	1	1	1	1	1	1	1	1	1	1	1	1	1	1
	Neb. Dept. of Revenue	13										1		1																												
Processing Institutions for Regulations and Requirements	Fall Membership	14															1																									
	Formula Students	15																1			1	1						1														
	Weighted Formula Students	16																					1						1					1								
	Limited English Proficiency	17																					1						1													
	Indian Land Factor	18																					1						1													
	Remoteness Factor	19																					1																			
	Proverty Factor	20																					1						1													
	Adj Weighted Formula Stu	21																													1											
	Excluded TGFOE Accts	22																									1															
	Transportation Allowance	23									1																1					1							1	1	1	
	Special Receipts	24									1																1					1					1		1	1	1	
	Adjusted GFOE	25																												1												
	Cost Factor Growth	26																												1												
	Aggregate Stu w/o Remoteness	27																												1												
	Cost Group Cost/Student	28																													1				1							
	Cost/Stu X Local Students	29									1																					1							1	1	1	
	Temporary Aid Adj	30									1																								1	1			1	1	1	
	Yield from Local Tax	31									1																												1	1	1	
	Net Option Students	32																																	1							
	Net Option Funding	33									1																									1			1	1	1	
	Allocated Income Tax Fund	34									1																												1	1	1	
	Processing Actual Receipts	35									1																												1	1	1	
	Minimum Levy Adj	36									1																									1			1	1	1	
	Lop Off	37									1																													1	1	
	Small Sch Stabilization Adj	38									1																														1	
	Stabilization Factor	39									1																															
	Prior Year Deficiency & Correction	40									1																												1			

Figure 4.4 Social fabric matrix of Nebraska state aid for a local K-12 public school system, 2006–7

to end at the delivery cell. For example, as stated above, in Figure 4.4 regulations and/or requirements are delivered from the Nebraska Department of Education row to cells in columns 14 through 40. If the columns of those cells do not, in turn, become rows 14 through 40 *that make further deliveries*, the amount of state monies would not be calculated and delivered to school districts.

System differentiation and elaboration and the SFM

A basic characteristic of systems is differentiation and elaboration (D&E) – that is, change. Because D&E is a basic principle of all systems, all systems have to react to change, especially with regard to the evaluation of the change in order to make decisions about whether the change is good and welfare-enhancing or bad and welfare-deteriorating. Social systems do this on a regular basis, and in modern societies change is continuous. The instrumental-ceremonial dichotomy literature of OIE is concerned with that evaluation and decision-making, and OIE's dichotomy literature emphasizes that optimality or welfare enhancement should not be expected from such decisions (Elsner, 2012). Different interpretative approaches for observing and explaining system D&E include evolution, self-organization, production, and emergence, with numerous models and different subcategories for each approach.

Limited analytical possibilities of Darwinian evolution

The majority of OIE interpretations of D&E in sociotechnical systems has been Darwinian evolution, used mainly as an analogy rather than as an analytical tool because Darwinian evolution has limited analytical possibilities for guiding the understanding of sociotechnical systems for the following reasons.

First, an inspection of the integrated system model in Figure 4.3 clarifies that Darwinian evolutionary theory is concerned with an explanation of a small bit in the component titled ecological systems. Although an important explanation for the evolution of species, one should not expect a theory about such a minute part of the whole to serve as a paradigm for the analysis of D&E for the components of the integrated system in Figure 4.2. Furthermore, such an approach is inconsistent with OIE rejection of reductionist modeling.

Second, although different scientific disciplines should borrow whatever is relevant from other disciplines, one should not expect biological models to provide much explanatory power about social systems. Economists have suffered embarrassment because of inappropriate borrowing in the past, most notably from Newtonian physics. Thus, we should not expect biological evolution theory to offer much more than an analogy for the analysis of social system change.

Third, the conceptualization of evolution in various scientific disciplines has been varied and diverse both within and across disciplines, but a general belief that has been prominent across disciplines has been the spirit of progress proclaiming that evolution is good – survival of the fittest, technological advancement, social progress, creative destruction, and so forth. Darwinian evolution models play into the ideological commitment to automatically conduct biased analysis with the idea that system D&E is good.

Fourth, Darwin's approach to evolution is inconsistent with what OIE has stressed, that is the importance of institutions and technology. Because Darwin did not incorporate either institutions or technology, his analysis with regard to species and soil has failed to indicate how we got to our current inventory of species and condition of soil. Today, the inventory of species cannot be understood by Darwin's paradigm because the exponential rate of destruction of species is a result of institutional and technological processes, simply stated. Likewise, this is true with regard to soil creation and erosion. Darwin drastically underestimated the years that it would take for the destruction of the mountain tops of the Appalachian Mountains in the US because corporate institutions have used mountain-destroying technology to get to the coal in the mountains more quickly because of the social criteria they used to judge success of their corporate institutions.

To explain D&E for complex socioeconomic systems as displayed in Figure 4.2, Geoffrey M. Hodgson and Thorbjørn Knudsen have argued for the relevance of a Darwinian sequence of variation, inheritance, and selection as an abstract universality (Hodgson, 2002: 259–60 and 269–73, and Hodgson and Knudsen, 2006: 2 and 14). The problems with this approach include the following. First, Darwin did not have an explanation for variation. Second, as clarified in the 1940s, Darwin's simple explanation of inheritance and selection was no longer accepted as sufficient in biology, and, in addition, an explanation for variation had been added. Today, the theory of biological evolution has progressed beyond the 1940s understanding – even further from Darwin's theory. Third, as explained above, knowledge obtained about only one concern in the ecological system of Figure 4.2 is of little assistance in the modeling of real-world systems as outlined in Figure 4.2. Finally, the insistence on universality is considered fallacious reasoning, and the adoption of universality forced Hodgson and Knudson to adopt other fallacious reasoning as well.[4]

D&E in the SFM

This author has explained how D&E can be expressed in general with the SFM by showing the gain and/or loss of rows and columns in the SFM and the gain and/or loss of deliveries between rows and columns (Hayden, 2006: 180–1). D&E can come about with any change in the socioecological system, thus making it more complex than for a biological species or ecological habitat alone. If, for example, an institution creates a new technological combination, that means there will be a new technological criteria being delivered to the institution(s). In turn, that means new rules, regulations, and requirements, which generate new processes that, in some cases, can impact on the ecological system and lead to consequences that are inconsistent with belief criteria. It is necessary to monitor and record such change in an SFM in order to be able to judge whether it is deleterious and, if so, to design policy to prevent it. Or, stated differently, when the SFM-A for socioecological analysis is used for policy analysis, it tends to emphasize precautionary principles. If precautionary monitoring is not implemented with a systemic analysis like the SFM, change will take place that is not monitored and may be impossible to reverse. It is not enough to just record the system. Given the potential powerful forces that can develop in modern society that make it very difficult and expensive to reverse harmful processes, analysis, monitoring, and precautionary action guided by complex system models become more important.

A general expression of D&E is not sufficient for the identification and explanation of change in the SFM. It is necessary to specify the detailed changes responsible for the D&E. For example, if there is a change in an institutional organization, that institution's changes in specific row delivery or deliveries to the columnar cells should be specified. If an invading army specifies new rules and regulations, those should be specified in the appropriate SFM columnar cells, along with the new institutional rows that need to be added to carry out the intent of the rules and regulations, along with the resulting deliveries to traditional-columnar institutions from the new institutions. If institutions deliver high volumes of greenhouse gases, new deliveries are made to ecological components from the resulting climate change, so those changed components need to be specified in the appropriate cells. This clarifies that D&E is complex; thus, its specifics and consequences need to be included in the SFM. It also clarifies why recognition of the complex systems principles is so important. The integration of the principles and the SFM characteristics is crucial for pragmatic analysis. This also clarifies why the work regarding complex systems and the instrumental-ceremonial decision-making process within complex social systems is so important.

Summary

We may summarize as follows:

- OIE needs to deal with complexity concerns, as it now emphasizes system complexity.
- The SFM-A and the SFM are different. The former can exist without the latter; the latter cannot exist without the former; but the former cannot be fully utilized without the latter.
- The early representation of the SFM-A digraph (see Figure 4.1) misled analysts with respect to deliveries and feedback. It is corrected in Figure 4.2.
- As a general practice, the SFM diagonal should be kept free of entries.
- Social systems are not agent-based. That is, systems and their processes are not based on agents, which are defined as particular entities in the system. Agents enter the social system as principal–agent relationships, and agents are entered as institutional deliveries in the cells in the SFM.
- It is important to make the SFM-A consistent with the open systems principle by: (a) adding a row and column (or rows and columns) to the SFM for the system's environment; (b) having deliveries from the environment indicated in the columns which represent the components to which the deliveries are

made; (c) having criteria from the environment delivered to institutional columns; and (d) recognizing that deliveries can be delivered from the environment to deliveries that can be registered with components.

- The problem to be solved must be defined before it is possible to construct a meso model for solving it.
- Socio-ecological systems contain variant criteria that require systems to process inconsistent with legitimate normative criteria.
- Rules, regulations, and requirements are delivered among institutional components, and those deliveries need to be registered in SFM cells. The entry of a rule, regulation, and/or requirement in a cell requires that its recipient column in the SFM become a delivery row and make additional deliveries, otherwise the influence of rules, regulations, and requirements ceases in the SFM.
- D&E is a basic principle of systems, and is more complex in social systems than in biological systems. Darwinian evolution offers limited assistance for the analysis of D&E. The existence of D&E requires precautionary monitoring with systemic analysis in order to judge whether particular D&E changes are beneficial.

Notes

1 When completing an SFM, the only matrix cells in which a delivery is to be indicated are cells in which there is a direct delivery from the row component to the column component, not an indirect delivery.

2 The 600-page continuous algebraic formula that was generated from the SFM is available at: http://cba.unl.edu/academic-programs/departments/economics/sfm/. For an example of an SFM that emphasizes rules from contracts, see the study completed by F. Gregory Hayden and Steven Bolduc (2000).

3 When there are new rules and regulations as outlined in Figure 4.4, there is an inevitable pushback from some institutional organizations because institutional organizations often do not possess the appropriate skills, technology, labor and/or budget to adequately complete the tasks consistent with the laws and requirements.

4 The dependence on the fallacy of universalism by Hodgson and Knudsen forced the adoption of other fallacies to include essentialism (Hodgson, 2002: 259–60 and 269–73; Hodgson and Knudsen, 2006: 2 and 14); tautological arguments (Hodgson, 2002: 267 and 274–5; Hodgson and Knudsen, 2006: 8); and equivocation (Hodgson, 2002: 267 and 269; Hodgson and Knudsen, 2006: 1–2 and 14).

References

Adkisson, Richard V. (2009) "The economy as an open system: an institutionalist framework for economic development," in Tara Natarajan, Wolfram Elsner, and Scott Fullwiler (eds), *Institutional Analysis and Praxis: The Social Fabric Matrix Approach*. New York: Springer, pp. 25–38.

Becker, Howard (1952) "Science, culture, and society," *Philosophy of Science*, 19 (4): 273–87.

Dewey, John (1979 [1909]) "The influence of Darwin on philosophy," in Philip Appleman (ed.), *Darwin: A Norton Critical Edition*. New York: W. W. Norton, pp. 305–12.

Dopfer, Kurt, Foster, John, and Potts, Jason (2004) 'Micro-meso-macro," *Journal of Evolutionary Economics*, 14 (3): 263–79.

Elsner, Wolfram (2007) "Why meso? On 'aggregation' and 'emergence,' and why and how the meso level is essential in social economics," *Forum for Social Economics*, 36 (1): 1–16.

Elsner, Wolfram (2012) "The theory of institutional change revisited: the institutional dichotomy, its dynamic, and its policy implications in a more formal analysis," *Journal of Economic Issues*, 46 (1): 1–44.

Elsner, Wolfram and Heinrich, Torsten (2009) "A simple theory of 'meso,' on the co-evolution of institutions and platform size – with an application to varieties of capitalism and 'medium-sized' countries," *Journal of Socio-Economics*, 38 (5): 843–58.

Elsner, Wolfram and Schwardt, Henning (2015) "From emergent cooperation to contextual trust, and to general trust: overlapping meso-sized interaction arenas and cooperation platforms as a foundation of pro-social behavior," *Forum for Social Economics*, 44 (1): 69–86.

Fullwiler, Scott T. (2009) "The social fabric matrix approach to central bank operations: an application to the Federal Reserve and the recent financial crisis," in Tara Natarajan, Wolfram Elsner, and Scott Fullwiler (eds), *Institutional Analysis and Praxis: The Social Fabric Matrix Approach*. New York: Springer, pp. 123–69.

Fullwiler, Scott T., Elsner, Wolfram, and Natarajan, Tara (2009) "The social fabric matrix approach to policy analysis: an introduction," in Tara Natarajan, Wolfram Elsner, and Scott Fullwiler (eds), *Institutional Analysis and Praxis: The Social Fabric Matrix Approach*. New York: Springer, pp. 1–22.

Gräbner, Claudius (2016) "Agent-based computational models: a formal heuristic for institutionalist pattern modeling?," *Journal of Institutional Economics*, online 12(1): 241–61.

Gray, Matthew and Gill, Roderic A. (2009) "Tackling 'wicked' problems holistically with institutionalist policymaking," in Tara Natarajan, Wolfram Elsner, and Scott Fullwiler (eds), *Institutional Analysis and Praxis: The Social Fabric Matrix Approach*. New York: Springer, pp. 87–102.

Hayden, F. Gregory (1989) *Survey of Methodologies for Valuing Externalities and Public Goods*, Report for Contract Number 68-01-7363. Washington, DC: US Environmental Protection Agency.

Hayden, F. Gregory (2006) *Policymaking for a Good Society: The Social Fabric Matrix Approach to Policy Analysis and Program Evaluation*. New York: Springer.

Hayden, F. Gregory (2009) "Utilization of the social fabric matrix to articulate a state system of financial aid for public schools and to derive conceptual conclusions," in Tara Natarajan, Wolfram Elsner, and Scott Fullwiler (eds), *Institutional Analysis and Praxis: The Social Fabric Matrix Approach*. New York: Springer, pp. 209–36.

Hayden, F. Gregory (2011) "Integrating the social structure of accumulation and social accounting matrix with the social fabric matrix," *American Journal of Economics and Sociology*, 70 (5): 1208–33.

Hayden, F. Gregory (2015) "Using the social fabric matrix to establish corporate accounting consistent with normative criteria regarding climate change," *Forum for Social Economics*, online DOI: 10.1080/07360932.2014.1002517.

Hayden, F. Gregory and Bolduc, Steve (2000) "Contracts and costs in a corporate/government systems dynamics network: a United States case," in John Groenewegen and Wolfram Elsner (eds), *Industrial Policies After 2000*. Dordrecht: Kluwer Academic, pp. 235–84.

Hodgson, G. M. (2002) "Darwinism in economics: from analogy to ontology", *Journal of Evolutionary Economics*, 12 (3): 259–81.

Hodgson, Geoffrey M. and Knudsen Thorbjørn (2006) "Why we need a generalized Darwinism, and why generalized Darwinism is not enough," *Journal of Economic Behavior and Organization*, 61 (1): 1–19.

Natarajan, Tara, Fullwiler, Scott T., and Elsner, Wolfram (2009). *Institutional Analysis and Praxis: The Social Fabric Matrix Approach*. New York: Springer.

Neale, Walter C. (1980) "Market capitalism as dispute resolution: the loss of legitimacy and the problems of the welfare state," *Journal of Economic Issues*, 14 (2): 391–8.

Parto, Saeed (2005) "Economic activity and institutions: taking stock," *Journal of Economic Issues*, 39 (1): 21–52.

Polanyi, Karl (1957) "The economy as instituted process," in K. Polanyi, M. Arensberg, and H. Pearson (eds), *Trade and Markets in Early Empire*. Glencoe, IL: Free Press, pp. 243–70.

Valentinov, Vladislav (2013) "Veblen and instrumental value: a systems theory perspective," *Journal of Economic Issues*, 47 (3): 673–88.

Valentinov, Vladislav (2014) "The complexity-sustainability trade-off in Niklas Luhmann's social systems theory," *Systems Research and Behavioral Science*, 3 (1): 14–22.

van Staveren, Irene (2001) *The Values of Economics: An Aristotelian Perspective*. New York: Routledge.

Zhu, Lin, Qualls, Whitney A., Marshall, John M., Arheart, Kris L., DeAngelis, Donald L., McManus, John W., Doumbia, Seydou, Schlein, Yoseph, Müller, Günter C., and Beier, John C. (2015) "A spatial individual-based model predicting a great impact of copious sugar sources and resting sites on survival of Anopheles gambiae and malaria parasite transmission," *Malaria Journal*, 14 (1): 1–15.

5 Themes in an institutionalist theory of economic policy

Paolo Ramazzotti

Introduction

The aim of the present paper is to discuss the ends and scope of economic policy from an institutionalist perspective. My point of departure is Wolfram Elsner's (2012) contention that "progressive institutional change remains an issue of proper deliberate, discretionary policy action, as institutionalists have always argued" (ibid.: 33). I elaborate on this claim by focusing on how complexity characterizes the economy we live in. In particular I stress that, given the different types of coordination that exist within the economy, no pattern of economic evolution can be taken for granted. I then discuss how economic coordination and change by a public agency can be conceived of. I point out that, owing to the complex features of the economy, two issues must be jointly discussed. The first is what ends policy-makers should pursue. This involves the formulation of moral value judgments concerning what the ends are, thus what change is required. The second is how policy-makers should frame the economy in order to devise the means to pursue those ends. This involves the formulation of cognitive value judgments, concerning how technical, historical, social, and political circumstances determine what can and cannot change.

The conclusion this discussion leads to is that it is not possible to conceptually separate economic theory from economic policy. Only when we properly identify what the societal priorities are is it possible to provide an outline of an economy's and of a society's evolution, and only when such an outline is available are choices actually possible. Thus, only through the interaction between moral value judgments and cognitive value judgments can we provide a means to adequately deal with economic complexity.

In the next section, I briefly discuss complexity. I distinguish diachronic and synchronic complexity, laying special emphasis on the latter in relation to the systemic openness of the economy. In the subsequent section I examine how coordination occurs in an economic system characterized by these two dimensions of complexity. I take into account relative prices and institutions but also purposive actions that actors take to change the rules of the game to their advantage. Given this multifarious coordination, the evolution of the economy may follow many different paths which depend on policy choices. The final section of the paper deals with the implications that this framework has for a proper understanding of how economic theory and economic policy relate. Some brief concluding remarks end the paper.

Diachronic and synchronic complexity

Complexity is a multi-faceted phenomenon and a detailed discussion of its characteristics lies beyond the scope of this chapter. I wish to point out here only some of its key features, along with their implications for economic analysis and economic policy.

Simon (1981) described complexity as "many variables interacting in a non-simple way." The non-simple way often depends on changes in the way a variable interacts with others, so that the interaction can never be taken for granted. These changes may result from endogenous processes that lead to the emergence of new variables or new patterns of interaction which are different from the past to the point that they could hardly be predicted beforehand. Intuitively, this is what seems to precede phenomena such as the oil shocks of the 1970s, the fall of the Berlin Wall, the 9/11 attack on the Twin Towers.

The above examples refer to specific historical events, "black swans" that appear to be unpredictable because of their uniqueness. More common phenomena abound, however, including hyperinflation, core–periphery relations within and among countries, different rates of innovation and growth among industries, and financial instability. In order to deal with these kinds of "non-simple" interaction in the real-world economy, scholars need to appropriately frame the problem. Thus Elsner (2015: 285) provides a list of properties that usually characterize complex systems. At a strictly microeconomic level they are (a) composed of huge numbers of similar entities, with (b) simple patterns of interaction among entities in connection with the (c) adaptiveness of entities. At a macro level these features lead to (1) limited predictability of future states and limited reconstructability of past states by means other than those involving exact representations of the system; (2) nonergodicity; (3) the emergence of structure, patterns, and behaviors that are stable but not explicitly and trivially encoded into the systems' micro-level.

Compared to conventional models, this framework allows a richer view of the economy in that it provides for a variety of possible outcomes that a given group of interacting entities may lead to, with equilibrium being only a very special case. It is flexible enough to accommodate different assumptions on the patterns of interaction, thereby allowing for a range of subdisciplinary inquiries (e.g. industrial organization, economic policy, etc.) as well as for approaches centered on different views of evolution (institutionalist, Austrian, etc.). It provides an account of why and how institutions emerge through interaction. Although it is not restricted to dynamic systems, it provides conceptual and formal tools to investigate what we may refer to as diachronic complexity.

When we assume that we are dealing with dynamic systems, the usual *ceteris paribus* assumption – i.e. that all other things remain the same – is obviously useful in order to allow tractability but it is even more unrealistic than in conventional economics. In general, the entities of a system, or the system as a whole, may react to external events or even interact with other entities or systems within a higher-order system. This not only suggests that there are higher orders of complexity. It also stresses that a distinctive feature of the real-world economy is what Kapp (1976) referred to as sequential interaction within a cumulative process. It ultimately provides the key elements of a research program centered on evolution.

There is another notion of complexity that I would like to focus on, however, which I will refer to as synchronic complexity. Going back to Simon's definition, the "non-simple way" that variables interact may depend not only on the number and types of interaction and on the types of adaptiveness of the entities but on systemic openness (Boulding, 1956; Georgescu-Roegen, 1976; Kapp, 1976; Chick, 2004).[1]

An open system is here defined as one that interacts with its surrounding environment in a way that is not knowable. Openness means that we do not know the actual boundaries of the system. Since everything is, in some way or other, connected to everything else, we are bound to assign a boundary to something we wish to investigate and, to this end, we may resort to heuristics. Whatever boundaries we choose to delimit the subject of our inquiry, however, are based on a discretional decision. This means that there may always be something we do not take into account that may be relevant.

Note that this has nothing to do with the above mentioned removal of the *ceteris paribus* assumption. What is at issue is neither that there may be external shocks nor that a system may be part of a higher order one. The issue is that, depending on the non-simple way that social variables interact at every point in time – gender relations, industrial relations, or the more or less extended nature of the family, just to mention a few examples – they may affect the economic system in a variety of ways. This is what makes it so difficult to draw a clear-cut distinction between economic and non-economic welfare. Moral sentiments (Smith, 2005) affect the quality of life by regulating procurement in one way or other. The clash that sometimes occurs between an individual's preferences and her values (Hirschman, 1984) suggests that the way ethics impinges on economic conduct is far from clear. At a macro level, when people react to the inconsistency between profitability and serviceability (Veblen, 1904), how this occurs depends on how effective ideologies, myths, and ethical values are (Dugger and Sherman, 2000) in justifying or, obversely, in denouncing the negative effects that contracted exchange has on society and social cohesion (Polanyi, 1944).

The boundary problem is accentuated by changes that may occur over time. What is irrelevant now may become relevant at some time in the future. Openness may depend on changes determined by the very processes that underlie diachronic complexity. Consider how the expanded use of petroleum as a key energy input for transport, for electricity, and for heating, eventually changed the extension of these markets around the world, thus the type of interaction within and among them. Changes such as these affect relative prices but also the balance of power within society. A new industry such as the oil industry leads to the insurgence of vested interests in the exporting as well as in the importing countries. It is likely to affect the political regimes of the countries involved, either by empowering those vested interests within those countries or subjecting those countries to the economic and political will of foreign vested interests. These changes feed back on the cultural and religious values of the populations, sometimes determining radical changes in the polity, in international relations, in the balance between both domestic and international power groups. As we look at these historical processes, we are obliged to acknowledge that they affect the economic performance of the oil market, of a great many other markets, of trends in growth and in income distribution, etc.

These examples suggest that variables that are of minor relevance at some point in time may subsequently become more relevant. Thus, although the distinction between synchronic and diachronic complexity is useful on conceptual grounds the two types of complexity often are interdependent in the real world.

This brief outline of the key features of complexity raises the issue whether, and to what extent, there is a way to coordinate such a complex environment, possibly attaining order out of chaos. This is the topic of the next section.

Variety in coordination

Relative prices associated with contracted exchange are generally considered the typical coordinating instance in a capitalist market economy. This claim needs to be qualified, however. It is fairly easy to acknowledge that the economies we live in are indeed coordinated by prices but also by a range of institutions. The role that institutions play remains an open issue among economists, however. New Institutionalists such as Coase (1937, 1960) and Williamson (1975, 1993a, 1993b, 2000) point out that the market operates in a relatively costly fashion, whereby it is possible to devise institutions that reduce those costs. Institutions therefore may allow a relatively more efficient allocation of resources, where efficiency is cost-effectiveness.

"Efficiency" as cost-effectiveness should not be confused with overall (Paretian) allocative efficiency. Cost-effectiveness only means that a single actor can reduce her costs. For instance, firm A may cut its transaction costs by taking over a company – firm B – that carries out R&D and sells it on the market. While this is convenient for firm A, it restricts the very scope of the market. The resulting firm (A + B) will avoid disclosing what presumably provides it with a competitive advantage. Furthermore, following the takeover, firm (A + B) may have less incentive to innovate since it can outcompete other firms through lower transaction costs, without any need to focus entirely on a nevertheless risky qualitative upgrading of its products and/or production processes. It may remain competitive, but in the context of a "low road" to development (Sengenberger and Pyke, 1992; Milberg and Houston, 2005).

The above considerations apply even if we accept the (mostly implicit and rather unrealistic) assumption that markets are impersonal. Economic actors, however, do not merely react to prices. They purposively interact – through rivalry, cooperation, imitation, predation – in order to change not only prices but the bargaining power between firms and workers as well as among firms within the production chain. As a result they preclude the ideal competitive environment where relative prices ought to carry out their coordinating function. Indeed, the firms who act this way affect the decisions of other actors, so that they exert a coordinating action which cannot be separated from other transactions-centered relations. This effect is, generally, greater as their size increases.

An important implication is that markets are not independent of the action of the firms. They may well operate as selection mechanisms but the nature of such a selection depends on the action of those very firms that should be selected (Ramazzotti and Rangone, 2002). Markets do not provide independent terms of reference to assess whether what firms do is efficient or not for the economy as a whole. Both the distinction between the market and institutions and the distinction between efficiency-centered and strategizing behavior turn out to be impracticable under these circumstances.

While the Coase-Williamson tradition focuses on institutions that make up for the inefficiency of the market, North (1990, 2005) focuses on extra-economic institutions such as, for instance, religion. It is these institutions that, in his view, may be a major cause of inefficiency in terms of low rates of growth. The reason is that they may provide behavioral rules that preclude maximizing behavior. Since these institutions are strongly related to beliefs, changing them is not an easy task.

Both of these New Institutionalist accounts of the role of institutions assume that the market is the logical point of departure for any inquiry. Institutions may increase or reduce its efficiency and this is how their economic relevance is assessed. An alternative strand of thought, centered on Original Institutional Economics, but which can be traced back to Adam Smith and his theory of moral sentiments, denies this centrality of the market. It argues that, historically, not all types of economy have been coordinated through contracted exchange and the relative prices that it leads to. Quite the contrary, since all economies are a subsystem of society, they are all regulated in one way or another. They all need some kind of institutional setup to coordinate activities, with or without the concurrent action of relative prices (Polanyi, 1957).

Following this perspective, let us consider the economy we live in. No price system may exist unless it is backed up by a set of rules that allow it to function. More specifically, all sets of relative prices depend on some legal-economic nexus (Commons, 1924; Schmid, 1987; Bromley, 1989; Samuels *et al.*, 1994; Samuels and Schmid, 1997). Property rights need to be assigned, appropriate behavior – hence also misbehavior – among actors must be defined, possible sanctions must also be identified, and some organization has to inflict those sanctions. Furthermore, the very extension of coordination by relative prices has to be decided. For instance, human beings as well as parts of their bodies may or may not be subject to contracted exchange.

The above institutions require some ethical system to exist, i.e. criteria that determine how they are to regulate (economic) activity. For instance, the assignment of property rights may be based on efficiency criteria – however defined – but also on distributional equity, or historical accident, war, force, and fraud. The extension of the price mechanism may depend on the importance assigned to alternative criteria in the production and distribution of resources, as in the case of the welfare state. The organization of production may depend on what is most profitable but other criteria may hold: consider the protection of social rights as they appear in a range of important charters such as the Universal Declaration of Human Rights (1948).

There would seem to be a common ground for discussion between those New Institutionalist scholars who, like North, emphasize the importance of beliefs – and, more generally, mental models (Denzau and North, 1994; North, 2005) – and Original Institutionalist scholars who stress the relevance of ethics. Indeed, these appear to be different ways to look at the same phenomenon (Dequech, 2002). What beliefs, ethics, and institutions in general imply for the functioning of the market should be clearly stated, however. They determine rights for someone, thus duties for someone else (Commons, 1990). They determine the choice sets of economic actors, thus what they can do and what they cannot do. Precisely because they determine "who may do what to whom" (Bromley, 1989: 49), they are a prerequisite for the market, thereby undermining the latter's presumed centrality. Truly, a given institutional setup may deter economic growth. But the contention that this is tantamount to inefficiency reflects an implicit assumption: that growth is more important than the institutions that "constrain" the market. While the value judgment underlying this assumption is legitimate, it is no more so than the value judgments underlying the establishment of the "growth-deterring" institutional setup. It is indeed a consequence of the systemic openness of the economy that such a clash in value judgments may occur.

Systemic openness implies that the economy does not just reflect the institutional setup determined by society. It also feeds back, thereby affecting society and how it changes over time. The output produced, the techniques used, the labor relations established: these and other circumstances affect the organization of society, how it functions and how it pursues both its economic and not economic ends. Thus, how people work – the number of hours, the stress, the safety conditions – as well as the income they receive, affects how they live in general, how they take part in other dimensions of their societal life, how they understand the world that surrounds them and that they are a part of (Scott, 1995; Dequech, 2014).[2] This understanding, in turn, feeds back on how people deal with that world, i.e. the extent to which they (intend to) accept it as it is or, alternatively, attempt to change part or all of it. Ultimately, it affects the way they contribute to the formation of the institutions that guide their lives (Hodgson, 2002).

This leads us to the conclusion that the beliefs people have, their understanding of the world they live in and the ethics that derives from this understanding affect the institutional setup that underlies the economy. Knowledge in this broad sense is as much a coordinating instance as those mentioned above. It is not independent of them, however, since the economy affects how people behave, what they choose and how they learn.

The above discussion stresses that coordination in the economy we live in involves markets, institutions, and knowledge. This is generally consistent with the so-called micro-meso-macro framework, whereby:

> We define micro as the level of individual agents and their interactions. As soon as some "structure" (institution) has emerged that exists independently from individual agents, we understand this to belong to the meso level if a "meso"-sized "carrier group" has been co-evolving with that structure. A meso-sized group, in turn, is defined in our model as any group of a size smaller than the whole population involved. The latter, finally, may be considered then to reflect the macro level, mirroring the real-world "national" level mentioned (considered as the space of more formal institutions and agency).
>
> (Elsner, 2010: 449)

The distinction between these three levels may be useful from a heuristic point of view. It has also been used to provide an account of coordination that would support a *general* theory of economic evolution (Dopfer and Potts, 2009). It is therefore important to assess whether and how the framework actually provides insights on coordination.

Let us focus on the micro level. Two apparently opposite features have to be pointed out. The first is that, in so far as economic actors pursue their specific goals, they are likely not to appreciate what happens at the macro-level. A typical example is the paradox of thrift whereby, if individuals attempt to increase their savings, the aggregate outcome is a fall in output but no change in overall saving. This unawareness of the consequences of one's individual action accounts for the independent status of the micro-level. It also justifies the existence of an agency that operates at the aggregate level.

The second feature is that economic actors may well be aware of potentially undesired outcomes. They may consequently act in order to avoid them. They may act in two distinct ways. The first is to adapt to circumstances in order to achieve a better outcome. This is what underlies a lot of game theory. As Loasby (1991: 44) points out, however:

> Nash equilibria constrain each individual as tightly as perfect competition, and have the advantage that the discovery of such equilibria apparently require neither an auctioneer nor any transactions which might disturb the outcome, but simply individual ratiocination. All actions are therefore equilibrium actions, as a rigorous insistence on optimization demands. However, each Nash equilibrium requires all players to be smart enough to work out the implications of the rules of the game, but not smart enough to recognize the potential advantages of varying them. They are only boundedly rational after all.

The second type of conduct, therefore, is to proactively change those very circumstances, that is, to vary the rules of the game.

In terms of the micro-meso-macro framework, economic actors may not only abide by the existing rules of the game and, through interaction, generate new rules. They may also purposively act on the trajectories that allow a rule to spread out in the economy. A meso level – where such trajectories occur – must obviously exist but the rules that will eventually prevail and play a significant role at the macro level will not necessarily result from an unintentional diffusion. Single actors may play a coordinating role that interferes and downplays the impersonal one that independent actors would allow for.

Independently of how they behave as economic actors, individuals are not only that. Because of systemic openness, they can hardly be reduced to that feature. As mentioned above, they are able to transcend their conventional economic goals when it comes to assessing their quality of life and the quality of life of the people around them. For instance, although, based on their specific economic activity, they may be unable to understand the causes of such appalling circumstances as unemployment or poverty, they may nonetheless feel that something is going wrong and think about how to fix the situation. They may therefore act as citizens – as opposed to single economic actors – so that a public agency may take appropriate measures. Little matters that the measures they ask for may be successful or not. What is relevant is that individuals may broaden the scope for institutions: the meso need not be conventionally economic.

Since the set of institutions that emerge at the meso-level may or may not fit together, the macro-level should ensure an adjustment process. Economic activity cannot be isolated from the rest of human concerns, however, so institutions have to do with many, if not all, of such concerns. There is no a priori reason to believe that they will eventually fit together. The typical Hayekian contention that markets self-organize is of little use here, not only because self-organization cannot be taken for granted but, above all, because markets are intermingled with a great many other societal variables.

These features allow us to look at the macro-level as the outcome of a range of actions that often are proactive, may be strategic and are not necessarily restricted to conventional economic variables. Consequently, coordination cannot be restricted to the economy – not to mention the market. It has to do with whatever individuals deem so relevant that it affects their actions. Furthermore, it occurs not only in a bottom-up fashion – from the micro to the meso and, finally to the macro – but also the other way round, in a top-down fashion.

Summing up, there are various coordinating instances that act upon the economy and the society it is a part of. To some extent, this accounts for the complexity described in the first section of this paper. On the other hand, owing to some balance of power or temporary convergence of interests, some dominant institutions may emerge and ensure an order out of what would otherwise be total chaos. This may account for the persistence of the institutional setup that is generally labeled "capitalism" as well as for the persistence, within capitalism, of periods of relative stability. A full picture, however, requires us to look at the last coordinating instance: government action.

Given the above discussion on complexity and coordination, two issues should be pointed out. First, just as economic actors try to influence the way they are supposed to interact, so may a government. The second issue is that, whatever the ends government action pursues, policy-makers must somehow make sense of a complex environment. These issues are discussed in the section that follows.

Public action

The discussion of complexity and of coordination leads to the conclusion that there is no general law that we can rely on when we try to describe the economy and the society we live in. The attempt to somehow regulate or direct the evolution of the economy is just as problematic. This does not mean that the conclusions lead us nowhere, however. It simply tells us that no mechanistic description or policy is available (Sotolongo, 2004).

One key point that arises from the discussion is that coordination occurs in at least three distinct, but interactive, ways: through prices; through institutions; through the proactive and strategic action of single actors. Institutions and the structure of knowledge consist of enabling constraints for economic actors. They provide for some stability in the economy because they usually tend to change slowly. The conditions they determine allow actors to choose according to relative prices. It is precisely because of their enabling and constraining function, however, that actors often try to change them. The evolution of financial markets in the USA over the past decades is a case in point (Varoufakis, 2011). Coordination is a contested process: different economic actors try to direct the economy in one way or other. They do so within an institutional setup that reflects but also feeds back on that interaction.

Can a policy-maker act in a consistent way upon this complex reality? Can she make sense of economic change? Doubtless, the issues discussed above provide tools for the economist's toolbox but they do not provide an explanation. Indeed, if the term "explanation" refers to a fairly accurate description of the economy and of how it evolves, a range of problems arise.

The systemic openness of the economy raises a key issue. How should the economy be circumscribed? What does it consist of? Is it the market as it is described by standard microeconomics textbooks? Is it the market plus government agencies and, perhaps, non-profit organizations? Does it include unions, lobbies, political parties, religious organizations? Openness implies that we cannot trace a once and for all boundary. It also suggests that when we do trace a boundary – possibly because we choose to focus on a specific issue – we are not only leaving some variables out of our inquiry; we are assuming away possible interactions between what we include and what we leave out. Only to some extent can we rely on a subsequent extension of our model and inquiry. As the boundaries change, the nature of the interactions – not just their extension – may change as well. Complexity hardly allows for reductionist practices that merely add up the results of distinct inquiries.

Given their different concerns and their bounded rationality (Simon, 1976), economic actors are likely to formulate different assumptions with regard to the boundaries of the economy. Thus, in order to plan its business activities, a local construction company may focus on information concerning local income growth and on what building areas will be made available by local authorities. A local importer of foreign cars and a multinational company are likely to be less concerned about how those authorities manage the local territory than about changes in the exchange rate, thus about monetary policy. All these companies, however, share a common goal: making money. There are different ways to go about doing this but the goal is fairly clear.

Individuals may want to make money just like any economic actor but, unlike business, they may pursue other goals as well. As we mentioned above, the quality of life may involve more than money. Given these premises, their notion of the economy is less straightforward than that of businesses.

Policy-makers try to make sense of reality in much the same way as individuals. They must decide what their policy goals are. They must subsequently understand how to achieve them. As far as the first issue is concerned, systemic openness suggests that no once and for all distinction is possible between economic and non-economic ends and that there is no reason to give precedence to conventionally economic ones. There is a broad range of policy perspectives that governments can choose from. Which one they do choose depends on the ultimate end that they pursue. Examples of such ends include Sen's (1999) development as freedom, Layard's (2005) and Kahneman's (Kahnemann *et al.*, 1997; Kahnemann, 1999) notion of happiness, the forceful establishment of the institutions required for a neoliberal market (Foucault, 2004; Brown, 2005; Ramazzotti, 2014a), or the straightforward protection of some vested interest. Choosing among these and other options obviously involves moral value judgments: deciding how the economy and society should be, i.e. what values should be assigned a priority.

Given an end, how can policy-makers choose the appropriate policy? In order to deal with this question it is necessary to qualify the economy they are referring to. The issue is not only that, given systemic openness, everything is connected to everything else. The issue is that it is necessary to decide what is deemed constant and what is deemed subject to change. Consider, for instance, a prisoners' dilemma. The decision to identify and pursue the appropriate way to achieve a Pareto optimal outcome sounds reasonable. It implicitly assumes, however, that the payoffs are given. In broader terms, here, just as in any case where the goal is a Pareto improvement, the extant distribution (usually, the endowments) is taken as given. This is a legitimate value judgment but nothing else. One might just as well consider the possibility of changing the existing distribution.

A decision such as this one – whether distributional conditions are potentially subject to change – actually involves two different interconnected value judgments. The first one is whether such an action is feasible, i.e. whether there are institutional, political or other circumstances that preclude such a change, at least in the time interval that is relevant for the policy-maker. The second one is up to what point should policy attempt to change a given situation. Since it is generally the case that someone benefits from a policy but someone else is damaged, when is this policy deemed appropriate?

Although the two value judgments are linked, the first relates to how the economy is understood to be structured and to function whereas the second has to do with how costs should be shared within society. The first is a cognitive value judgment whereas the second is a moral value judgment.

The two steps outlined here – identifying a goal and circumscribing the economy – are not the end of the story. Once the economy is properly depicted, only a proper inquiry will provide an understanding of whether and how the goal may actually be achieved. In turn, the resulting knowledge may lead to a reassessment of the goal, thus to a reassessment of the boundaries of the economy, and so on in an iterative process.

There is more to the value judgments discussed so far. Leaving aside the restrictive case of Pareto optimality, consider a policy – e.g. the introduction of a new technology – that is expected to make everybody better off, independently of any ceremonial valuation. The problem is how this specific end in view – making people better off – relates to the ultimate ends outlined above. If the new technology increases the income available to everybody but reinforces an undesirable division of labor among genders or among social classes, should it be valued positively in instrumental terms? The answer cannot be given a priori. It involves answering a question concerning the possibility of actually changing – possibly with some alternative policy – the existing division of labor. We are back to the combination of moral and cognitive value judgments.

The objection that the answer depends on what people want in a deliberative democracy is not a convincing one. As Sen (1999) argues with his example of the Indian woman – who is unaware that her subordinate position in the family and in society precludes her from living a better life – people may well internalize the values underlying the organization of the economy and of society. What is at issue is that any instrumental valuation reflects the status quo. More specifically, as Samuels (1977: 882) argues, "'Efficiency' is a function of power and the valuational process (governing whose interests count) which operates through the power structure." Thus, no instrumental valuation is possible unless one clearly distinguishes what can and should change from what cannot and/or should not.

On more methodological grounds, what I am suggesting is that, while it is reasonable to conceive of models that focus on specific aspects of reality and deal with them according to whatever tools the scholar deems appropriate, the true issue is how and where to identify and circumscribe them. Conventional economic analysis conceives of the economy as a closed system. It starts out with a set of axioms and elaborates on them by deducing economic laws and applying them to general and special cases. The complexity discussed so far, however, suggests that you cannot proceed this way. An alternative approach, therefore, consists of formulating a discretionary judgment concerning what is relevant, quite independently of axioms.[3]

Relevance here has two interdependent dimensions. The first is that the questions underlying the inquiry should be made explicit.[4] They include the ultimate end pursued which, when we focus on a policy perspective, inevitably involves a moral value judgment. The second is that the categories used and the theory they lead to must be grounded in a methodologically rigorous procedure. By this I mean that it must be possible to understand the assumptions – as well as the arguments - underlying the inquiry.[5] This involves another type of value judgment – a cognitive value judgment – which has to do with the general idea one has of how the economy is and of how it should be investigated.[6]

Although complexity hardly allows for clear-cut economic laws, the above approach does allow the tools in the economist's toolbox to grow and to provide insights. These insights may not lead to a fully-fledged theory but they may reduce the degree of uncertainty that any policy decision involves.

I have already pointed out that, contrary to conventional views, policy is not constrained by relative prices alone. It is constrained by the institutional setup, which determines how transactions occur and how relative prices are determined. It is also constrained by the conduct of other actors and by the patterns of change this conduct may determine. Policy has to cope with actors who contrast any measure that clashes with their, actual and potential, vested interests as well as with their views of what is appropriate. From this perspective, policy cannot be envisaged as a set of fixed institutions and incentives that allow the market to operate successfully, thereby making economic actors behave in a desired fashion. Rather, it is a continuous process where vested interests try to contrast public action, thereby forcing government to counter-react, only to be followed by a new reaction, etc. Public action obviously involves recourse to the economist's toolbox, with a clear understanding of the cognitive value judgments that underlie it. It also involves an ongoing interaction with other actors since, as Stanfield and Carroll (2009: 11) point out, "[w]hile it is true that any regulatory scheme tends to bring forth efforts to evade control, this only means that regulation must be continuously reformed not that it must be abandoned."

The denial of a mechanistic account of how the economy works suggests that, as a general rule, policy cannot consist of switching a structural model of the economy into its inverse reduced form. This difficulty arises because any (structural) model is not only an approximation in the sense that it abstracts from trivial issues, i.e. issues that are not important for a correct understanding of a core issue. It is an approximation because – owing to complexity – it cannot definitely distinguish core issues from trivial ones.[7] This approximation can be improved upon but it cannot be overcome. The gap between a model and reality is not filled with more information. It requires greater understanding. Contrary to what is likely to occur in a closed system, uncertainty does not necessarily fall as you increase the available information. Uncertainty may increase because the new information suggests that aspects of the core issue were not taken account of. The decisions concerning the boundaries, the heuristics and the time devoted to the inquiry may prove to be inappropriate, thereby undermining the previous understanding.

Concluding remarks

Contrary to the impression that one might get from a cursory look at the previous sections, the aim of the paper is not to argue that any policy is doomed to failure because of the absence of appropriate terms of reference such as a clear-cut theory of how the economy is coordinated. It is that policy-makers should free themselves of the bounds that a simplistic view of the economy suggests. By simplistic view I refer to the belief that there is an automatism that coordinates the conduct of economic actors. The complexity of the economy depends on the coexistence of diverse, and sometimes inconsistent, coordinating instances. This results in economic and social outcomes that most often reflect the predominant role of sectional – vested – interests. It also results in a difficulty – for all actors – to single out a pattern of behavior and performance of the economy, i.e. to formulate reliable expectations about the future.

The policy implications are that the pursuit of some sort of social welfare implies dealing with the strategies of the sectional interests as well as reducing the degree of uncertainty in the economy. The actual policies, however, cannot be devised in the conventional way, which consists of taking a model from political economy and identifying the appropriate objective and instrumental variables. The reason for this is that an important gap exists between any model and historical reality.

To some extent this is consistent with David Colander's (2014) claim that "policy search requires a practical sense of real-world institutions, a comprehensive knowledge of past literature, familiarity with history, and a well-tuned sense of nuance" (ibid.: 489). My point, however, is that, economic knowledge depends on the questions we ask and on the assumptions we make concerning what is given and what can be changed. Policy-makers cannot simply add extra-economic knowledge to (neutral) economic models.

In a general context of uncertainty policy-makers must formulate a decision concerning what societal problems should be addressed. This involves asking whether a change is possible that solves those problems. In turn, this leads to the use of the economist's toolbox in order to frame the problems in an account of how the economy is working. The resulting account of the economy allows the policy-maker to assess the original problems in the light of what appears to be possible. The assessment is the starting point for a recursive process which eventually will allow the policy-maker to formulate an educated guess over what to do.

Complexity means that the economic and extra-economic dimensions cannot be conceptually separated. Consequently, the scope of economic knowledge cannot be defined a priori. It is the result of a sequential interaction between the identification of the ends to be pursued and an appropriate understanding of what issues, boundaries, variables and forms of interaction are relevant to those ends.

Acknowledgments

I wish to thank two anonymous referees for their comments and suggestions. The usual disclaimer applies.

Notes

1 I do not consider, here, non-dynamic types of complexity, such as fractals, that are not specifically associated with systemic openness.

2 Needless to say, advertisements are another important example in that they do not merely inform but exert their power of suggestion, they act upon the perception that people have of (sections of) reality and, consequently, the interpretations and explanations they subsequently elaborate.
3 A more detailed discussion of these themes may be found in Dow (1996, 2008).
4 This a key theme in Myrdal (1978, 1998).
5 This issue is at the origin of Delorme's (2010) discussion of deep complexity and how it can be anchored.
6 A more detailed discussion of moral and cognitive value judgments may be found in Ramazzotti (2014b).
7 Following Musgrave's (1981) taxonomy, it is not possible to properly distinguish between "domain" and "heuristic" assumptions.

References

Boulding, Kenneth E. (1956) "General systems theory – the skeleton of science," *Management Science*, April, pp. 197–208.

Bromley, Daniel W. (1989) *Economic Interests and Institutions: The Conceptual Foundations of Public Policy*. New York: Blackwell.

Brown, Wendy (2005) "Neoliberalism and the end of liberal democracy," in *Edgework: Critical Essays on Knowledge and Power*. Princeton, NJ: Princeton University Press, pp. 37–59.

Chick, Victoria (2004) "On open systems," *Brazilian Journal of Political Economy*, 24 (1): 3–16.

Coase, Ronald H. (1937) "The nature of the firm," *Economica*, 4 (16): 386–405.

Coase, Ronald H. (1960) "The problem of social cost," *Journal of Law and Economics*, 3: 1–44.

Colander, David (2014) "The economics of influence," *Journal of Economic Issues*, 48 (2): 485–92.

Commons, John, R. (1924) *Legal Foundations of Capitalism*. New York: Macmillan.

Commons, John, R. (1990) *Institutional Economics: Its Place in Political Economy*. New Brunswick, NJ: Transaction Publishers.

Delorme, Robert (2010) *Deep Complexity and the Social Sciences: Experience, Modelling and Operationality*. Cheltenham: Edward Elgar.

Denzau, Arthur T. and North, Douglass C. (1994) "Shared mental models: ideologies and institutions," *Kyklos*, 47 (1): 3–31.

Dequech, David (2002) "The demarcation between the 'old' and the 'new' institutional economics: recent complications," *Journal of Economic Issues*, XXXVI (2): 565–72.

Dequech, David (2014) "The institutions of economics: a first approximation," in *Journal of Economic Issues*, XLVIII (2): 523–31.

Dopfer, Kurt and Potts, Jason (2009) *The Theory of Economic Evolution*. London: Routledge.

Dow, Sheila C. (1996) *The Methodology of Macroeconomic Thought*. Cheltenham: Edward Elgar.

Dow, Sheila C. (2008) "A future for schools of thought and pluralism in heterodox economics," in John T. Harvey and Robert F. Garnett, Jr (eds), *Future Directions for Heterodox Economics*. Ann Arbor, MI: University of Michigan Press, pp. 9–26.

Dugger, William, H. and Sherman, Howard, J. (2000) *Reclaiming Evolution. A Dialogue Between Marxism and Institutionalism on Social Change*. London: Routledge.

Elsner, Wolfram (2010) "The process and a simple logic of 'meso'. Emergence and the co-evolution of institutions and group size," *Journal of Evolutionary Economics*, 20: 445–77.

Elsner, Wolfram (2012) "The theory of institutional change revisited: the institutional dichotomy, its dynamic, and its policy implications in a more formal analysis," *Journal of Economic Issues*, XLVI (1): 1–43.

Elsner, Wolfram, Heinrich, Torsten, and Schwardt, Henning (2015) *The Microeconomics of Complex Economics. Evolutionary, Institutional, Neoclassical and Complexity Perspectives*. Amsterdam: Elsevier/Academic Press.

Foucault, Michel (2004) *Naissance de la biopolitique. Cours au Collège de France 1978–1979*. Paris: Seuil/Gallimard.

Georgescu-Roegen, Nicholas (1976) "Process in farming versus process in manufacturing: a problem of balanced development," in *Energy and Economic Myths. Institutional and Analytical Economic Essays*. New York: Pergamon Press.

Hirschman, A. O. (1984) "Against parsimony: three easy ways of complicating some categories of economic discourse," *American Economic Review*, 74 (2): 89–96.

Hodgson, Geoffrey M. (2002) "Reconstitutive downward causation: social structure and the development of individual agency," Edward Fulbrook (ed.), *Intersubjectivity in Economics. Agents and Structures*. London: Routledge.

Kahneman, Daniel (1999) "Objective happiness," in D. Kahneman *et al.* (eds), *Well-Being: The Foundations of Hedonic Psychology*. New York: Russell Sage Foundation.

Kahneman, Daniel, Wakker, Peter P., and Sarin, Rakesh (1997) "Back to Bentham? Explorations of experienced utility," *Quarterly Journal of Economics*, 112 (2): 375–405.

Kapp, Karl W. (1976) "The open-system character of the economy and its implications," K. Dopfer (ed.), *Economics in the Future: Towards a New Paradigm*. London: Macmillan.

Layard, Richard (2005) *Happiness: Lessons from a New Science*. New York: Penguin.

Loasby, Brian J. (1991) *Equilibrium and Evolution. An Exploration of Connecting Principles in Economics*. Manchester: Manchester University Press.

Milberg, William and Houston, Ellen (2005) "The high road and the low road to international competitiveness: extending the neo-Schumpeterian trade model beyond technology," *International Review of Applied Economics*, 19 (2): 137–62.

Musgrave, Alan (1981) "'Unreal assumptions' in economic theory: the F-twist untwisted," *Kyklos*, 3.

Myrdal, Gunnar (1978) "Institutional economics," *Journal of Economic Issues*, 12 (4): 771–84.

Myrdal, Gunnar (1998) *Value in Social Theory*. London: Routledge.

North, Douglass C. (1990) *Institutions, Institutional Change and Economic Performance*. Cambridge: Cambridge University Press.

North, Douglass C. (2005) *Understanding the Process of Economic Change*. Princeton, NJ: Princeton University Press.

Polanyi, Karl (1944) *The Great Transformation*. New York: Holt, Rinehart & Winston.

Polanyi, Karl (1957) *The Economy as Instituted Process. in: Trade and Market in the Early Empires: Economies in History and Theory*, eds Karl Polanyi, Conrad M. Arensberg, and Harry W. Pearson. Glencoe, IL: Free Press, pp. 243–70.

Ramazzotti, Paolo (2014a) "Technocratic consensus, institutional change and questionable ends. Remarks on Italy's economic policy," in Roy Cerqueti (ed.), *Polymorphic Crisis. Readings on the Great Recession of the 21st Century*. Macerata: EUM, pp. 122–52.

Ramazzotti, Paolo (2014b) "Shared economic thought and the neglect of social costs. Reflections on why progressive economists often stick to conventional wisdom," *Journal of Economic Issues*, XLVIII (4): 1113–32.

Ramazzotti, Paolo and Rangone, Marco (2002) "Firms and selection: possible features of innovation processes," *RISEC – Rivista Internazionale di Scienze Economiche e Commerciali*, 49 (1): 55–79.

Samuels, Warren (1977) "Technology vis-à-vis institutions in the JEI: a suggested interpretation," *Journal of Economic Issues*, 11: 871–95.

Samuels, Warren J. and Schmid, Allan A. (1997) "The concept of cost in economics," in Warren J. Samuels, Stephen G. Medema, and Allan A. Schmid (eds), *The Economy as a Process of Valuation*. Cheltenham: Edward Elgar, pp. 208–98.

Samuels, Warren J., Schmid, Allan A., and Shaffer, James D. (1994) "An evolutionary approach to law and economics," in Richard W. England (ed.), *Evolutionary Concepts in Contemporary Economics*. Ann Arbor, MI: University of Michigan Press.

Schmid, Allan A. (1987) *Property, Power, and Public Choice. An Inquiry into Law and Economics*, 2nd edn. New York: Praeger.

Scott, W. Richard (1995) *Institutions and Organizations*. Thousand Oaks: Sage.

Sen, Amartya K. (1999) *Development as Freedom*. New York: Alfred Knopf.

Sengenberger, Werner and Pyke Frank (1992) "Introduction: research and policy issues," in Frank Pyke and Werner Sengenberger (eds), *Industrial Districts and Local Economic Regeneration*. Geneva: International Institute for Labor Studies, pp. 3–29.

Simon, Herbert A. (1976) "From substantive to procedural rationality," in S. J. Latsis (ed.), *Method and Appraisal in Economics*. Cambridge: Cambridge University Press, pp. 129–48.

Simon, Herbert A. (1981) "The architecture of complexity," in *The Sciences of the Artificial*. Cambridge, MA: MIT Press.

Smith, Adam (2005) *The Theory of Moral Sentiments*. São Paulo: Metalibri. Online http://www.ibiblio.org/ml/libri/s/SmithA_MoralSentiments_p.pdf.

Sotolongo, Pedro L. (2004) "Complexity and TINA," *E:CO*, 6 (4): 58–65.

Stanfield, James R. and Carroll, Michael C. (2009) "The social economics of neoliberal globalization," *Forum for Social Economics*, 38 (1): 1–18.

Universal Declaration of Human Rights (1948) online at http://www.un.org/en/documents/udhr/.

Varoufakis, Yanis (2011) *The Global Minotaur: ·America, the True Causes of the Financial Crisis and the Future of the World Economy*. London: Zed Books.

Veblen, Thorstein (1904) *The Theory of Business Enterprise*. New York: Scribner's.

Williamson, Oliver E. (1975) *Markets and Hierarchies: Analysis and Antitrust Implications*. New York: Free Press.

Williamson, Oliver E. (1993a) "Contested exchange versus the governance of contractual relations," *Journal of Economic Perspectives*, 7 (1): 103–8.

Williamson, Oliver E. (1993b) "Transaction cost economics and organization theory," *Industrial and Corporate Change*, 2 (1): 107–56.

Williamson, Oliver E. (2000) "The new institutional economics: taking stock, looking ahead," *Journal of Economic Literature*, XXXVIII: 595–613.

6 On the evolutionary foundations of the dynamic capability view

An exercise using the methodology of isolation

Kalevi Kyläheiko

Introduction

In this paper the methodological foundations of economics-based strategy research are analyzed through the lens of the *methodology of isolation*. During recent years the dynamic capability view (DCV) has challenged the resource based view (RBV) as the leading background theory within strategy research. There are, however, contradictory interpretations of the true nature of DCV. I claim that the main reason is the lack of clarity concerning the methodological underpinnings of the DCV. Hence I will scrutinize the cognitive, behavioral, time-related, and ontological assumptions used in different DCV and RBV versions and show that the newer DCV 2.0 version seems to be the most promising for a coherent strategy framework. However, its micro foundations have to be opened up to more efficiently utilize its evolutionary foundations. This means that the cognitive limitations of the decision-makers, the fundamental role of radical uncertainty, and the key role of entrepreneurship have to be taken seriously.

Modern economics-based strategy research looks for strategies that allow a firm to obtain sustainable competitive advantage (SCA), i.e. the situation in which the firm earns supra-natural rents over time. According to Winter (1995) there are actually three main sources for sustainable extra profits. They can be either: (1) monopoly profits based on entry barriers and economies of scale and scope; (2) Ricardian rents based on the use of non-replicable and unique resources; or (3) Schumpeterian rents based on innovations.

The first attempt to explain SCA was launched by Porter's (1980, 1985) five forces model that rests on the Bain-Mason structure-conduct-performance paradigm. The message of this paradigm was that the supply and demand conditions in a particular industry determine the market structure, which affects the conduct of the firm, which, in turn, determines the performance of firms. The emphasis is at the *industry* level and the goal is to increase social welfare. Porter's clever idea was to combine this paradigm with the business strategy by turning the normative social welfare message upside down. Porter (1980) focuses on the strategic issue of how to position a company so that it can sustain extra returns on investments (at the cost of social welfare, of course). Porter's CA-*generating* strategies form a device through which a firm's *internal* strengths and weaknesses can be effectively adapted to the opportunities and threats provided by its environment. The performance of a firm depends on its external environment that can be characterized by the five forces: bargaining power of suppliers and buyers, threat of new entrants and of substitute products or services, and rivalry among current competitors. The main strategies to gain SCA are either to establish entry barriers to rivals or to exploit the economies of scale and scope.

The second approach is the resource-based view (RBV) launched in the mid-1980s. It rapidly became a dominant view within economics-based strategy research. It challenged the received Porterian view by looking at firms *internally* in terms of their resources/capabilities rather than *externally* in terms of their products/market structures (see Wernerfelt, 1984; Rumelt, 1987; Barney, 1986, 1991; Peteraf, 1993). RBV has its roots both in strategy and economics. Such strategy classics as Barnard, Selznick, and Chandler emphasized the role of a strategy as a device which facilitates the development of internal capabilities so that externally determined opportunities can be obtained. In economics the roots of RBV can be traced to the works of Ricardo, Chamberlin, and especially Penrose (1959). They focused on capturing rents on firm-specific resources and emphasized the primacy of *firm heterogeneity* as a source of CA. The firm differences depend partly on *tacit* and *idiosyncratic* resources, which cannot be easily or at all replicated. Hence, these resources are valuable, *rare*, inimitable, and non-substitutable (VRIN) in the sense of being able to exploit opportunities (Barney, 1991: 106). Together VRIN resources constitute the set of core capabilities that form *isolating mechanisms* (Rumelt, 1987), which are supposed to be able to protect the CA against rivals' attacks thus making it sustainable.

It soon became evident, however, that when trying to understand the evolution of modern companies in real time, RBV is too static. The view had to get dynamized to be able to explain the rise of SCA especially in rapidly changing industries. DCV launched by Teece *et al.* (1997) was an attempt to tackle this problem. They defined "... dynamic capabilities as the firm's ability to integrate, build, and reconfigure internal and external competences to address rapidly changing environments" (ibid.: 516). Because the DC's are deeply embedded in organizational path dependencies they are tacit and therefore hard to imitate and substitute, thus constituting a dynamic counterpart for static VRIN attributes (Collan *et al.*, 2014). This first version of DCV can be viewed as a dynamized version of retrospective RBV. The problem was the lack of micro-foundations and the inability to explain the role of entrepreneurship. The second version of DCV (DCV 2.0) launched by Teece (2007) made an attempt to contribute to these issues. I will argue that this is possible but only when strategy research takes a more evolutionarily inclined methodological stance.

How to use the methodology of isolation as a tool to reveal the methodological underpinnings of different approaches

Isolation – what it is all about in scientific explanation

To explore the underlying explanatory structures of rival theoretical approaches Mäki (1990, 1992, 2004) has developed a useful methodological device called *the methodology of isolation* (see also Kyläheiko, 1995, 1998). The idea is that to make sense of the complexity of the real world, the theoreticians are forced to focus on a small number of items (things, properties, events, processes, relations, mechanisms). The most relevant items are rearranged and included in the domain of a theory and the rest of the items are excluded. This determines the explanatory limits of each theoretical approach. The *methodology of isolation* is a device developed to analyze this continuous process of (de)isolative rearranging and categorizing. It helps shed light on implicit metaphysical underpinnings of different types of explanations. Focusing on isolative inclusions and exclusions as well as techniques through which they have been obtained enables us to reveal strategic points at which theoretical controversies are most likely to occur.

I start my appraisal by first introducing the so called *formal isolations*, which lay the foundations for further comparisons. The basic category, *isolation*, simply means that a set of items is cut off from the rest, thus constituting an isolated field of included items. *De-isolation*, in turn, means that an isolated field is supplemented with some formerly excluded item(s). A typical method in economics is to isolate *theoretically* by using "intellectual experiments." An example of a theoretical isolation is a neoclassical textbook firm interpreted as a twice differentiable concave production function. All the other items relating to a real firm (resources, capabilities, entrepreneurial motives, etc.) have been excluded.

Another relevant distinction is made between *internal* and *external* isolations. *Internal isolation* means that the inner structure and influences coming from inside (= *intrinsic factors*) are excluded. *External isolation*, in turn, is used to eliminate *extrinsic factors*. Again, a neoclassical firm viewed as a concave production function illustrates an internal "black box" isolation in which, for example, entrepreneurial alertness is excluded.

In terms of internal and external isolations one can open an important methodological perspective by focusing on the role played by internal and external *closures* in theoretical explanations. The system can be characterized as "closed" in the specific sense that a researcher can anticipate predictability and stability of empirical and/or theoretical regularities, if and only if (1) *external closure* and (2) *internal closure* are simultaneously satisfied (Mäki, 1992). Taken together, these two closures constitute a methodological stance known as *the norm of full closure*. The situation where internal and/or external closures do not hold can be characterized by *the norm of no (full) closure*. Here we have an important divide between neoclassically and evolutionarily inspired modes of explanation to be analyzed later.

The triumph of the use of the full closure norm was classical Newtonian particle mechanics. Recalling the Newtonian scientific ideals of mainstream economics, it is not surprising that the norm of full closure is used in neoclassical economics. Agents are treated as atomistic, fully isolated from the complex internal structures of different beliefs and motives held by real individuals. The *advantage* of the use of full closure is the opportunity (1) to analyze the behavior of (representative) agents as *passive reactions* to changes of singular extrinsic factors in terms of *causal* "laws", (2) to utilize case-by-case optimization, and (3) to derive theorems concerning regular economic phenomena using *the assumption of equilibrium*. The main *disadvantage* of the use of full closure is the impossibility of coping with open-ended, emergent, and partly unpredictable historical *processes* of the real world. Innovative entrepreneurial behavior can genuinely be analyzed only in the open-ended context. In addition, the norm of full closure ontologically excludes *qualitative changes*, such as the emergence of new techniques, new products, new organizational solutions and new institutions.

Vertical (de)isolation means that universal aspects of things are cut off from particularities that instantiate them. *Vertical de-isolation*, in turn, means that an abstraction is enriched by increasing more particularities that exemplify it. Since every theory is bound to vertically isolate and, consequently, to be unrealistic, the real issue is not (un)realisticness per se, but whether the abstractions used are appropriate or inappropriate in some well-defined methodological sense. Mäki's (1990) *essentialist realist* ideas give an interpretation of this idea. The point of departure is the ontologically inspired notion of *essentialist isolation* whereby the essential entities are isolated from the observational surface.

From the *essentialist realist* point of view, it is important that the chosen level of abstraction is supported by a process of abstraction that gives rise to an essentialist interpretation. For instance, the criticism of Nelson and Winter (1982: 7–10) against the claimed "unrealisticness" of the neoclassical production function explanation can be re-read from this angle. They argue that the black box explanation cannot be used as an *essential* representation and legitimate abstraction because it cannot be obtained by abstracting from well-documented empirical evidence, which, for example, could reveal the important path-dependent firm-specific routines and capabilities.[1] In brief, the production function abstraction cannot capture the essence. Nelson and Winter's methodological postulate *appreciative theorizing* can be understood from this essentialist realism perspective.

Ontological isolations used in rival approaches

To understand the formation of theoretical isolations in different approaches one has to look at their *ontological* isolations as well.

Ontological justification based on the norm of full closure

Although there is no methodological consensus among neoclassical economists there seems to be a common denominator for many of them from hard boiled deductivists to Friedmannian predictivists, namely the methodological commitment to *the norm of full closure*. This norm enables the production of theoretical regularities, often characterized as steady-state equilibria, which are realized by the actions of well-informed maximizing agents and disturbed by no innovations. The full closure norm ignores those open-ended processes, which are created by the agents who make *real* decisions in the sense that any agent could also have acted differently.

Ontological justification based on the denial of the norm of full closure

Evolutionary economists base their isolations on the explicit refutation of the *full closure* norm. The refutation of *internal* closure rests on the analysis of agents' open-ended behavior in the conditions of radical uncertainty and the refutation of *external* closure rests on the in-depth understanding of underlying knowledge structures (embedded in first- and higher-order routines and capabilities) and evolutionary mechanisms, which maintain them and govern the interplay between agents and selection environments. Taken together, these two conditions result in the heterodox methodology and in the *ontological position*, which comes close to basic ideas of *essentialist realism*.[2] This view regards scientific endeavors as attempts to reveal enduring tendencies governed by causal mechanisms and deep structures. This can be done by using *essentialist isolations*, which are needed to separate real "deep" features from accidental "surface" features. Essentialist realism understands *causality* in terms of entities equipped with *causal powers* and necessarily starts from the idea of an open system. Through causal powers *causal agents*, such as *entrepreneurs*, can bring about effects and transmit influences, e.g. information or signals. These two elements constitute the core of the so-called *causal process theory* (Mäki, 1990, 1992) whose acceptance can be regarded as an important explanatory divide between orthodox and heterodox economics. This division can also be found between the Porterian five forces model and RBV and DCV 2.0 as will be later shown.

The characteristics of the *causal process theory* differ from the *ideal type* characteristics used by orthodox economists. To put it roughly, the standard neoclassical models assume that economic systems are in the equilibrium state where there is no ongoing processes (i.e. no causal agents bring about effects) and all the actors have full information. By contrast, at least the neo-Austrian approach belongs to the category of causal process theories. The Kirznerian idea of *entrepreneurial alertness* or *Schumpeterian innovativeness* incorporate the idea of causal agency capable of bringing about effects (e.g. through arbitrage and innovations) while the Hayekian idea of *markets as discovery mechanisms* incorporates the idea of causal propagation where the substance being propagated is price information. Interestingly, both *entrepreneurial alertness* and *markets as discovery and selection mechanisms* are also essential elements of the evolutionary theory of strategy. Hence, I interpret evolutionary approaches as manifestations of the causal process theory.

In order to reveal causal tendencies *essential* in the context of strategic change, many evolutionary economists assume that agents have abilities to learn through reinforcement mechanisms, which lead to path-dependent behavior. Agents function in a complex and radically uncertain environment and interact with other agents and institutions that constrain their behavior. In such conditions, creative causal acts generate *variation* through innovations, their unintended consequences, errors, and stochastic elements. The role of internal and external *selection mechanisms* is to propagate information and to alter the relative economic importance of rival innovations thus determining the direction of economic development at the micro as well as macro level.

Isolative techniques and strategies

When choosing between isolative strategies every theorist has to solve both *the ontological problem* of what the isolated field will be and *the methodological problem* of how isolations will be done. The *ontological* question deals with the substance of isolations, whereas the *methodological* question deals with the isolative techniques and strategies. Following the lead of Nelson and Winter (1982) I will start by dividing economic theorizing into two different but linked categories, called *formal* and *appreciative theorizing*. In light of these definitions the distinctions shown in Table 6.1 can be made.

The distinction between these two types is not clear-cut and most theoretical approaches use both of them. The hallmark of *formal* isolative techniques is that the issue of including and excluding items is primarily determined by *methodological* criteria, such as analytical tractability or elegance, whereas *appreciative* techniques emphasize *ontological* criteria and theorizing rests upon *essentialist isolations* which try to reveal underlying structures and mechanisms. The choice between the norm of *full closure* or the norm of *no full closure* reflects this divide.

To conclude, the *methodological* (how to isolate) and *ontological* (what and why to isolate) aspects of *an isolative strategy* determine the research practices followed by economists. The first position, held by most neoclassical economists, is based on the methodological choice in favor of formal theorizing at the expense of appreciative theorizing, i.e. *the ontological choice is more or less subordinated to the methodological choice*. The stronger the methodological preferences for formal theorizing are, the more limited the set of potential explanatory items and the less ontological criteria, such as essentiality, affect the choice. The second basic position, favored by most evolutionary economists, emphasizes *appreciative theorizing*. Here, the essentiality criterion plays a more decisive role and *ontological choices are no longer subordinated*.

Now we can go to the issue of how to de-isolate existing theoretical frameworks. This connects *the issue of isolation* to *the issue of explanation* (Mäki, 2004; Kyläheiko, 1998). De-isolative strategies are as follows: (1) *to de-isolate by*

Table 6.1 Distinctions between appreciative and formal theorizing

	Appreciative theorizing	*Formal theorizing*
General nature	Rich, often verbal and subject to logical inconsistencies.	Narrow but logically consistent.
Empirical nature	Close to empirical substance.	In some well-defined cases econometric fits, in other cases only stylized facts, if any.
Focus	To apply theoretical tools to articulate what is *essential*.	To improve a theoretical tool itself to explore logical connections.
Causal nature	Explicit causal argument(s).	Not necessarily causal arguments.
Type of theoretical isolation utilized	Essentially inspired theoretical isolation. No full closure.	Analytically inspired theoretical isolation. Full closure.

Source: Kyläheiko (1995).

supplementation; (2) *to de-isolate by replacement*; (3) *to de-isolate by ad hocness*. These strategies deal with such issues as how to react when an existing theoretical framework faces a situation where it has to explain new phenomena revealed by, say, empirical observation, appreciative theorizing, or rival theories. If one cannot convincingly explain them in terms of an existing theory, one can try to relieve the dilemma either by *supplementing* or *replacing* an existing theory or by using *ad hoc assumptions*. The supplementing strategy means that the existing explanans will be supplemented by means of new theoretically consistent explainers. Replacement means that some explainers of the explanans set are replaced by another explainer(s). The third (and unfortunately mostly used method in strategy research) is based on ad hocness and simply means that one utilizes auxiliary *"ad hoc" assumptions* in addition to the original explanans set to produce seemingly plausible explanations.

Towards substantive isolations used in strategy research

A step from the metatheoretical level to explanatory theories requires *substantive isolations*, which define the scope and substance of each particular theory. In my view (Kyläheiko, 1998), the most important substantive isolations used in economics-based strategy research are:

(Cx): *Cognitive isolations related to the degree of uncertainty and complexity faced by an agent*

(Bx): *Behavioral isolations relating to the way how the agent, especially an entrepreneur, behaves under cognitive constraints*

(Tx): *Temporal isolations relating to the static, stationary, dynamic nature of the models used (logical vs historical)*

(Ox): *Ontological and methodological isolations relating to the norm of full closure and appreciative theorizing*

I will start from the *cognitive* substantive isolations. The very idea of strategic change implies that there have to be innovative activities which are related to *uncertainty* and *complexity*. Without uncertainty and complexity there are no real economic problems either and the main goal of strategy research, i.e. obtaining SCA, could be calculated as a solution of constrained optimization. Unfortunately, the entrepreneurs are always faced by complexity and uncertainty i.e. they are cognitively incompetent. Hence, they cannot always optimize and their decisions may prove to be false. On the other hand, only uncertainty makes it possible to profit from innovations and to obtain extra profits. Following Kyläheiko (1995, 1998) and Collan *et al.* (2014). I use the following uncertainty and complexity characterizations:

(C1): *Parametric uncertainty* is based on the agent's subjective degree of belief with regard to the probability of events and the consequences of his/her actions. The probability function and the decision situation are assumed to be known. An agent has *certain* knowledge as to *the structure of the decision problem*, but *uncertain* knowledge as to the (probability) *parameters* of the decision problem. This *parametric uncertainty* concept can easily be combined with neoclassical assumptions concerning profit maximization.

(C2): A more de-isolated concept, *structural uncertainty*, is based on imperfect knowledge of the structure the future can take. Most relevant entrepreneurial decisions no doubt take place under structurally uncertain circumstances.

(C3): The lack of sufficient cognitive capabilities of a decision-maker when facing a complex decision situation results in the "competence gap"; this complexity-related concept of uncertainty is called *procedural uncertainty* (Simon, 1976).

(C4): The most de-isolated uncertainty concept is called *radical uncertainty*. Here it means that there exist at the same time both parametric, structural, and procedural uncertainties faced by a decision-maker.

Standard neoclassical economics has tried to overcome these problems by filling the information and competence gaps in terms of an *omniscient optimizer* and using only parametric uncertainty in their formalisms. This is far from the entrepreneurial reality and does not pass the essentialist realism test. To be serious the *evolutionarily inspired view of strategy* has to start from the radical uncertainty concept. Here the key concept is the "routine." It captures the idea of "what is regular and predictable about business behavior" from operative tasks to strategic management heuristics (Nelson and Winter, 1982: 15).

Our next substantive isolations are called *behavioral* isolations (Bx). They relate to the notion of *rationality*. One of the "hard-core" assumptions of the neoclassical research program concerns the maximization behavior of economic agents. According to Langlois and Czontos (1993: 120) such a "thin conception of rationality" which could lead to calculative maximizing behavior involves (1) almost perfect information, (2) continuous, reflexive, transitive, and complete preference orderings, and (3) constrained optimization of an objective function.

While many neoclassicians emphasize a thin conception of rationality just because it excludes psychological behavioralist commitments and transforms the choice into an exercise of pure logic, heterodox economists regard this behavioral sterilization as a failure that hinders *essential* and *realistic* theorizing (Nelson and Winter, 1982: 30–3). The criticism against the purely logical conceptualization of rationality can be traced back to Simon who 1947 introduced the notion of "bounded rationality" as a characterization of behavior that is "intendedly rational, but only limitedly so." Later Simon (1976) launched the distinction between *substantive* and *procedural rationality*. *Substantive rationality* refers to the outcomes of rational choices, whereas *procedural rationality* deals with the effectiveness of the choice process that depends on the cognitive "competence"-gap. By connecting these rationality notions with the cognitive isolations (Cx) one can introduce *behavioral (de)isolations (Bx)*:

(B1): *Parametric uncertainty and no competence gap* → *(thin) bounded rationality*

(B2): *Structural uncertainty and no competence gap* → *(thick) bounded rationality*

(B3): *Structural uncertainty and competence gap → (thick) bounded procedural rationality*

(B4): *Radical uncertainty and proactive alert innovative behavior → innovative rationality*

In the case of *(thin) bounded rationality* (B1) the outcome can be formulated in terms of subjective probability distributions and there is no procedural uncertainty that could result in complexity. Hence, a decision-maker could be replaced by an omniscient calculator who utilizes constrained optimization methods within a given means-end framework. Deliberate idiosyncratic business strategies are neither allowed nor needed because, in the same situation, each firm always makes the same optimal decision. This means, of course, that *variation* among firms is excluded.

However, to be able to explain the essential element of entrepreneurial endeavor it is necessary to *thicken* the concept of rationality at the expense of the explanatory power of the maximization rule. This brings us to the notion of (thick) *bounded rationality* where there are two versions based on the concepts of either *substantive* or *procedural* uncertainty. *Bounded (substantive) rationality* (B2) can be achieved by accepting *structurally imperfect knowledge* in the explanans set but by retaining the idealization of procedural certainty (non-complexity) at the same time.

If the explanans set is de-isolated so that *cognitive limits of agents* are recognized as well, the answer to the question of learning possibilities becomes crucial (Simon, 1976: 132–3). This brings us to *bounded procedural rationality de-isolation* (B3). When compared to de-isolation of bounded substantive rationality (B2) now a decision-maker's responses to environmental shocks are different (Kyläheiko, 1995). In (B2) de-isolation, environmental uncertainty results in a more constrained optimization rule that strengthens the need for cognitive abilities, whereas in procedural de-isolation (B3) environmental uncertainty results in a growing competence gap, which triggers off search procedures to produce more predictable and stable satisficing *routines*. Using routines often economizes on scarce decision-making resources and makes it possible to learn by modifying these routines in terms of new information and past experiences. There are also other crucial differences between (B2) and (B3) de-isolations as well. One important difference deals with the role of the *time* factor. Because backward-looking routines are based upon repeated experiences in the past, it is necessary to take *historical time* into account when utilizing the concept of procedural rationality. The most de-isolated concept, *innovative rationality* (B4), is based on the idea of *radical uncertainty* and *proactive learning*, thus implying that it is not enough to overcome solely the problems of procedural uncertainty. Even if the environment were so stable that the competence gap could be bridged, it would always be possible to create novelties which would generate radical uncertainty and so on. Consequently, the creative mind of an individual alone can break down a steady-state situation and, most importantly, trigger off new developments. Procedural rationality de-isolation (B3) emphasizes adaptive information processing behavior through *reactive, "passive" learning*, whereas innovative rationality de-isolation (B4) stresses the role of *proactive, creative learning* through search processes. The former focuses on *threats* while the latter on *opportunities*.

Next we can have a brief look at *temporal isolations* used in strategy research. *Temporal modeling idealizations* concern the rates of change in a factor or its features and play an important role in economic reasoning. *Static* (T1) analyses are based on the idealization that the time factor does not count. Comparative statics means nothing but comparing different timeless equilibria, as Joan Robinson always used to remind us. The Newtonian-inspired full closure thinking allows the treatment of time as just another logically consistent variable with other variables of models and allows the extension of the static optimization analysis to the intertemporal dynamic optimization analysis. *Steady-state* (T2) *models* rest on the idealization of equal and constant rates of "change" in each included factor. Nothing in this *logical time* construct distinguishes past from future. Difficult problems of structural changes and disequilibrium processes can be avoided by idealizing the speed of adjustment to be infinite and adjustment costs to be nil, or simply by postulating equilibrium steady-states. Thus, *irreversible historical time* can be transformed into *reversible logical time* (cf. Robinson, 1974). Through this device, the pervasive uncertainty of future events can be excluded. Since the evolutionary approach regards radical uncertainty as its ontological furniture, it tries to de-isolate the standard neoclassical set of temporal assumptions which prevents the analysis of historical time.

A typical temporal idealization used in *dynamic* models (T3) can be formulated so that no new variables (for instance, no innovations) appear in the system and the causal relations within the model do not change endogenously. In the context of strategic change, these idealized assumptions are problematic, since they treat agents as identical particles that deterministically obey fixed predetermined laws of motion (as celestials). An exit could be a de-isolation where innovators and learning agents endogenously generate changes through self-organization (T4). Interestingly, this step has already been taken in post-Newtonian *far-from-equilibrium* physics and chemistry, which use ideas of chaos and complexity theories (Elsner, 2010).

The last substantive isolation category refers to *ontological* and *methodological isolations* used and their justifications. We have already touched upon this issue and here we can only state that there are two basic ontological isolations to be done: one can choose either the norm of full closure (O1) that also dictates the formal methodological stance or the norm of no full closure (O2) that allows the use of more elements of appreciative theorizing based on the essentialist realism.

Economics-based strategy approaches in light of methodology of isolation

Porterian five forces model

Now we are able to look different rival approaches from the perspective of the methodology of isolation, focusing on their substantive isolations.

Porter's five forces model's message is that a firm should position itself so that it maximizes its bargaining power by means of entry barriers and economies of scale. The Porterian rents are monopoly rents. Porter's idea of SCA is strongly *externally determined*. The firms within an industry are idealized to be *homogeneous* in terms of their strategically relevant capabilities. In addition, Porter uses an idealization that industry level forces have similar effects on each firm and that all the firms react predictably. The substantive isolations used in Porter's model are as follows:

(C1) & (B1): Behind the Porterian model is a neoclassical monopoly model with all its typical idealizations, i.e. uncertainty is assumed to be *parametric* and the agents are able to optimize since they are (thinly) *boundedly rational*. The *ontological* stance is the *norm of full closure* (O1) and the *methodological* stance is based on *formal theorizing*, even if Porter's illustrations are fairly informal.

The temporal isolation (T1) used is *static*. Therefore Porter cannot give any good explanation of the *sustainability* of monopoly rents. The analysis of the *internal organization* is extremely thin. Entrepreneurial innovating behavior is not actively taken into account when formulating the competitive strategy.

Porter's "upside-down" neoclassicism gives rise to interesting theoretical ambiguities because of its "full closure nature." In general, neoclassical optimization logic postulates calculatively strong agents who do not have any causal power to deliberately influence their environment. Porter, however, postulates *rational agents with causal power* (= with the ability to capture SCA). This strong combination (rational and causal power) makes some firms almost omnipotent. One can only ask through which kind of selection mechanisms these omnipotent firms have been selected. If every firm is assumed to be omnipotent, one cannot easily see how only some lucky firms can base their strategic logic on obtaining SCA based on monopoly power. One possible reason may be economies of scale and scope, which give rise to natural monopolies. If that is the case, we are in a neoclassical world, where extra strong technology determinism rules. Only the firms with economies of scale and scope can succeed. Behind this explanation the only explainer is good luck! Paradoxically, this is an even narrower stance than standard neoclassical *external determinism* and does not leave much scope for discretionary business strategies.

From the explanatory perspective, even worse is that the Porterian "upside down" logic with imperfect competition leaves the question of full closure open. Whereas the neoclassical models typically look for the conditions of the existence of the unique market equilibrium, Porter's strategy concept rests on the existence and viability of the imperfect competition equilibrium. However, he does not characterize the connections between different firms and does not tell us how this equilibrium could ever be achieved, let alone how monopoly rents could be sustained. He only *postulates* his answer.

Later Porter (1991) tries to go further through de-isolating by supplementing and takes into account the criticism that he overlooks innovation. What is new is the emphasis on *dynamics* and *internal* innovation *processes*, which result in continuous upgrading of the sources of CA. In fact, Porter now seems to adopt some Schumpeterian elements. New opportunities are created, imitated, and de-stroyed and CA is only provisionally sustained if the firms are not ready to renew their capabilities. However, these *ontological* properties (e.g. a causal process view based on bounded procedural rationality) cannot be reconciled with his basic model. They offer a good example of the art of *de-isolating by ad hocness* at its worst. In brief, Porter's *no full closure* emphasis clearly contradicts the premises of Porter's old framework, which was based on the static but theoretically well-founded matching of external and internal factors using the equilibrium explanation and profit maximization hypothesis.

Resource-based view focusing on firm internal resources

The resource-based view (RBV) challenged the Porterian view by looking at firms *internally* in terms of their resources that are partly *tacit* and *idiosyncratic* and therefore hard to replicate. The resources are *rare* and *valuable* in the sense of being able to exploit opportunities and/or neutralize external threats. Together these characteristics constitute the set of core resources which give a firm an SCA. From this angle, one can regard RBV as an attempt to *vertically de-isolate the Marshallian representative firm* and to derive strategic conclusions from this endeavor. One can see RBV as an example of de-isolating by supplement in a way that allows the firm *internal* factors to be taken into account.

Wernerfelt (1984) and Rumelt (1987) brought the many former strategy strands (Chamberlin, Selznick, Chandler, Penrose) together by using formal methods to complete RBV. Wernerfelt developed a dual to the Porter-inspired SCA theory by noticing that "for the firm, resources and products are two sides of the same coin". Indeed, one can find many dual similarities in the strategic views of Wernerfelt and Porter. Only the implications derived from the typical neoclassical model are different, since Wernerfelt focuses on *resource market imperfections* and Porter on *product market imperfections*. Interestingly, Wernerfelt uses such concepts as "rational," "optimal," and "maximization," and clearly his cognitive and behavioral isolations are typically neoclassical. It is a question of a *static equilibrium model* with the emphasis on resources. From the dual theory perspective Wernerfelt's and Porter's results are actually identical. The basic RBV uses similar cognitive (C1) and behavioral (B1) isolations as Porter. However, Wernerfelt's (1984: 174–79) practical examples and strategy formulations crucially differ from Porter's strategy options. The only way to coherently draw these different conclusions would have been to abandon the static equilibrium framework actually used by RBV. This is due to the simple fact that a firm's superior capabilities based on the critical pool of resources (leading to core capabilities with VRIN attributes) are inherently *dynamic* and cannot be dealt with statically. Firms are heterogeneous because they have an irreversible history of their own based on accumulated tangible and intangible resources and on organizational capabilities of tacit learning. This view would have been fully in accordance with empirical innovation studies. However, to be able to answer this challenges RBV should have been able to get rid of its static maximization-based framework as well by replacing it by a real *dynamic (or evolutionarily grounded) RBV*. This could have been done only by de-isolating the full closure norm and by accepting the use of the no full closure norm with all its problems. However, Wernerfelt and later Barney (1991) and Peteraf (1993) did not take this route. They just gave lip service to this de-isolations and used the static formal basic equilibrium model.

The main problem of the standard RBV is its inability to deal with competition and internal and external selection mechanisms, i.e. to deal with *historical* time. RBV seems to take firm-specific resources for granted, not as outcomes of a careful efficiency- or evolutionary-based reasoning. A more detailed and disaggregated picture is needed and one has to acknowledge that there is no single success formula or strategy but that the innovating firm is in a continuous state of flux where the myopic decisions depend on firm-specific resources as well as on complementary assets, radical uncertainty, the appropriability regime, and the rate of environmental change. It is clear that RBV cannot offer any useful strategy framework that could be able to explain how CA can be sustained outside a fictitious stationary state. In such conditions it would be enough to have resource with VRIN attributes but unfortunately we are not living in a stationary world. It is clear that RBV has to be radically de-isolated in a way that makes it possible to replace the full closure norm by the no full closure norm. Interestingly and symptomatically, the protagonists of RBV were silent on the role of entrepreneurs and left open the crucial question of where the VRIN resources come from and how.

Dynamic capability view as a method to dynamize the strategy framework

It is clear that when trying to understand the evolution of modern business firms in real time, the snapshot given by RBV is too static. It has to be de-isolated by supplementing its explanans set so that SCA can be explained as an outcome of entrepreneurs' proactive decisions in historical time. The first version of DCV, launched by Teece *et al.* (1997), was a modest attempt in this direction. According to Teece (2012: 1395) "DC's are higher-level competences that determine the firm's ability to integrate, build, and reconfigure internal and external resources/competences to address, and possibly shape, rapidly changing business environments." The firm was seen as bundles of routines that generate (first-order) ordinary capabilities (Winter, 2003) that are able to replicate the existing organization in stationary conditions but not any more when the environment is in flux (Zollo and Winter, 2002). Then the firm needs higher-order DCs to be able to change existing resources/capabilities.

A crucial element of DCs is that they are not available in the markets but have to be generated within the firm. Since the market for DCs is thin or non-existent their generation is pervasively uncertain and costly. Because of their path-dependent nature the DCs are tacit and therefore hard to imitate and substitute, thus constituting a dynamic counterpart for static VRIN attributes. This first version of the DCV can be interpreted as a dynamized version of the RBV. Now the impact of environmental changes within the ecosystem has been taken into account by supplementing the explanans set with DCs that explain the changes of existing resources/routines/capabilities. However, this first-generation DCV model does not yet clearly articulate its cognitive and behavioral isolations and also leaves unclear what exactly its ontological and methodological stance is. Interestingly, Teece *et al.* (1997) and Winter (2002) clearly refer to evolutionary thinking and use routines as basic constituents of capabilities thus giving this approach a flavor of the no full closure. Nevertheless, the way DCs are to be interpreted remains a little unclear. For instance, one influential strand of DCV research, based especially on Eisenhardt and Martin (2000), interprets DCV simply as an extension of RBV in the context where the external environment is changing. In this quasi-dynamized view, the DCs are regarded as best practices that promote efficiencies. According to this view, no more crucial methodological de-isolations are needed. It is enough to de-isolate the RBV idealization of no external factors in a way that allows the capabilities to change. In sum, the original Teecean first DCV version uses cognitive isolation that at least allows structural uncertainty (C2), even if this is not explicated, and allows also routine-based behavior instead of optimizing behavior thus using procedural behavioral de-isolation (B3) as well, whereas Eisenhardt and Martin's "best practice" approach can be interpreted only as a de-isolation that allows reflection of the changing environments. It is still based on maximization logic and clearly utilizes the norm of full closure as its forerunner RBV.

The next step towards a well-defined theoretical framework, called DCV 2.0, was taken by Teece (2007), Helfat *et al.* (2007), and Helfat and Peteraf (2009) who started to search for the micro-foundations of DCs. Based on this de-isolation project, Teece (2007) recognized that the DCs consisted of capacities: (1) to identify an opportunity or strategic option ("sensing"), (2) to exercise the strategic option by means of real investment in tangible or intangible assets ("seizing"), (3) to transform the resource- and knowledge bases, the routines/ordinary capabilities of the firm, in a way that gives the best strategic fit with the changing ecosystem and the strategy followed ("reconfiguring") (Collan *et al.*, 2014). This means that now the DCs were first time ever seen as outcomes of intentional entrepreneurial/managerial actions. They were no longer based solely on ordinary routines/capabilities as Winter (2003) seemed to think. The "sensing" link now also de-isolated the explanans so that it included the ability to sense weak signals, which is an essential part of the entrepreneurial function. This activity cannot be based on firm internal routines/capabilities but is something that really distinguishes between firms (think about the fate of Nokia, Motorola, and Apple in the ICT).

Teece (2012) emphasized that top management's entrepreneurial competencies relating to sensing, seizing, and reconfiguring are necessary when sustaining CA (see also Zahra *et al.*, 2006; Helfat and Peteraf, 2015). Teece (2012: 1398) concludes as follows:

> Entrepreneurship is about sensing and understanding opportunities, getting things started, and finding new and better ways of putting things together [...]. Entrepreneurial management has little to do with standardized analysis

and optimization. It is more about figuring out the next big opportunity or challenge and how to address it – rather than maintaining and refining existing procedures.

The new DCV 2.0 takes these aspects into account, even if it does not yet offer any real process theory of entrepreneurial action (let alone the emergent repercussions between companies and institutions – see Elsner, 2010).

This means that new de-isolations of the explanans set made it possible, first, to take into account the ecosystem where the firm functions in an exact way through sensing. This means that the basic idea of RBV to ignore the role of external factors was denied. Second, the new DCV 2.0 made it possible to take into account the role of an entrepreneur as a proactive agent. Third, DCV 2.0 includes at least a (rudimentary) theory about *entrepreneurship*, which is based on the ideas of Kirzner, Schumpeter, and Penrose. It clearly distinguishes between *managerial* and *entrepreneurial competencies* and emphasizes the interplay between them. As Penrose (1959) stresses, the growth of firms is, however, more dependent upon the latter, upon the ability to create and discover new opportunities and to make them come true. Rumelt (1987: 143) connects this idea with the concept of evolution and defines the Schumpeterian "rent as the difference between a venture's ex post value (or payment stream) and the ex-ante cost (or value) of the resources combined to form the venture." This definition neatly brings together the aspects of radical uncertainty and discovering new combinations. If we were living in a stationary neoclassical RBV world there would be an expectational equilibrium where "ex post value = ex ante cost" and no entrepreneurial rent and hence no incentives for growth either. In order to be motivated to seek extra profits (Kirzner) and to be able to sustain them, at least the following preconditions have to exist: *radical uncertainty* (C3); *proactivity innovational rationality* (B4); *disequilibrium historical processes based on routine/capabilities to overcome difficulty gaps* (T4); *causal ambiguity* (*tacitness, specificity, complexity*); and *entrepreneurial alertness.*

Conclusions

After this methodological reappraisal of strategy research approaches I am ready to conclude that DCV 2.0 effectively utilizes the *sensing-seizing-reconfiguring* triad and the idea of *intentional entrepreneurial behavior* is a giant step towards an evolutionarily inspired theory of strategy suitable also for turbulent conditions characterized by keen competition. However, as showed by Collan *et al.* (2014) this development is still in its infancy both theoretically and especially empirically. DCV 2.0 is not yet genuinely forward-looking, since the important role of expectations and managerial guesses and hunches is overlooked and there is no real theory of entrepreneurship based on causal process theory. The next step should be to further develop the cognitive and behavioral de-isolations and to try to formalize them by using modern complexity-based methods following, for instance, the learning and network-based ideas put forward by Professor Elsner (2010). Another necessary step would be to find out routine/capabilities-based de-isolations that can be operationalized (see, however, Danneels, 2015) so that DCV 2.0 could be either econometrically justified or suitable for field experiments. Even if I am a dedicated follower of appreciative theorizing it is quite clear that to be successful every theoretical framework has to be able to get corroborated in the reality check.

Notes

1 See Nelson and Winter (1982: 8): "It is a caricature to associate orthodoxy with the analysis of static equilibria, but it is no caricature to remark that continued reliance on equilibrium analysis, even in its more flexible forms, still leaves the discipline largely blind to phenomena associated with historical change."

2 Nelson and Winter (1982: 134): "Theorists should aim to tell the truth in their theorizing, but they cannot aim to tell the whole truth. For to theorize is precisely to focus on those entities and relationships in reality that are believed to be central to the phenomena observed – and largely to ignore the rest."

References

Barney, J. B. (1986) "Strategic factor markets: experience, luck and business strategy," *Management Science*, 32 (10): 1231–41.

Barney, J. B. (1991) "Firm resources and sustained competitive advantage," *Journal of Management*, 17 (1): 99–120.

Collan, M., Freiling, J., Kyläheiko, K., and Roemer, E. (2014) "Entrepreneurship and the art of tackling technological crises: a strategic real options framework," *International Journal of Technology Intelligence and Planning*, 10: 166–85.

Danneels, E. (2015) "Survey measures of first- and second-order competences," *Strategic Management Journal* (accepted 29 July 2015 for publication).

Eisenhardt, K. and Martin, J. (2000) 'Dynamic capabilities: what are they?', *Strategic Management Journal*, 21 (10/11): 1105–21.

Elsner, W. (2010) "The process and a simple logic of 'meso.' Emergence and the co-evolution of institutions and group size," *Journal of Evolutionary Economics*, 20 (3): 445–77.

Helfat, C. E. and Peteraf, M. (2009) "Understanding dynamic capabilities: progress along a developmental path," *Strategic Organization*, 7 (1): 91–102.

Helfat, M. and Peteraf, M. (2015) 'Managerial cognitive capabilities and the microfoundations of dynamic capabilities', *Strategic Management Journal*, 36 (6): 831–50.

Helfat, C. E., Finkelstein, S., Mitchell, W., Peteraf, M. A., Singh, H., Teece, D. J., and Winter, S. G. (2007) *Dynamic Capabilities – Understanding Strategic Change in Organizations*. Malden, MA: Blackwell.

Hine, D., Parker, R., Pregelj, L., and Verreyne, M.-L. (2013) "Deconstructing and reconstructing the capability hierarchy," *Industrial and Corporate Change*, 23 (5): 1299–325.

Kyläheiko, K. (1995) *Coping with Technology*, Research Papers 48. Lappeenranta University of Technology, Lappeenranta.

Kyläheiko, K. (1998) "Making sense of technology: towards a synthesis between neoclassical and evolutionary approaches," *International Journal of Production Economics*, 56–7: 319–22.

Langlois, R. N. and Czontos, L. (1993) "Optimization, rule-following and the methodology of situational analysis," in U. Mäki, B. Gustafsson, and C. Knudsen (eds), *Rationality, Institutions and Economic Methodology*. London: Routledge, pp. 113–32.

Mäki, U. (1990) "Scientific realism and Austrian explanation," *Review of Political Economy*, 2: 310–44.

Mäki, U. (1992) "On the method of isolation in economics," in C. Dilworth (ed.), *Idealization IV: Intelligibility in Science*, Poznan Studies in the Philosophy of the Sciences and the Humanities 26, pp. 317–50.

Mäki, U. (2004) "Theoretical isolation and explanatory progress: transaction cost economics and the dynamics of dispute," *Cambridge Journal of Economics*, 28 (3): 319–46.

Nelson, R. R. and Winter, S. (1982) *An Evolutionary Theory of Economic Change*. Cambridge, MA: Harvard University Press.

Penrose, E. T. (1959) *The Theory of the Growth of the Firm*. Oxford: Basil Blackwell.

Peteraf, M. A. (1993) "The cornerstones of competitive advantage: a resource-based view," *Strategic Management Journal*, 14: 179–91.

Porter, M. E. (1980) *Competitive Strategy: Techniques for Analyzing Industries and Competitors*. New York: Free Press.

Porter, M. E. (1985) *Competitive Advantage*. New York: Free Press.

Porter, M. E. (1991) "Towards a dynamic theory of strategy," *Strategic Management Journal*, 12: 95–117.

Robinson, J. (1974) "History versus equilibrium," *Indian Economic Journal*, 21: 202–12.

Rumelt, R. P. (1987) "Theory, strategy, and entrepreneurship" in D. J. Teece (ed.), *The Competitive Challenge: Strategies for Industrial Innovation and Renewal*. Cambridge, MA: Blackwell, US, pp. 137–58.

Simon, H. A. (1976) "From substantive to procedural rationality," in S. Latsis (ed.), *Method and Appraisal in Economics*. Cambridge: Cambridge University Press.

Teece, D. J. (2007) "Explicating dynamic capabilities: the nature and microfoundations of (sustainable) enterprise performance," *Strategic Management Journal*, 28 (13): 1319–50.

Teece, D. J. (2012) "Dynamic capabilities: routines versus entrepreneurial action," *Journal of Management Studies*, 49 (8): 1395–401.

Teece, D. J., Pisano, P., and Shuen, A. (1997) "Dynamic capabilities and strategic management," *Strategic Management Journal*, 18 (7): 509–33.

Wernerfelt, B. (1984) "A resource-based view of the firm," *Strategic Management Journal*, 5: 171–80.

Winter, S. (1995) "Four Rs of profitability: rents, resources, routines and replication," in C. A. Montgomery (ed.), *Resource-based and Evolutionary Theories of the Firm: Towards Synthesis*. Boston: Kluwer Academic.

Winter, S. G. (2003) "Understanding dynamic capabilities," *Strategic Management Journal*, 24 (10): 991–5.

Zahra, A., Sapienza, H., and Davidsson, P. (2006) "Entreprenurship and dynamic capabilities: a review, model and research agenda," *Journal of Management Studies*, 43 (4): 917–55.

Zollo, M. and Winter, S. G. (2002) "Deliberate learning and the evolution of dynamic capabilities," *Organization Science*, 13 (3): 339–51.

7 The enduring tension

The political economy of industrial policy

James I. Sturgeon

Introduction

Tension and conflict are an enduring thread in the fabric of human association, complicating the arts of associated living. In this chapter the concept of enduring tension, defined below, is used to interpret a strand of economic thought related to the organization of production. The chapter begins with a sketch of early modern western views of conflict related to the social control of production. The purpose of this sketch is limited to illustrating how the enduring tension may shine a somewhat different light on this strand of economic thinking. It is then used in analyzing industrial policies aimed at easing the tension. Selected policies which illustrate reasons and circumstances for the social control of production are examined.[1] In particular, the dual policy approach of direct regulation and anti-monopoly are discussed and critiqued including a sketch of the theoretical roots of these approaches. The chapter concludes with an examination of a policy alternative derived from institutional theory. First is a short discussion of the enduring tension.

The concept of enduring tension

Enduring tension is used to describe the conflict between what is good for individuals and what is good for society. It is a tension between private and public interests. The proposition here is that people live together neither in natural harmony nor perpetual conflict, but in a durable and enduring tension created as they seek to resolve the problems brought on by the evolving forces of the life process. Drawing on the arts of associated living humans can control the tension and prevent the tearing of the social fabric. Like the industrial and ceremonial arts, these arts are learned, evolve, and accumulate.

The enduring tension has long been part of human association. For purposes here the gist of the problem came into stark relief when the "organic" society of the Middle Ages began to give way to the more "interdependent" society that followed. In a production-for-use handicraft system, there was little question as to what was being traded. The gradual decline of the handicraft system was followed by an increase in monetary valuation exchange. Hence additional and powerful avenues to heighten the enduring tension were introduced. In money societies individuals can do well if they have money, sometimes with little concern for how they acquire it. For the group, which includes those associated with the interdependent network of economic relations, the problem is different. At bottom some in the group must be capable of provisioning the means of life, as a matter of both skill and permission.

Economic thought and the enduring tension

Of course an "enduring tension" is not explicitly found in the history of economic thought. Here it is used to examine the competitive market, which several writers in the past half millennium have developed to analyze the organization of production. This strand has influenced production organization policy and there is little doubt that standard economic theory from Smith through Marshall and beyond sanctioned the market as the principal organizing mechanism for production. Competition was the force believed capable of disciplining "individual" producers' actions.

The following is a brief and simplified survey of the "modern" intellectual history related to social conflict and tension related to this strand. It dates to Machiavelli (2013) and can be traced to contemporary thought. Adam Smith (1937) framed it as private vice/public virtue and sought an alternative economic order to replace mercantilism. Malthus (1967) and Ricardo (1969) followed suit but turned it into a prescription for economic stagnation and bare subsistence. Marx (1970) saw the problem as an inevitable struggle between the haves and the have nots, a class struggle leading inevitably to the promises of the Enlightenment. Veblen (1904) framed the problem as a stream of distinctions between science and superstition, or more specifically between industrial and pecuniary habits. Keynes saw the problem as a series of fallacies of composition that led to an internal breakdown of economic order; individual rationality leading to irrational group outcomes. Galbraith (1952) used the concept of countervailing power to explain why both liberals and conservatives have problems explaining the large corporation and to show why government activity was needed to help close the gap between the power of the corporation and the ability of the individual to bargain over wages.

Niccolò Machiavelli – self-interest and the state

Machiavelli was the first student in early modern Western Europe to write systematically about the problem of the state, the nation, and conflict. He was concerned with the new state primarily oriented toward commerce, and represented the point of view of the rising middle class[2] that was beginning to emerge in the fifteenth and sixteenth centuries. He wrote when the rise of manufacturing and commerce and of the middle (capitalist) class coincided with the rising individualism of the Renaissance. Machiavelli (2013) wrote of humans as motivated by self-interest and power. Further, he was aware of the struggle to overcome the vested interests of those seeking to maintain their power and position.

> It ought to be remembered that there is nothing more difficult to take in hand, more perilous to conduct, or more uncertain in its success, that to take the lead in the introduction of a new order of things. Because the innovator has for enemies all those who have done well under the old conditions, and lukewarm defenders among those who may do well under the new.
>
> (Machiavelli, 2013)

With these words Machiavelli succinctly grasped one of the more durable sources of resistance to change and of social tension.

The most enthusiastic followers of this philosophy included the rising urban population anxious to acquire political and economic power and position, yet suffering under the rule of agriculturally orientated aristocrats. The interests of the general public were not considered because it was assumed that what was good for the ruling class was good for the remainder of the population. Machiavelli wrote about self-interest in such narrow and sometimes uncomplimentary terms that the analysis repels some, but the fact remains that he was saying in his way what Smith and the eighteenth-century philosophers later said in a more honorific manner.

Adam Smith – the joy of natural law and social harmony

Smith tended to see conflict in individual terms. He too believed individuals were motivated by self-interest, but in a world of strenuous market competition it would be impossible to make an income in except by producing goods of high quality as cheaply as possible. He relied upon competition, a particular form of conflict, to harness the tension among individuals and force them to promote the public welfare. Smith's "law of markets" was revolutionary because it applied the Newtonian concept of the natural order to the economic system.

The natural order concept captivated the imagination of philosophers because it supplied a model for replacing the mercantile/monarchial system which they saw as inefficient, oppressive, and obstructive of further industrial progress. Like the Physiocrats he argued that if the artificial regulations of monarchy and mercantilism were swept away the natural economy would come into its own. Smith's economics, in the context of a larger natural order, helped to supply the intellectual ideas necessary to give people enough confidence to overthrow the old order. The concept was almost tailor-made for the needs of the eighteenth century. It said, in effect, that there must be laws governing the social organization of mankind similar to those governing the physical universe. Accordingly, the monarchies and church had enslaved the minds of men and substituted an artificial and unnatural set of laws in place of natural laws.

Smith gave conflict a new turn. Before him it was customary for those with a pessimistic philosophy to follow Machiavelli and Hobbes in declaring that conflict was inevitable, if not beneficial. Smith visualized conflict at the level of competitive individuals engaged in small-scale methods of production beneficial to the wealth of the nation. The eighteenth century's social philosophers were optimistic nearly to the point of foolishness and soon a strong reaction set in against this optimism. Perhaps one of the reasons was the shock associated with the violence of the French Revolution. When the British middle class saw this it occurred to them that the English working class might do the same. The promises of competitive market control of power had not been realized and some in England argued that the suffering was due to the undesirable institutional arrangements that were still persistent.

Thomas Malthus and David Ricardo – end of joy

Few have thought Malthus and Ricardo to harbor an optimistic outlook. For them bare subsistence was the plight of most. The population doctrine of Malthus and the wage doctrines of Ricardo proved emotionally satisfying to the British middle class. Poverty was due to inexorable laws of nature and not to the existence of defective social arrangements. Class conflict had grown since the time of Smith's *Wealth of Nations* in part due to the repressive measures the ruling classes imposed upon the rank and file of laborers. There was also a very sharp class conflict between businessmen and landowners.

Malthus saw poverty as a stimulus to the production of wealth and as a natural phenomenon that could not and should not be cured. Indeed, what was bad for the masses, poverty, was good for the society because it provided the incentive to work. This ironic reversal of the effects of the enduring tension is notable. The poverty of the masses, while unfortunate, was the natural order and government attempts to improve the condition of individuals would only harm the group. The atomistic world could also explain population pressure and wages and it was a world in which human atoms acted as they did because they were more or less naturally forced to do so. There were not only predictable relationships between individuals but also between economic classes.

Thus at the beginning of the nineteenth century not only economists but much of the population was deeply and emotionally involved in the problems of social conflict that raged around them. Not surprisingly much of the reaction was emotional and one of the deep ironies of the situation is that Ricardo, in particular, was accepted as readily as he was because he seemed to be the embodiment of pure logic, unsullied by emotional preconceptions. Malthus was nevertheless correct implying that population, poverty, and depression were problems that deserved the best thought that people could give them. While Ricardo was mistaken in opposing Malthus on the problem of depression he was correct in saying that income distribution, high prices, and the behavior of monopolistic landlords created a serious problem for society. By the beginning and early years of the nineteenth century, economists had turned pessimistic and rejected the idea of economic progress and economic improvement. This denial of the hopes and promises that had been raised by the social philosophers of the eighteenth century came as a blow.

It is probably a mistake to credit Malthus and Ricardo for being able to convince the world that the optimistic prophesies of Smith regarding the future of industrial society were really "a fool's paradise" (Heilbroner and Milberg, 2002). A better explanation of the pessimism that set in toward the end of the eighteenth century was the traumatic shock that people received from the French Revolution and the wave of Red hysteria that followed. The fear of radical reforms swept over England perhaps to a greater extent than the fear of communism in the US after the World Wars. The British Parliament passed laws forbidding laborers from organizing unions and they legislated the wages of labor in a way that worked hardships on them. They set their faces sternly against social reform legislation. And, of course, by repealing a series of anti-competitive acts and passing other acts they sought to institute the promise of the competitive market. These events also increased the suffering of the masses and caused an upsurge in social discontent, class hostility, and conflict. This era of hysteria and pessimism was tailor-made for the acceptance and glorification of the kind of pessimistic ideologies that Malthus and Ricardo offered.[3]

Karl Marx – joy returns

Marx was perhaps the most effective spokesman for the working population in factories and mines. He vigorously reaffirmed the hopes and prophesies of the eighteenth-century philosophers and tried to direct the attention of economists to social, political, and economic problems, as had Smith. One of the important contributions of Marx was to make cultural change a systematic and integrated part of his theory of human affairs. In fact, his theory of the cumulative development of economic life may be his most important contribution to a systematic analysis of social change. The attempt to unify theory and historical events and to create an awareness of economic change and of the conflict of values of an increased number of groups helped make it possible to have a better understanding of the past.

Marx's theory of conflict was a continuation of the theory of conflict which came to occupy a dominant part in the thinking of Western Europe from at least the time of Machiavelli. Whereas some classical economists had seen the conflict working itself out primarily through individual rivalry, Marx saw it in terms of both individual competition and class conflict, with the latter overshadowing the former in importance. Marx's theory of class conflict was valuable in counteracting the excessive emphasis that economists in the liberal classical tradition placed upon harmony.[4] He understood conflict and transposed it to serve his purposes and his conception of the science of history. He believed that capitalism concentrates class conflict more clearly than previous systems and that it creates and educates the proletariat that will rise and overthrow it. The selfish capitalist had no intention of playing a role in helping to usher in the desirable socialist system Marx wanted, but yet was an active agent in this process.

Thorstein Veblen – evolutionary tension

Veblen's theory of the economy is lodged in the Darwinian concept of cumulative change and adaptation. In tracing the evolution of production from handicraft to machine process he concluded that production became separated into two interrelated activities: industrial and pecuniary. To this basic distinction he added ancillary ones: serviceability distinct from vendibility, making goods versus making money, the machine process versus business enterprise, and more (Veblen 1904). Industrial activities are related to workmanship, serviceability, to making goods. Pecuniary activities are distributional, predatory, related to vendibility, to making money. Veblen's theory is that business controls the industrial arts for pecuniary purposes. The creation of the industrial arts, though, was due to the cumulative evolution of the community's stock of knowledge, and thus due to the community as a whole.

One may argue that Veblen's distinction is an expression of the tension between the social interest of making goods and the "individual" interest in making money. Veblen's theory of modern welfare involves two degrees of separation. The first degree is in the real sector. This separation emerged as the machine process came to dominate the productive apparatus and be controlled by the demands of pecuniary valuations. The purpose of production is as a means to consumption, but when making goods is a by-product of making money this is a separation of a key part of the life process – consumption – from production. Yet, even as business enterprises manipulate prices, engage in adroit salesmanship, and much else, they do produce goods and sell them to an end consumer.

The second separation occurs as the money/commercial economy evolved more and more into the pecuniary/credit economy. The manipulation of business capital became more important, ordinary, and common, as a business activity. Prices of business capital – stocks, bonds, and their derivatives, became the principal concern. This concern is added to the process of making money, not via the vendibility of goods, but by manipulation of financial capital. Making money shifts more to the manipulation of financial asset values, mostly based on intangible property, rather than production of goods and manipulation of product prices. This is a process of "producing," buying and selling business capital. For this activity there is no end user; business capital is bought to be resold. Hence there occurs another degree of separation between production and consumption. The greater the separation of means and ends the greater the pressure on the enduring tension. In the case of economic activity this emerged as a separation of production from its purpose, consumption.

John Maynard Keynes – tension through fallacies of composition

Perhaps the ultimate political economist was Keynes. After all, with his work the explicit role for the polity is justified. His basic insight was that the economy can suffer a breakdown of internal coordination. Contrary to the classical view, especially J. B. Say, there are no laws equilibrating individual actions with economic aggregates such that full employment is achieved. Keynes' theory rests in part on fallacies of composition that create tension between individual rationality and social good.[5] These fallacies may be seen as an expression of the enduing tension analyzed using the force of aggregates to drive the wedge and exacerbate the tension.

Keynes argued, for example, that the interest rate and the marginal efficiency of capital should tend to zero, bringing about the decline of the rentier class. Clearly high interests rates are good for capital rentiers, but discourage investment, often in the form of new machinery. Keynes, like Veblen, argues the latter is good for society.

John Kenneth Galbraith – power and the corporation

Galbraith focused attention on the modern corporation in a way compatible with Veblen's view. He argued that the economic policies embodied in anti-trust could not properly control the dominant producers, that concentrations of economic power (blocs) exerted pressure on each other, and that the free market economy was a myth. His concept of countervailing power, much derided by standard theorists, pointed to a tension between those capable of holding their own, i.e., in possession of a differential advantage, in the "competition" among blocs of economic power and those needing institutional adjustments to allow the development of enabling institutions to create their countervailing power.

This did not necessarily mean the elimination of competition from the economy but a recognition that the competitive sectors of the economy have steadily declined and are relatively less important than those areas already subject to decentralized corporate planning. Power resides in this system with the organization and specifically the technostructure, the technical and managerial experts of modern corporations. However, technostructure planning is not coordinated with the rest of the economy, lacks a public purpose, and has never been systematically thought out. This system, Galbraith said, obsessed with the production of goods, created an artificial demand for many products and under-invested in the public sector. He argued, not unlike Veblen, that a class of intellectuals, experts and professionals should design industrial policy.

Production, income distribution, and the enduring tension

A clear indicator of the enduring tension may be found in the distribution of income. For our purposes here the importance of income distribution is that as it becomes more unequal the tension increases and that a theory of income distribution is often implicit in a theory of production. In standard economic theories it usually turns out that the capitalist, or entrepreneur, is the agent responsible for creating and animating the productive forces in the economy, a confusion of social traditions with the factors necessary for the production of goods. A somewhat corresponding confusion may be found in the standard theory of income distribution. It teaches that income inequality is functional and results from proportional productive contribution.

The classical economists and their neoclassical followers denied that their theories justified existing income distributions. They were simply the laws of economics. True, Smith saw the income of landlords as being exploitative and was also critical of the mercantilists because they were making profits as a result of monopoly positions in the economy. He was also cynical in his attitude toward the business community.[6] The activity that he approved of was the businessman's thrift and parsimony. This behavior, refraining from spending all his income, saving some of it, and putting it back into industry, was the embodiment of virtue for Smith. Thus he tended to glorify thrift and saving and assert that capital and thrifty businessmen make industrial growth possible. Industrial growth is responsible for a high standard of living, making cultural heroes of thrifty businessmen and entrepreneurs. Marginal productivity analysis concluded that in a market economy under competitive conditions everybody received an income proportional to the value of their productive contributions. Consequently, this meant that the incomes of laborers were unavoidably low and the incomes of businessmen were necessarily high.

John Stuart Mill was alone in the eighteenth-century intellectual tradition in seeing a possibility of social improvement in the nineteenth century. He had a glimpse of what the democratic aspect of a system could be, yet recoiled from the necessary social legislation to usher in such a system due to his fundamentalist education which told him that government ought not interfere with the lives of individuals. It was clear that none of the social improvements he wanted could be achieved unless institutional adjustments, probably initiated by government, were instituted.

Marx, Veblen, and Keynes perceived that income distribution was critical to the ability of the economy to maintain stability and understood that mal-distribution of income leads to insufficient aggregate demand and hence exerts pressure that increases the chance of conflict.

Economic thought and economic policy

The efforts of economic philosophers are not idle speculation. They lie behind the formation and practice of the social control of production. The idea of a natural order carried with it the idea of inevitability. Newtonian mechanics, when applied to the economy, suggested there were forces parallel to the laws of gravitation in physics. This emerges, for example, as the "law" of supply and demand in economics. Both the liberal classical economists and Marx shared a belief that the future was predictable because of such laws and these views carried over to shape policy prescriptions. Smith visualized conflict as competitive individuals engaged in small-scale methods of production with such a large number of producers that no one or no small group could come to control the market and thereby take unfair advantage of the public. It would, therefore, be impossible for them to get together to control production and prices.

It is particularly important to notice that the doctrines of laissez-faire and competitive markets, when united with population theory, provide an intellectual position from which to resist factory welfare legislation. The individual must indeed be harnessed and prevented from charging the public unfair prices and making unfair profits but price competition would automatically take care of this matter. Malthus, along with perhaps most other believers of the time, argued that self-interest was the will of God. By placing the prestige of science behind it, Malthus was able to conclude:

> He [God] has enjoined every man to pursue as his primary objective his own safety and happiness … By this wise provision the most ignorant are led to promote the general happiness, and end which they would totally fail to attain if the moving principle of conduct had been benevolence.
>
> (Malthus, 1967: 128)

The Malthusian/Ricardian doctrine was used to repeal the poor laws and to move England rapidly toward a policy of less governmental intervention in economic affairs. This made it possible to argue against laws that would aid the poor, improve their wages, reduce hours of labor, require more safety devices in factories, and generally improve the conditions under which laborers worked. For example, child labor was taken for granted on the farm and while often oppressive, it was not usually as oppressive there, where the child lived with its parents, as when it was introduced in factories and mines.

Both the liberal classical economists and Marx were correct in finding a place for conflict in their analysis. Both, however, had a fictional idea of its consequences. The classical notion that conflict will usher in public welfare and a market economy is not borne out in experience. Marx's postulate about the universality of class conflict was based upon fragmentary information obtained from a limited history of Western European society. History is not necessarily a history of class conflict although it is filled with conflicts and warfare primarily between ambitious ruling groups in different classes and societies.

Veblen noticed that the analysis of Smith *et al.*, was deficient for understanding an economy that had evolved under the pressure of technology. He created a new theory by looking at what was going on with business conditions. Two concepts, intangible property and credit, emerged for analysis. Intangible property, the most common form of which is goodwill, while of scant use to the general community, is valuable to the business that has it. More precisely intangible property is the right to fix prices by withholding from others what they want but do not own (Commons, 1934). This ability in turn stems from a differential advantage, in part rooted in the extension of credit. Credit, mostly in the form of bonds and stocks, permits control of tangible property, the industrial apparatus of production. In his analysis the first degree is problematic, but capable of being controlled and directed if restrained by social controls policy. The second degree consolidates the monetary production system so that it is animated by making money through effort that is of no use to the life process, and more likely detracts from it. The means/ends continuum is distorted beyond reasonable tolerances and social control falls to the imbecilic institutions of the financial system. This ushers in expanded avenues for predation and fraud. Veblen mostly eschewed polices[7] for social change yet it is clear that his theory implies a different policy tract.

The competitive market in a capitalist system of production is a mechanism that increases class conflict and creates forces leading to group control of the productive means. This is an argument consistent with Marx, Veblen, and Keynes, though arrived at through rather different theories. For Marx the tension is relieved by the historical process of moving from capitalism to socialism. Veblen argued that a class of technical experts, engineers, would be the logical agents to control an industrial (machine process) economy if the continuity of means and ends was to be restored. For Keynes the consequences of tension, brought on by the fallacies of composition, are such that they cannot be resolved by the internal working of the economy, only by the society, i.e., an external force applied by government policy. There is no necessity that these polices will be perceived as necessary and hence the economy suffers a lack of coordination and depression in the form of involuntary unemployment.

Public control of production – the old order

The self-regulating market is a social mechanism believed able to control production via competition provided the proper "institutions" are in place. This leads to the idea that through the use of pro-competition (anti-trust) policies and public utility regulation the market can be made to yield better results than those gotten with the pure self-regulating market. These are arguments most consistent with the liberal classical position. As new technologies evolved in the nineteenth and twentieth centuries so too did new industries. In the United States these were mostly organized by privately owned companies, though much government assistance in the form of subsidies, land grants, patents, and new legal forms was prominent.[8] Driven by technologies and companies, the tension between the public and private domains was especially taut. Economic competition was often so strenuous that it created anti-social conflict. After the Civil War in the United States railroads sometimes reduced freight rates to the point they lost money, causing the bankruptcy of some and the consolidation of several by the victors. The Standard Oil Trust used methods of economic warfare to eliminate or buy up competitors as did many trusts and companies. This was common for the time and a consequence of this competition was that oligopolies and other concentrated forms of organization emerged. Existing controls were not up to the task of constraining private interests to serve the public good. As the tension increased, pressure increased to seek adjustments.[9] There were, in fact, adjustments in the nineteenth and twentieth centuries to address these outcomes. Indeed there were adjustments along the way. It was a period in which there were a few minor upswings of reform. There was coordination and agreement as to the goals of society and both the mores and the technology were imposing a considerable degree of planning and teamwork. As these new rules were instituted to deal with these tensions[10] they fell into two fairly distinct tracks, anti-trust and public regulation. These two general policy tracks have formed the basis of US policy since the late nineteenth century. Table 7.1 presents a selection of the laws that form the legal foundation for the policies.

In their time these adjustments helped ameliorate the enduring tension, but they became less effective as the economy evolved. The economic theory

Table 7.1 Selected pro-competition and regulatory laws of the United States

Name of law	*Purpose*	*Year*
Interstate Commerce Commission	Public regulation	1887
Sherman Anti-trust Act	Antitrust/pro-competition	1890
Food and Drug Act	Public regulation	1906
Federal Reserve Act	Banking regulation	1913
Clayton Act	Anti-trust/pro-competition	1914
Federal Trade Commission Act	Anti-trust/pro-competition	1914
Federal Water Power Act	Public regulation	1920
Securities Act of 1933	Financial regulation	1933
Banking Act of 1933 (Glass-Steagall)	Banking regulation	1933
Robinson-Patman Act	Anti-trust/pro-competition	1936
Public Utility Regulatory Act	Public utility regulation	1934
Communication Act of 1934	Public utility regulation	1934
Civil Aeronautics Act	Air line regulation	1938
Wheeler-Lea Act	Anti-trust/pro-competition	1938
Celler–Kefauver Act	Anti-trust/pro-competition	1950
Telecommunications Act of 1996	Public utility regulation	1996
Dodd-Frank Wall Street Reform and Consumer Protection Act	Financial regulation	2010

Source: Compiled from selected texts and economic history sources.

informing these polices is the pro-competition policy of the liberal classical and neoclassical tradition. The United States Federal Trade Commission and Justice Department explicitly take this position: "Free and open markets are the foundation of a vibrant economy. Aggressive competition among sellers in an open marketplace gives consumers– both individuals and businesses – the benefits of lower prices, higher quality products and services, more choices, and greater innovation."[11] Yet, in modern times the view that the market controls the firm is largely a myth. It may be widely held and deeply believed, but widespread belief is not necessarily proof that a proposition is warranted.

Ironically, the enforcement of these policies frequently spawns movements to deregulate and to less vigorously enforce pro-competition laws. Some assert that technologies have created opportunities for competition where once natural monopolies prevailed. It is the case that these regulations and laws, based on economic theory of the old order, are insufficiently equipped to deal with problems and may even contribute unduly to conflict. This does not lead to the conclusion that competitive markets are the means to resolve issues created by the changed conditions of production. Practices and rules to deal with economic power, patents, public utilities and a wide variety of other sources of differential advantage need to evolve as technology evolves or they become a contributor to economic and political tension, rather than the reverse.

Keynesian type reforms were useful, though spotty and fragmented. Yet while the reform movement should have shown something like an accelerating trend, it showed no such thing. If anything, there was a powerful counter-movement that sought a return to the views of social control based on classical/neoclassical theory.

The result has been to leave production decisions in the hands of those concerned most with pecuniary valuation. This means then, that the intellectual reform movement had run out of steam and there was scant possibility of it reviving until some sort of new intellectual synthesis was forthcoming.

The modern era of business organization requires new and innovative forms of social control. New technologies have also created a necessity for different types of social control. New tensions have emerged. How to handle "intellectual" property, for example, is a source of tension. New social experiments in control are warranted and a new intellectual perspective lodged in instrumentalist and institutional economics is a candidate to address these circumstances and provide a basis for new forms of social control.

Institutional economics and the social control of enduring tension

For institutional economics the Veblenian dichotomy embodies the enduring tension by casting it as the tension between the instrumental and ceremonial aspects of economic life. The tension waxes and wanes under the force borne of technological change and the requisite adjustment of other aspects of behavior to it. The attempt in the early nineteenth century to implement the utopian idea of a self-regulating market economy threatened upheaval in the economies of the UK and the US (Polanyi, 1944). The institutional approach was and is an opportunity to move away from ideas of the past to ideas lodged in an evolutionary perspective.[12] The Institutional philosophy of social control is based on the fact that economic activities take place in a cultural context and as such are subject to the instrumental and ceremonial aspects of a culture. The most dominant instrumental aspect of the modern era has been the widespread use of machine process production and consumption. The most dominant ceremonial aspects have been the belief in the application of individual rights to the concept of the self-regulation of economic activity.

Institutional political economy advances the proposition that business activity is better understood as the existing organizational mechanism that controls the industrial process and that the application of organized intelligence (planning) can improve the outcome of these activities compared with the unfettered market and individual self-interest. The practical ability to control the activities of business is bounded by the intensity of the ceremonial belief in the "natural right" of the individual to control the use of property. It may be painful to give up old habits of thinking and acting, but it is also true that this is a prerequisite to creating new patterns of thinking and new philosophies.

Policy, planning, and tension

Institutionalists argue that under proper management industrial production could make possible a reasonable standard of living for all. Veblen (1904) argued that the techniques of planning are a logical extension of modern technology. Polanyi (1944) points out that modern economies are mixed which means there are gradations of planning involving government at the national, state, and local levels, as well as planning by business enterprises at different levels. The planning of such groups has gone so far that it is misleading to think about the way in which the market economy controls economic activities. A step forward is to recognize that it is not a question of plan versus market or no plan – it is a question of what kind of planning. Such planning as exists in the US today has the disadvantage that it plans for instability and is out of step with the needs of modern technology (Ayres, 1951). Maladjustments between ideology and technology create social tensions. Modern technology requires coordination and teamwork and these are susceptible to technological organization from the simple cooperation of driving spikes in railroad ties to the complicated organization of an entire economy in times of war.

Once we face this fact the problem would necessarily arise as to the kind of controls and planning appropriate to the problem and the method to be used. We would confront the problem that past planning has rested upon ideologies whose foundations have irrational material and which, therefore, cause maladjusted economies. Contemporary opponents of planning point to the failures of centrally planned economies such as the former USSR. They neglect to notice that ideology played an important and possibly fatal role in those economies and that planning is successfully operational in other economies.

The alternative to the planning we have had in the past may be described as instrumental planning. It undertakes to apply the critical and experimental methods that have proved successful in the sciences and use these on the problems of economic society. Instrumental/experimental planning is based on an application of the methods and tools of institutional analysis and requires an experimental habit and a genuine interest in data. This is the type of planning embedded in the institutionalist theory of instrumental logic.

Institutional economics has developed theory, tools, and evaluative processes to apply to industrial planning. These include the principles of institutional adjustment, the means-ends continuum, the Veblenian dichotomy, the social fabric matrix, the skills matrix, evolutionary game theory (strategic interaction), and instrumental value theory (see Foster, 1981; Sturgeon, 2009; Waller, 1982; Hayden, 2006; Sturgeon and Bowles, 1997; Bowles, 2013; Elsner *et al.*, 2015). Other technical planning instruments, including input/output analysis, stock flow modeling, and sector balances analysis, enhance the institutionalist's theoretical base. Unlike the market-based approach of standard theory which leaves social value out of the process except where it enters via individual judgment, institutional theory makes a cornerstone of the analysis. Specialists, including economists, can play a part in showing which patterns of the past have been responsible for the maladjustment of the present, and thereby help to reconstruct the values of society which will make it possible for the ideals as well as the facts to have a chance to operate. A guiding principle in this would be the means-ends continuum.

The means–ends continuum is an endless succession of means which become ends. Means and ends are inseparable because the arrival at an end has consequences for what happens next. It is a truism that means are ends and their continuum is based on seeking to understand the consequences stemming from choosing alternative means. The value of production is as a means to consumption which is a means to the growth and maintenance of the life process. An economic system which uses its production system as the means of making money creates a tension in the production/consumption continuum, a degree of separation in Veblen's term. Planning policies would be concerned with the continuity of means and ends. One consequence of this would be to mesh the distinction between the macro/group and micro/individual levels of planning and in turn help ease the enduring tension.

Another characteristic of instrumental planning is to place less emphasis on the monetary unit in making economic comparisons and more emphasis on the actual physical units of kilograms, tonnes, standards of efficiency, nutrients, rate of labor turnover, and things of this kind. The emphasis on finance tends to obscure the realities related to industrial growth. The fact is an industrial economy depends upon a broad spectrum of skilled workers. Money is not of decisive importance, rather scientific knowledge, the tools, and the machines are.

As things stand now, we have a double system of book-keeping in which we measure things in physical units and an elaborate system measuring things in monetary units. In an instrumental/experimental mode of operation there would be many more studies on specific problems and economic categories, for example more study about the economics of housing, transportation, communication, food production and distribution, public and private health. Planners would need to recognize that a study of money flows is not a reasonable substitute for physical planning because money flows often neglect important parts of the welfare of society. Further, under planning, a theory of social costs and social returns would rise in importance whereas it has been relatively unimportant in the older order. We know that investment in intellectual skills and the abilities of individuals bring bigger yields in terms of national income.

As pointed out by Machiavelli societies do not go smoothly or quickly from one perception of the proper policies to another. Institutional adjustments of an incremental nature are needed. What might proposals to initiate experimental/instrumental planning look like? Consider the following elements of an experimental planning logic. First the twin goals of increased educational opportunities and full employment would be established. These are not new by any means, but past policies to reach them have enjoyed but partial and infrequent success. The element missing from the standard "Keynesian" approach to full employment, aggregate demand management, has usually been a way to direct and control the spending necessary to meet the goal. The post-Keynesian employer of last resort proposal is one way to address this problem. However, it usually suffers a higher level of social ceremonial resistance than a proposal for community service. Thus another way that gets at both goals is a program requiring one year of community service, voluntarily extendable for up to six years. Service would carry a wage and health insurance, and each quarter would count toward Social Security coverage. Further, for each year of service participants would be eligible for a one-year educational scholarship at any public post-secondary educational institution. The community service and scholarships would be paid by federal block grants to state and local organizing units.

The proposal squares with an economic proposition of institutional economics: if it is technologically possible, it is financially possible. It also directs and controls the spending more specifically. The planning tools to help direct, control, and adjust the program are the social fabric matrix, input/output analysis, and sector balance coordination. These along with the principles of institutional adjustment allow a means to alter the plans and "experiments" as they evolve and encounter consequences in need of adjustment.

For industrial policy the proposal eases the tension involved in a shortage of consumer spending for the goods capable of being produced by a financially unconstrained production system. It also would help in the supply of skilled workers that better understand the importance of social planning and cooperation. It helps ease the transition from pecuniary logic and valuation of production to an instrumental logic and valuation. The ancillary improvement is that fewer resources need be turned to use to persuade consumers of a particular product.

We expect adjustments to be necessary as part of the planning process. Here is a role for the combination of evolutionary game theory (Elsner *et al.*, 2015), the principles of institutional adjustment (Foster, 1981; Bush, 1987), and the social fabric matrix (Hayden, 2006). The combination of these tools would be used to evaluate and understand the planning programs. They would identify problems and suggest adjustments. In short the tools of institutional economics would be employed to understand, liberate, direct, and control the evolutionary and dynamic forces of the economy.

A community with a reasonable understanding of planning involving instrumental logic would open up the possibility of creating an economy capable of achieving a dynamic and adjustable developmental path, one that continually adjusts to a changing technological and geographic environment. It would recognize that change, progress, and evolution are at the very heart of any conception of planning, and that human beings have the capacity to enrich their lives by using experimental methods. This kind of planning would lead to another conception of national objectives and the public welfare. A conception more likely to maintain a balance between the interests of the individual and the group and more likely to ease and control the enduring tension.

Notes

1 The scope of this is restricted to so called "industrial policy" which for present purposes means policies for pro-competition and its regulations and alternatives such as industrial planning. Space does not permit a broader scope that would include military/industrial relations, full-employment policy, environmental policy, and more. Each of these may be analyzed using the enduring tension but not in this chapter.

2 The reference here and elsewhere in the text is to the middle class as seen in these times, namely the rising industrialist, capitalist class that was between the landed aristocracy and the working class.

3 In trying to put the matter in perspective we may notice that moveable type printing was known to Europeans by 1450 or earlier. Thus by the time of Malthus and Ricardo its

potential benefits for mass education had been available for 350 years. Yet economists and other social scientists generally were still under the institutional preconceptions that were in conflict with the scientific way of thinking that printing made more available. Such education may well tend to calm the force of such emotion, enhance the arts of associated living, and ease the raging social tension.

4 This does not mean that Marx's theory of economic and class conflicts is satisfactory. As a matter of fact, practically the same criticisms that apply to the liberal classical tradition apply to the Marxian tradition of conflict.

5 These are well known and not repeated here.

6 This point is frequently overlooked, especially by those seeking to justify the position and income of the business classes.

7 The best known exceptions are his work with the Department of Agriculture during World War I and his recommendation for production to be organized and deployed by engineering values instead of pecuniary ones.

8 See Commons (1924) for an analysis of the last mentioned.

9 The history of the abuses by the early trusts and other businesses, and the reactions to them is well known and not repeated here. See Mitchell and Mitchell (1947) for one such history.

10 This is part of what Karl Polanyi has named the double movement (see Polanyi, 1944). The double movement is between the efforts to institute a self-adjusting market and the efforts to curb the social wreckage it creates.

11 https://www.ftc.gov/tips-advice/competition-guidance/guide-antitrust-laws

12 Institutional economics has played a significant role in the social control of business. Veblen, Hamilton, Clark, Galbraith, and others led the way in creating a theoretical analysis and Commons, Hamilton, and Witte, led the way in creating and applying controls. There are a host of laws and regulation born of this approach. In the early twentieth century this took the form of regulatory commissions designed to ensure that the public purpose of the telephone, electricity, natural gas, water distribution, and others be served.

References

Ayres, Clarence E. (1951) *The Industrial Economy: Its Technological Basis and Institutional Destiny*. Boston: Houghton Mifflin.

Bowles, Douglas (2013) "Toward an integrated theory of social stratification," *American Journal of Economics and Sociology*, 72 (1): 32–58.

Bush, Paul D. (1987) "The theory of institutional change," *Journal of Economic Issues*, 21 (3): 1075–116.

Commons, John R. (1924) *Legal Foundations of Capitalism*. New York: Macmillan.

Commons, John R. (1934) *Institutional Economics: Its Place in Political Economy*. Madison, WI: University of Wisconsin Press.

Elsner, Wolfram, Heinrich, Torsten, and Schwardt, Henning (2015) *The Microeconomics of Complex Economies: Evolutionary, Institutional, Neoclassical, and Complexity Perspectives*. Amsterdam: Academic Press.

Foster, J. Fagg (1981) "Syllabus for problems of modern society: the theory of institutional adjustment," *Journal of Economic Issues*, 15 (4): 929–45.

Galbraith, John K. (1952) *American Capitalism: The Concept of Countervailing Power*. Boston: Houghton Mifflin.

Hayden, Gregory F. (2006) *Policy Making for a Good Society: The Social Fabric Matrix Approach to Policy Analysis and Program Evaluation*. New York: Springer Press.

Heilbroner, Robert L. and Milberg, William (2002) *The Making of Economic Society*. Upper Saddle River, NJ: Pearson.

Machiavelli, Niccolò (2013) *The Prince*. Toronto: Prohyptikon Publishing.

Malthus, Thomas R. (1967) *An Essay on Population*. London: Everyman's Library.

Marx, Karl (1970) *Capital: A Critique of Political Economy*. London: Lawrence & Wishart.

Mitchell, Broadus and Mitchell, Louise P. (1947) *American Economic History*. Cambridge: Riverside Press.

Polanyi, Karl (1944) *The Great Transformation*. Boston: Beacon Press.

Ricardo, David (1969) *The Principles of Political Economy and Taxation*. London: Everyman's Library.

Smith, Adam (1937) *An Inquiry into the Nature and Causes of the Wealth of Nations*. New York: Modern Library.

Sturgeon, James (2009) "The social fabric matrix, individual action and the principles of institutional adjustment, in Tara Natarajan, Wolfram Elsner, and Scott Fullwiller (eds), *Institutional Analysis and Praxis: Interdisciplinary Applications of the Social Fabric Matrix*. New York: Springer, pp. 39–54.

Sturgeon, James and Bowles, Douglas (1997) "Class Structure and Relatively Homogeneous Labor Markets." New Orleans, LA: Allied Social Science Association, unpublished.

Veblen, Thorstein B. (1904) *The Theory of Business Enterprise*. New York: Charles Scribner's Sons.

Waller, William (1982) "The evolution of the Veblenian dichotomy: Veblen, Hamilton, Ayres, and Foster,' *Journal of Economic Issues*, 16 (3): 757–71.

8 Co-evolutionary processes in a model of long-run economic development

Andreas Pyka and Pier Paolo Saviotti

Introduction

There is now a large consensus about the role of innovation played in economic growth processes since the Industrial Revolution. Most of the existing growth theories acknowledge the role of technologically driven economic growth in models which, however, reflect only on the quantitative dimension of economic development, highlighting the impressive development of figures like income per capita over time. Obviously, this particular view neglects the most important and visible aspect of economic growth, namely structural change. Even if our income is in real terms four times the income of our grandparents, this does not mean that we consume four times the same goods and services they did. We do not have four Volkswagen Beetles in our garages and we do not spent only 25 percent of our working time in professions characteristic of mining and steel industries.

Without doubt, not considering structural change in models of economic growth and development prevents us from understanding what is really going on in the long run. Structural change manifests itself not only in changing weights of existing industries or in the obsolescence of skills and qualifications on the labor markets, but also in very drastic changes in the complete sectoral make-up of an economy. In Saviotti and Pyka (2004a) we developed an alternative model of economic growth and development – labeled TEVECON – which allows for the emergence of new industries as well as the decline of existing industries, which we together interpret as a realistic approximation for structural change. Since 2004, we continuously have extended this model to explore the relationship between creation and destruction in Schumpeterian economic development. The first extensions of the model were restricted on the supply side assuming a Says-Law relationship.

However, innovation on its own could never have had an impact on growth if the goods and services it produced had not been purchased by consumers and users or, in other words, if there had not been a demand for the new goods and services. Therefore, this crude treatment of the demand side was not adopted for further modifications of our model. To improve our understanding of long-run economic development – encompassing the period from the beginning of the Industrial Revolution until the present time – it is therefore not convincing to neglect the role of the demand side and the qualitative changes which also took place there. In his work, Wolfram Elsner is always emphasizing the complexity of economic systems. The development of complex economic systems must be a complex process in its own right, and without doubt a major source of economic complexity is the co-evolution of demand and supply. Various sources of self-reinforcing and mutual interdependent feedback effects are to be expected between the supply side offering new products and services, generating income for the employed workforce and the demand side composed of consumers with changing needs and wants and changing skills and competences. In Saviotti and Pyka (2012) we introduced for this purpose an explicit consideration of the demand side dynamics into our TEVECON model.

The emergence of such demand dynamics for novelties requires a disposable income with which consumers can purchase the new goods and services. In addition, a set of preferences, which made these goods and services also desirable, is required. So new goods are only appearing in the consumption baskets if extra income is available in addition to the one which consumers need to spend on previous goods and services. Furthermore, consumers need to be aware that the new goods and services contribute to the satisfactions of their needs and wants. Obviously, both conditions depend on the education level prevailing in an economy, which determines the income and the alertness and sensitivity towards novelties.

The Festschrift for our colleague Wolfram Elsner gives us the opportunity to summarize the major building blocks and outcomes of our TEVECON modeling trajectory, now more than ten years old, and to highlight our first findings concerning co-evolutionary processes. Wolfram Elsner is always interested in understanding and disentangling – but also in taking seriously – the complexities economists face in their analysis of economic behavior and processes. Without doubt, the degree of complexity is highest when it comes to co-evolutionary processes. Therefore, this Festschrift is the right place to summarize our recent findings.

Our starting point: structural change

It is one of the amazing performances of capitalistic organized economies that a very large number of different sectors has been created since the Industrial Revolution. Examples are sectors producing cars, aircraft, computers, radios, televisions, refrigerators, plastics, etc. Schumpeter (1912) had already made clear that a simple development path from horse-drawn carriages to modern railways does not exist but requires important structural changes and transformations. The appearance of the new sectors asks for an explanation in economic theory. No theory or model of economic development can escape this basic question: how and why did these sectors emerge?

Given that structural change and growth are related but not identical, the additional question of whether structural change contributes to growth arises. Structural change is a much broader phenomenon and many definitions are possible (see, for example, Silva and Teixeira, 2008). In literature, structural change is mostly studied as the changing weight of sectors defined at levels of aggregation encompassing primary, manufacturing, and services (see, for example, Baumol, 1967; Chenery, 1960; Kuznets, 1957; Cornwall, 1977; Salter, 1960; Fabricant, 1940; Pasinetti, 1981, 1993; Fagerberg, 2000; Verspagen 1993; Metcalfe *et al.*, 2005). This tripartite representation based on agriculture, manufacturing, and services, however, is far too rough in the light of the rich differentiation real economic systems are confronted with.

Our starting point is the historical fact that economic development has been very uneven. Observed growth rates varied substantially at a given time and in the course of time. In addition, the emergence of new sectors differed among countries, for example depending on their relative state of development. The two concepts of proportional and non-proportional growth (see Pasinetti, 1981; Chenery, 1960) are a useful starting point. When all sectors show the same productivity growth and demand growth rates, then proportional growth occurs. In this situation the economic system's composition, as represented by the relative employment and output of different sectors, remains constant. In other words, in situations of proportional growth there is no structural change. Most of the traditional models of economic growth rely on this unrealistic assumption of proportional growth. For that reason, we were interested in developing an alternative growth model, which goes beyond this simplifying assumption.

We designed our TEVECON model within an evolutionary economics framework comparable to, for example, Dosi *et al.* (2010) or Ciarli *et al.* (2010, 2012). TEVECON's emphasis on the endogenous change in composition of the economic system, and in particular the tendency towards a growing differentiation, or on the balance between growing output variety and growing sectoral quality and differentiation, can be considered as strong representations of the concept of non-proportional growth. In this chapter of the Festschrift for Wolfram Elsner we do not refer to any formal details but illustrate only the major building blocks. A detailed formal description of the model may be found in Pyka and Saviotti (2011). One aspect of non-proportional growth is the simultaneous existence of different sectors, which coexist at individually different development stages. In principle, our TEVECON model is generating a sequence of industry life cycles as shown in Figure 8.1, which displays the number of firms in five consecutively emerging industries. This first result has to be highlighted: without having assumed sectoral dynamics following archetypical industry life cycles, the cyclical development of sectors emerge from the interplay of supply and demand side dynamics.

From the development of industries and their production and innovation performance, we can derive macroeconomic figures such as income development (Figure 8.2) and employment development (Figure 8.3) which are the aggregate of the sectoral developments. In particular, a consideration of Figure 8.3 illustrates nicely that the development in different sectors can be extremely uneven: increasing employment in rising industries can compensate for declining development in mature industries with strong rationalization activities.

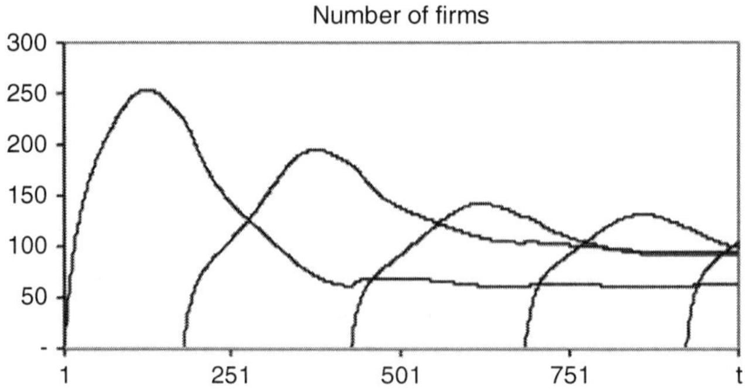

Figure 8.1 Number of firms

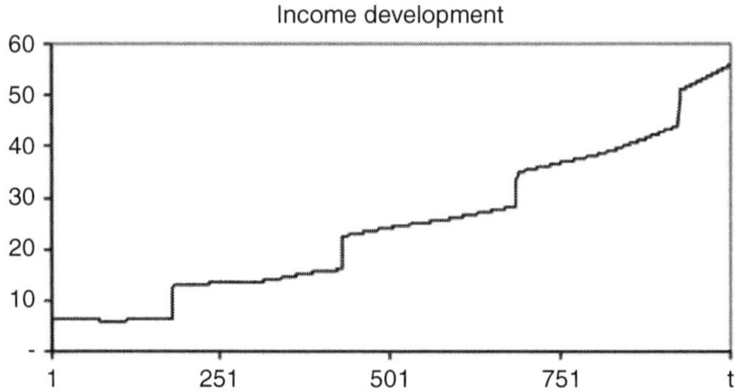

Figure 8.2 Evolution of macroeconomic income

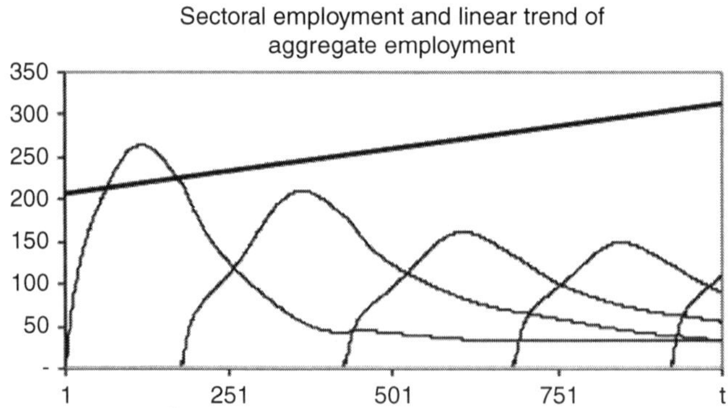

Figure 8.3 Sectoral and aggregate employment curves

Another strand of literature with which TEVECON has some similarities is the so-called unified growth theory (Galor and Weil, 2000; Galor, 2005). The similarity is the emphasis on the long run, although unified growth theory aims for an even longer time horizon extending back to the beginning of human history. As already pointed out, our intended time horizon is the period since the Industrial Revolution to the present, which is the *third period* in the unified growth theory. TEVECON not only stresses structural change but very importantly also its direction. Under a wide range of circumstances the model predicts a growing differentiation of the economic system or, in other words, output variety. The endogenously generated structural change in TEVECON, however, is a mechanism, which either did not exist or played a negligible role before the Industrial Revolution.

Trajectories and patterns of economic development

We claim that convincing models of economic development need to be able to explain patterns of long-run development and growth. Focusing on the period starting with the Industrial Revolution requires an understanding of the broad features, which occurred since the late eighteenth century. First, we had the emergence of the manufacturing industry. Second, within manufacturing itself, there was a progressive differentiation, beginning with sectors such as textiles, energy (steam engines), railways, and steel, following with chemicals, electricity, cars, planes, etc. This means that manufacturing became more and more differentiated in the period, which started a century after the Industrial Revolution began, with newer sectors coexisting with older ones. Third, in the most recent decades the employment share of services overtook that of manufacturing.

The fundamental ingredient which gives rise to growth and development is innovation. The emergence of innovations depends on search activities which provide the required knowledge. Innovations become effective and affect economic development because entrepreneurs found new firms to exploit the outcomes of search activities and because consumers and users purchase the products and services embodying such innovations. This is a process which makes the economic system increasingly differentiated. Therefore structural change is closely connected with increasing differentiation.

The above processes are composed of three different trajectories (Saviotti and Pyka, 2013) and two periods. The concept of the trajectory is among the most important in evolutionary economics (Nelson and Winter, 1977; Dosi, 1982). Our trajectories are slightly different: they are long and occur at high levels of aggregation like national economies. These trajectories are not specific to any particular technology, although new technologies are likely to emerge because they allow a faster movement along them.

- *Trajectory 1*. The efficiency of production increases in time. Here efficiency must be understood as the ratio of the inputs used to the output produced, when the type of output remains constant.

- *Trajectory 2.* The output variety of the economic system increases over the course of time. Here such variety is measured by the number of distinguishable sectors, where a sector is defined as the set of firms producing a common although highly differentiated output.
- *Trajectory 3.* The output quality and internal differentiation of existing sectors increases over the course of time. This means that if, during the period of observation, the type of output changes what we will observe is a combination of growing productive efficiency and quality change.

Within our three trajectories framework we can analyze an endogenous growing number of sectors producing completely different types of output and simultaneously each producing a highly diversified output. These two very different differentiation types are often described as vertical and horizontal differentiation.

Trajectory 1, productive efficiency, is the oldest and, until the Industrial Revolution, the most developed of the three trajectories. But, productive efficiency started growing in a cumulative fashion only after the beginning of the Industrial Revolution (Maddison, 2001). Since then, trajectory 1 can be summarized under the heading of rationalization.

Growing productive efficiency is certainly one of the factors which contributed to economic growth since the Industrial Revolution. However, with growing productive efficiency alone the rich patterns of capitalistic production systems we are interested in could not have emerged. With productive efficiency alone we would today be producing cars such as the Ford Model T with much smaller quantities of all the inputs required.

In the early phases of the Industrial Revolution, output differentiation (trajectory 2) was limited. It occurred mostly at the level of capital goods and only considerably later at the level of consumer goods. The increasing internal differentiation and output quality of consumer goods and durables (trajectory 3) started to take off after the beginning of the twentieth century, certainly in the period after World War II. Growing output variety is an intra-sector phenomenon. Cars, aircraft, televisions, computers, telecommunications, etc. constituted not only completely new sectors but also underwent an immense degree of internal differentiation.

The meaning of co-evolution is now the following insight: none of the three trajectories could have occurred alone without the other two. Thus continuous rationalization, if not complemented by the emergence of new sectors and by their internal differentiation and rising quality, would lead an economic system into a bottleneck in which all output demanded could have been produced by a declining proportion of the labor force and declining incomes from labor. Such a bottleneck is avoided only by the emergence of new sectors (Pasinetti, 1981). While the assumption of demand saturation and the neglect of the internal differentiation of sectors limit the possible generalization of Pasinetti's approach, we have shown that both the emergence of new sectors and their increasing quality and internal differentiation provided additional scope for further growth and allowed its continuation in the long run. In this context, full demand saturation is unlikely to occur within any sector as long as new sectors are being created (Saviotti and Pyka, 2008).

Furthermore, both the emergence of new sectors and their growing quality and internal differentiation can compensate for the diminishing capability of incumbent and maturing sectors to create employment (Saviotti and Pyka, 2004b).

The two periods

In a recent paper we (Saviotti and Pyka, 2013) hypothesized that during the period from the Industrial Revolution to the present a transition occurred from an economy in which most of the population could only purchase basic necessities to one in which most people could afford a much wider range of goods and services of higher quality. We called this transition from necessities to imaginary worlds. This description emphasizes that in the first century of industrialization most economic agents, even in the richest parts of the world, could not purchase anything besides bare necessities. In the first period, British working-class households spent about 90 percent of their income on food, clothing, and housing. It was only after the 1930s that the share of income spent on the above three categories started falling (Hobsbawm, 1968; see also Figure 8.4).

By the 1950s the share of necessities fell to about 60 percent, leaving about 40 percent to be spent on other, presumably higher, goods and services. The disposable income required to buy the new goods and services was generated by

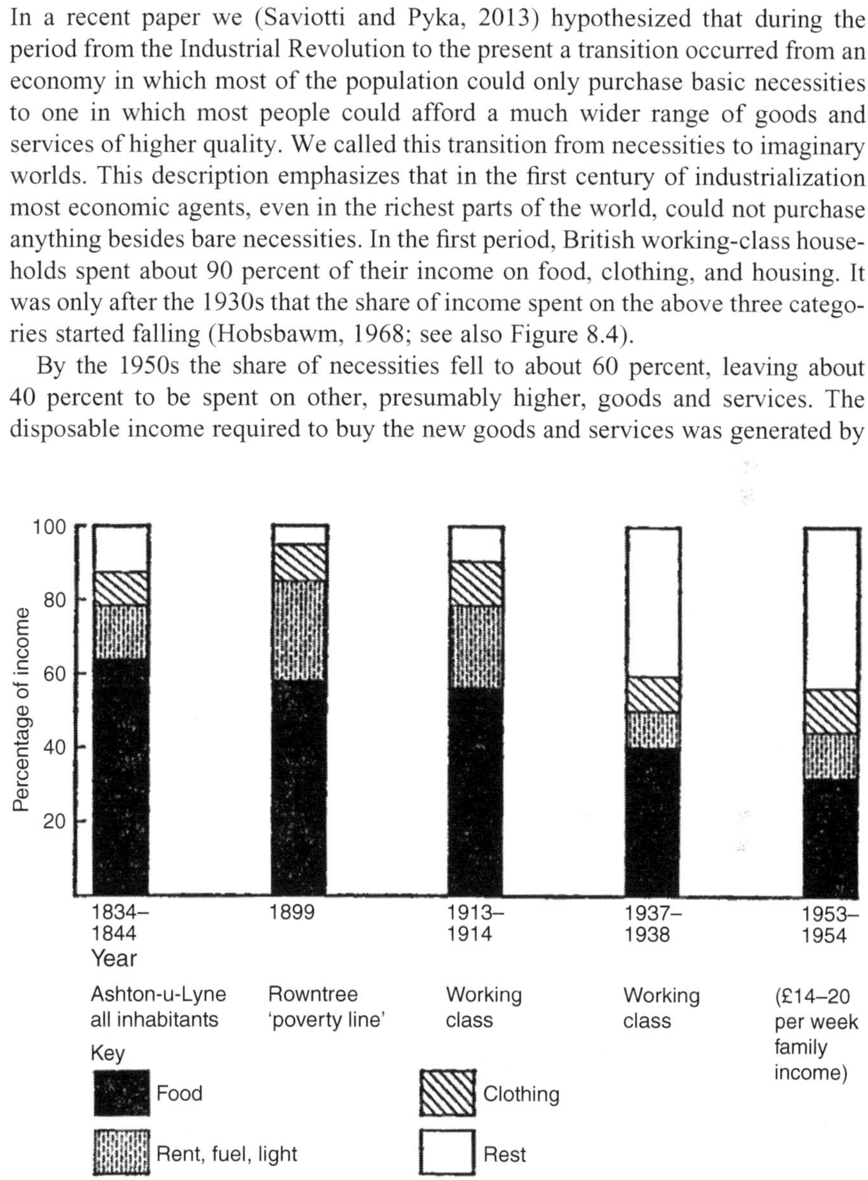

Figure 8.4 Family expenditures of workers (taken from Hobsbawm, 1968)

the combined effect of the growing efficiency in the production of necessities (trajectory 1), and the employment effect due to the emergence of new sectors (trajectory 2) and their growing differentiation (trajectory 3). Furthermore, education played an extremely important role by supplying the higher competencies required for the emergence of trajectory 2 and by contributing to the creation of additional employment and income. Historically, starting from the beginning of the twentieth century, new goods and services emerged (trajectory 2) and their quality and differentiation increased constantly (trajectory 3). This combination of trajectories contributed to a mechanism which allowed the capitalist economic system to create growing wealth for most of the population of industrialized countries.

Co-evolutionary processes in economic development

This brief illustration highlights the important co-evolutionary processes which connect industrial development and structural change with increasing welfare, increasing education levels, and an increasing awareness by consumers concerning to goods and services which no longer show a direct link to the necessities required for the satisfaction of biological needs, i.e. for survival.

Obviously, the analysis of these complex processes is far from being a trivial exercise: with our TEVECON model we can compare two scenarios, which we call in Saviotti and Pyka (2013) low quality (LQ) and high quality (HQ). In the LQ scenario, besides trajectory 1 we allow for trajectory 2 only. This means that new sectors are created but their output is not undergoing any quality improvement or increasing differentiation in time – in other words we do not allow for trajectory 3. In the HQ scenario trajectories 1, 2 and 3 co-evolve.

Our results displayed in Figure 8.5 show that the income created is initially higher for the LQ scenario but later in the HQ scenario is leapfrogging the LQ scenario with respect to income development. In early periods in the LQ scenario income rises faster due to a faster introduction of new sectors. However, due to the lower qualifications the technological opportunities of these industries are not exploited. In contrast, in the HQ scenario exploitation is done more efficiently, which leads finally to higher incomes. This corresponds with the historical development observed: in the early phases of economic development after the Industrial Revolution (say in the nineteenth century) the cost of producing high quality goods and services would have been too high given the purchasing power consumers had available at the time. In our calculations, purchasing power in the LQ scenario could not increase since both the quality of human capital and wages remained constant in the course of time. On the other hand, in the HQ scenario the purchasing power of consumers can increase because both the quality of human capital and wages increase in the course of time. Consequently, the income generated in the HQ scenario, while being initially lower, increased more rapidly and eventually overtook that of the LQ scenario.

In the early phases of the economic development – which means in our TEVECON model after the onset of the Industrial Revolution – the cost of producing high-quality goods and services was too high given the purchasing

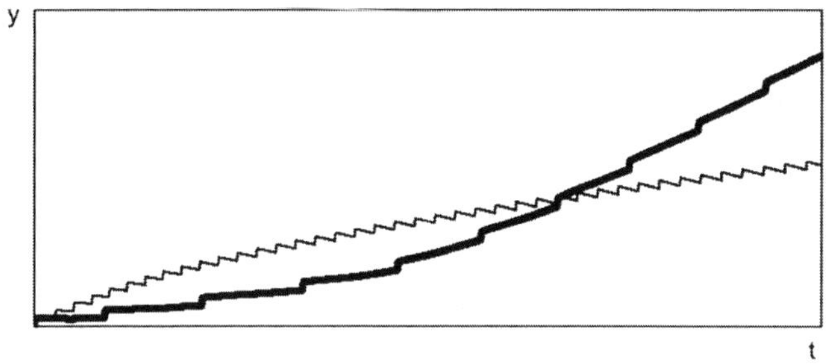

Figure 8.5 Effect of product quality on aggregate income Y. The vertical line indicates the time required for HQ income (bold line) to catch up with and to overtake LQ income (thin line)

power of contemporary consumers. In our simulation experiments, purchasing power in the LQ scenario is not increasing because both the quality of human capital and wages remained constant. This part of co-evolution is restricted by not allowing for developments triggered by trajectory 3. On the other hand, in the HQ scenario the purchasing power of consumers can increase because both the quality of human capital and wages increase in the course of time. The increasing demand for highly qualified labor and the corresponding increase in wages jointly enabled the production of higher quality and more differentiated goods and services and the emergence of markets for them. However, such outcome could not occur since the beginning of industrial development because initially the required income would not have been available. The transition occurred later when the income generated by the HQ scenario overtook that of the LQ scenario.

Based on our results we consider the observed historical development path as a combination of the LQ scenario in the initial period followed by the HQ scenario in the later years. Our explanation of the transition from necessities to imaginary worlds needs to be compared to another one, previously proposed by economic historians, according to which the high rate of population growth induced by the initial phase of the Industrial Revolution would have compensated for the growing productive efficiency that such a revolution had generated. Our explanation for the delay with which the onset of a more quality conscious and differentiated consumption emerged does not replace the answer of economic historians but reinforces it. Both a high rate of population growth and a low ratio of income per capita to the cost of HQ delay the onset of the transition from low to high quality. However, the mechanism we propose needs to be taken into account because even without a growing population it is impossible for economic development to be dominated immediately by a high-quality scenario.

The fundamental role of education in the transition from the LQ to the HQ scenario is closely related to the quality of human capital. Only in the HQ scenario does increasing output quality go hand in hand with an increasing quality of human capital and with increasing wages. In TEVECON the improvement in the quality of human capital stems from education. The mechanism is as follows: investment in education leads to higher wages and thereby increases the demand for higher-quality goods and services. Based on TEVECON experiments we propose the following mechanism to explain the path of economic development, which occurred in the more recent half of economic development, namely the HQ phase:

- The higher-quality output requires higher competencies. These competences are created by the education system.
- The higher competencies improve the human capital, which supports growth, increases investment in and growing diffusion of education, and slows down population growth.
- The higher competencies receive higher wages, which provide the increasing available incomes, which create demand for the higher priced goods and services.

This virtuous feedback loop leads to growing income per capita, and to the growing variety and quality of consumption (see Figure 8.6).

The above co-evolutionary mechanism is highly dependent on the role played by education in creating both the higher competencies and the income per head required for the observed path of economic development to occur. The above description implies that in our TEVECON model education is not conceived as a cause of economic development, but as a variable, which co-evolves with competencies, wages, demand, prices, output quality, growth, investment, and population growth. However, education is not available to everyone in the same quantity and quality. Thus, in Saviotti and Pyka (2015) we started distinguishing within our economic system two social classes, which could correspond to blue- and white-collar workers (henceforth blue and white collars). The two classes differ in the

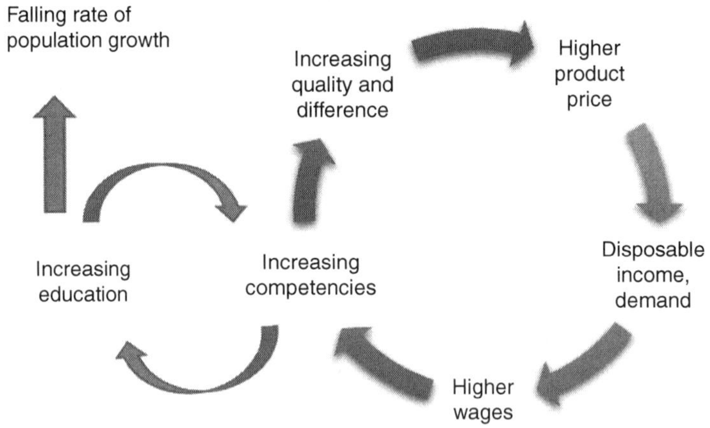

Figure 8.6 Co-evolution of education, product quality and differentiation, wages, disposable income, and demand

amount and quality of education they receive, which in turn leads to a different quality of human capital and to different wages.

In a series of simulation experiments, we varied the amount of total investment in education in the economic system (Saviotti and Pyka, 2015), the share of the education investment (s_{ED}) going to each of two social classes (white- and blue-collar workers), and the relative quality of the education each class received. We started the experiment with a very unequal population and education distribution: only 20 percent of the education investment is dedicated to blue collars, which initially accounted for 80 percent of the population. Henceforth we will call the blue collars L class and the white collars H class. The results we obtained are as follows:

1 There is a threshold in education investment below which economic development by the creation of new sectors does not occur. Only one sector is created and the subsequent economic growth is extremely limited. Above the threshold an increase in investment in education accelerates the rate of creation of new sectors leading to faster growth. This confirms the role played by education in the co-evolutionary process described above.
2 The higher the investment in education the faster the population share of the H class grows leading to a corresponding fall in the population share of the L class. This shows that education can be socially progressive and that it could have contributed to the emergence of a salaried middle class.
3 By making the initial 20:80 percent allocation of investment in education to the L and H classes more egalitarian, moving to 50:50 percent and 80: 20 percent), we find that such changes increase the income (Figures 8(a)–(c)) of the L class relative to that of the H class. However, the same change leads to a fall in average income. Thus, a trade-off exists between using education to achieve growth and an equitable income distribution.
4 Although during certain periods the income of the L class can be higher than that of the H class, the income of the latter grows faster and overtakes that of the L class. For the highest share of education investment allocated to the L class, the overtaking process is not yet complete during the period we explored but the trend is clear.
5 The previous conclusion is somewhat modified by taking into account the relative income per head of the two classes during the period we explored (Figures 8.8(a)–(c)). When the share of education investment of the blue collars (s_{ED}) is varied from 20 percent to 50 percent and 80 percent, the income per head for the L class (iphL), initially inferior, overtakes that of the H class (iphH) (Figures 8.8(a)–(c)). It must be observed that this relative gain of income per head of the L class is obtained more by a fall in the iphH of the H class than by an increase of iphL of the L class. In this experiment the average income per head for the whole labor force (iphA) displayed in Figure 8.9 falls by as much as the income per head of the H class. In other words, moving from a highly non-egalitarian allocation of educational resources to an egalitarian one it is possible to raise the income per head of the L class above that of the H class, but at the price of reducing the average

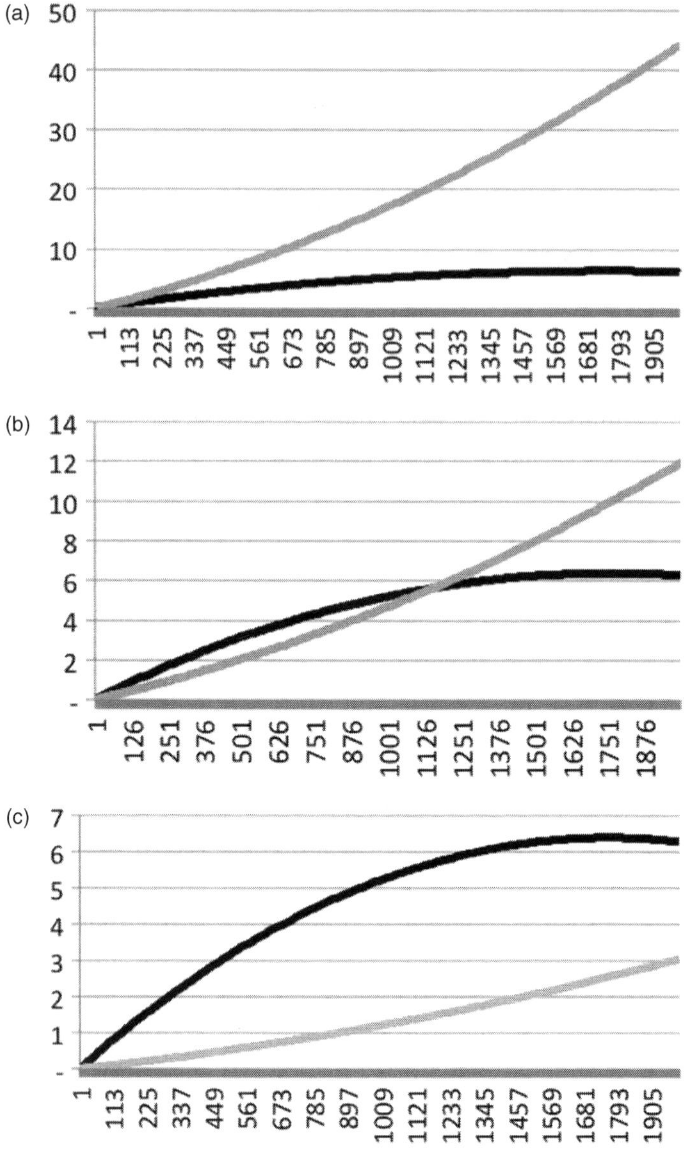

Figure 8.7 (a) Income evolution with 20% of investment in education allocated to the L (black) and 80% to the H (grey) class. Time on the horizontal axis; (b) Income evolution with 50% of investment in education allocated to the L (black) and 50% to the H (grey) class. Time on the horizontal axis; (c) Income evolution with 80% of investment in education allocated to the L (black) and 20% to the H (grey) class. Time on the horizontal axis

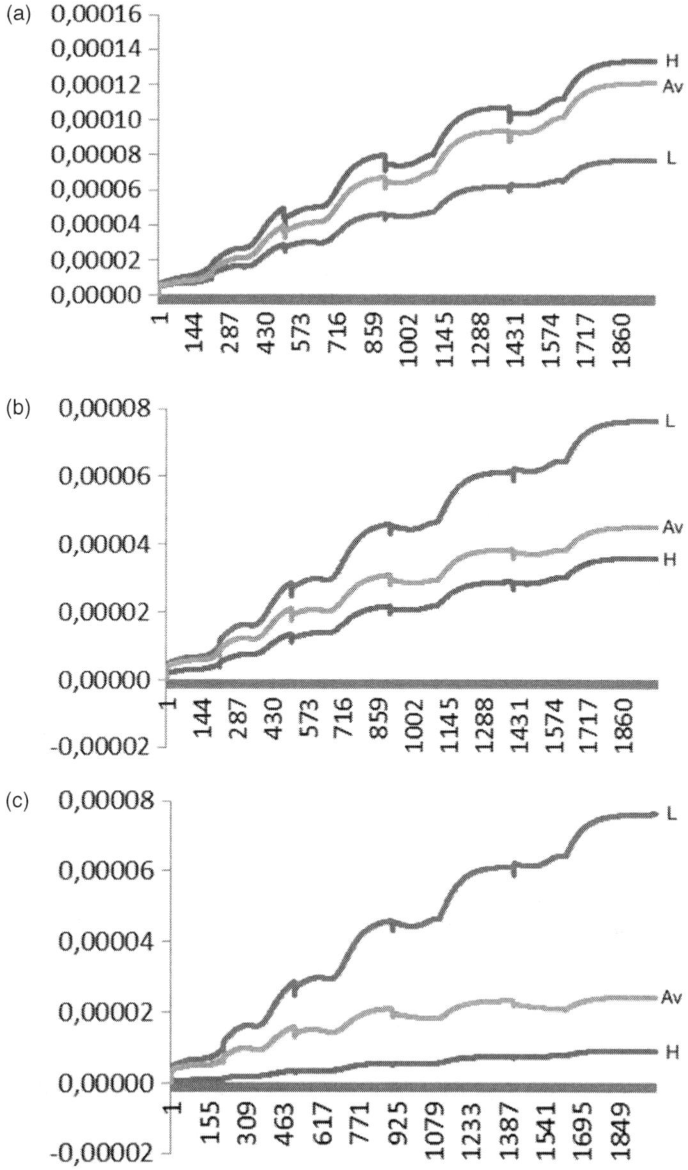

Figure 8.8 Evolution of the income per head for the L and H classes and of average income per head (A) when the share of education investment (s_{ED}) of the L class is varied from 20% (a) to 50% (b) and to 80% (c)

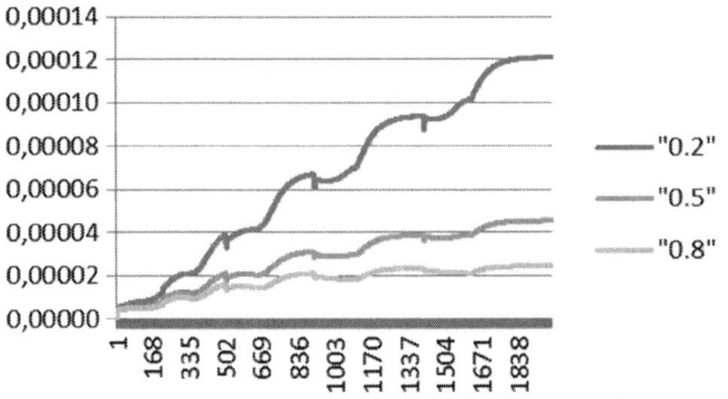

Figure 8.9 Effect of changing the share of investment in education allocated to the L class (s_{EDL}) from 20% to 50% to 80% on the average income per head

income per head. We can expect that any such allocation of educational resources by impoverishing the H class, which receives the higher-quality education, relative to the L class, which receives the lower quality education, leading to a fall in average income per head, is very unlikely to be implemented in any economic system. We expect the people receiving the best education, and therefore having the best human capital, to be paid higher wages than the people receiving a lower-quality education, although this difference needs to be limited to avoid the trend towards a growing inequality which is now prevailing in a number of developed economic systems.

Conclusions

In this chapter we have summarized some of our previous work and focused on the role played by co-evolutionary mechanisms in the pattern of economic development observed since the Industrial Revolution and in particular the twentieth century. We explored the joint effect of education, human capital, product quality, and wages on the creation of new sectors and thereby on economic development. As a result of this previous work we think that co-evolutionary mechanisms are not exceptional but occur quite frequently in economic development. In fact, we would go as far as to state that co-evolution is the rule and pair-wise cause-effect relationships are the exception, to be found in particular cases. Such pair-wise cause-effect relationships are likely to be important in economic systems in which most variables do not interact or interact very weakly and in which strong interactions are limited to pairs of variables. We expect this situation to occur more often in systems of limited creativity in the presence of low structural change. We expect the important transformations, which in the end give rise to the long-run persistence of economic development and growth, depend on the co-evolution of different variables. The existence of a positive feedback of the types described above can accelerate the emergence of new activities and sectors, thus very rapidly changing the composition of the economic system. Needless to say, no form of proportional growth in which all sectors grow at the same rate could give rise to similar types of structural change. An alternative interpretation would stress the existence of industry life cycles as a determinant of structural change. The existence of ILCs is predicted by TEVECON under a wide range of conditions. However, both the existence and the properties of ILCs (duration etc.) depend on the co-evolution of demand, competition, education, and other variables. Let us conclude this chapter on the importance of co-evolution by stating two things:

1 Co-evolution is obviously a form of complexity.
2 Without wishing to say that they are the same thing, we wish to point towards the similarity of co-evolution and auto catalysis (Prigogine and Stengers, 1985) since both of them have the capacity to accelerate processes leading to the emergence and growing importance of new system components.

References

Baumol, William J. (1967) "Macroeconomics of unbalanced growth: the anatomy of urban crisis," *American Economic Review*, 57 (3): 415–26.

Chenery, Hollis B. (1960) "Patterns of industrial growth," *American Economic Review*, 50: 624–54.

Ciarli, Tommaso, Lorentz, André, Savona, Maria, and Valente, Marco (2010) "The effect of consumption and production structure on growth and distribution. A micro to macro model," *Metroeconomica*, 61 (1): 180–218.

Ciarli, Tommaso, Lorentz, André, Savona, Maria, and Valente, Marco (2012) *The Role of Technology, Organisation, and Demand in Growth and Income Distribution*, LEM Working Papers 2012/06. Pisa: San'Anna School of Advanced Studies, Laboratory of Economics and Management

Cornwall, John (1977) *Modern Capitalism, its Growth and Transformation*. London: Martin Robertson.

Dosi, Giovanni (1982) "Technological paradigms and technological trajectories: a suggested interpretation of the determinants and directions of technical change," *Research Policy*, 11: 147–62.

Dosi, Giovanni, Fagiolo, Giorgio, and Roventini, Andrea (2010) "Schumpeter meeting Keynes: A policy-friendly model of endogenous growth and business cycles," *Journal of Economic Dynamics and Control*, 34: 1748–67.

Fabricant, Solomon (1940) *The Output of Manufacturing Industries, 1899–1937*. New York: National Bureau of Economic Research, pp. xxv and 685.

Fagerberg, Jan (2000) *Technological Progress, Structural Change and Productivity Growth: A Comparative Study*, Working Paper No. 5/2000. Oslo: Centre for Technology, Innovation and Culture, University of Oslo.

Galor, Oded (2005) "From stagnation to growth: unified growth theory," in P. Aghion and S. Durlauf (eds), *Handbook of Economic Growth*, Vol. 1. Amsterdam: Elsevier/North Holland, pp. 171–293.

Galor, Oded and Weil, David N. (2000) "Population, technology, and growth: from Malthusian stagnation to the demographic transition and beyond," *American Economic Review*, 90 (4): 806–28.

Hobsbawm, Eric J. (1968) *Industry and Empire*. Harmondsworth: Penguin Books.

Kuznets, Simon (1957) "Quantitative aspects of the economic growth of nations: II. Industrial distribution of national product and labor force," *Economic Development and Cultural Change*, 5 July, suppl., pp. 1–111.

Maddison, Angus (2001) *The World Economy*. Paris: OECD.

Metcalfe, J. Stan, Foster, John, and Ramlogan, Ronnie (2005) "Adaptive economic growth," *Cambridge Journal of Economics*, 30: 7–32.

Nelson, Richard R. and Winter, Sidney G. (1977) "In search of useful theory of innovation," *Research Policy*, 6: 36–76.

Pasinetti, Luigi L. (1981) *Structural Change and Economic Growth*. Cambridge: Cambridge University Press.

Pasinetti, Luigi L. (1993) *Structural Economic Dynamics*. Cambridge: Cambridge University Press.

Prigogine, Ilya and Stengers Isabelle (1985) *Order out of Chaos: Man's New Dialogue with Nature*. London: Flamingo, Fontana Paperbacks.

Pyka, Andreas and Saviotti, Pier-Paolo (2011) "Economic growth through the emergence of new sectors," in S. Mann (ed.), *Sectors Matter – Exploring Mesoeconomics*. Berlin: Springer, pp. 55–102.

Salter, Wilfried E.G. (1960) *Productivity and Technical Change*. Cambridge: Cambridge University Press.

Saviotti, Pier-Paolo and Pyka, Andreas (2004a) "Economic development by the creation of new sectors," *Journal of Evolutionary Economics*, 14 (1): 1–36.

Saviotti, Pier-Paolo and Pyka, Andreas (2004b) "Economic development, qualitative change and employment creation,' *Structural Change and Economic Dynamics*, 15 (3): 265–87.

Saviotti, Pier-Paolo and Pyka, Andreas (2008) "Product variety, competition and economic growth," *Journal of Evolutionary Economics*, 18: 323–47.

Saviotti, Pier-Paolo and Pyka, Andreas (2012) "On the co-evolution of innovation and demand: some policy implications," *Revue de l'OFCE*, Special issue: *Debates and Policies: Agent-based Models and Economic Policy*, eds Jean-Luc Gaffard and Mauro Napoletano, 124 (5): 347–88.

Saviotti, Pier-Paolo and Pyka, Andreas (2013) "From necessities to imaginary worlds: structural change, product quality and economic development," *Technological Forecasting and Social Change*, 80: 1499–512.

Saviotti, Pier-Paolo and Pyka, Andreas (2015) "On the co-evolution of innovation and demand: some policy implications," in Franceso Crespi and Francesco Quatraro (eds), *The Economics of Knowledge, Innovation and Systemic Technology Policy*, Routledge Studies in Global Competition. Abingdon: Routledge, pp. 15–47.

Schumpeter, Joseph (1934 [1912]) *The Theory of Economic Development*. Cambridge, MA: Harvard University Press.

Silva, Ester G., Teixeira and Aurora A. C. (2008) "Surveying structural change: seminal contributions and a bibliometric account," *Structural Change and Economic Dynamics*, 19: 273–300.

Verspagen, Bart (1993) *Uneven Growth Between Interdependent Economies*. Aldershot: Avebury.

Part III

Policy and crises

Finance, growth, and industry

9 Alternative policies after the financial crisis

New thinking from complex evolutionary economics

Ping Chen

Introduction

The 2008 financial crisis shocked the very foundation of neoclassical economics, since equilibrium models in neoclassical economics simply deny the possibility of endogenous business cycles and financial crises. During and after the crisis, many countries adopted monetary and fiscal policies for stabilizing and stimulating economies according to the textbook economics of the IS-LM model that resulted in widely different results. The critical role of structural reform is missing in the two-level framework of micro and macroeconomics.

In this article, we will discuss two main issues: first, the origin and nature of the crisis that reveals the fundamental flaws in neoclassical economics and demands a paradigm change in economic thinking; second, alternative policies in complex evolutionary economics, which is capable of understanding the changing world after the crisis.

Methodologically speaking, the mainstream economic thoughts have a common problem: linear one-way thinking with an equilibrium perspective. Mainstream economists often ignore economic complexity, including non-linearity, non-equilibrium, non-stationary, social interactions, and the large picture of ecological-industrial systems (Dopfer, 2005; Elsner, 2012). We have better alternatives both in theory and practice by means of the new perspective, since we live in a non-linear and non-equilibrium world under open competition (Chen, 2010).

Diagnosis of the cause of financial crisis

There are three questions related to the debate on this crisis. First, was the crisis caused by an endogenous mechanism or by external shocks? Second, can we identify warning signals for coming crises? Third, do we have any instruments to deal with financial crises? There are two competing approaches in addressing these questions.

Static statistics and equilibrium models have little understanding of market instability and financial crisis

The static methods of statistics in econometric analysis have no clear answers to the above questions. According to the efficient market hypothesis and rational expectation theory, there is little chance for market crises under the "invisible hand" paradigm if market fluctuations follow a random walk or Brownian motion. The Frisch model of noise-driven cycles was a perpetual motion machine that cannot maintain persistent business cycles (Frisch, 1933; Chen, 2010: chapter 12). The popular dynamic stochastic general equilibrium models are variations of the noise-driven model, including rational expectations, RBC models, and financial accelerators (Lucas, 1981; Kydland and Prescott, 1982; Bernanke *et al.*, 1996). The equilibrium theory simply rules out the possibility of endogenous instability because their market model is self-stabilizing under the equilibrium-optimization paradigm and attributes business fluctuations only to external shocks.

We found out that the noise component only accounts for 30 percent of market variance. We have solid evidence that financial market indexes are non-stationary and their main component can be explained by non-linear color chaos (Chen, 1996). Business cycles are mainly generated by non-linear endogenous mechanisms. Schumpeter's idea of the biological clock can be described by "color chaos" (Chen, 1988, 2005).

We should point out that the disequilibrium models do provide explanations for large business fluctuations, such as fractal Brownian motion and power law models in econophysics (Mandelbrot, 1997; Mantegna and Stanley, 2000). However, a static disequilibrium model has little power in analyzing non-stationary time series and historical events. We had little means to stabilize the market if market fluctuations were governed by fat tail, fractal Brownian motion, unit root, power law, or Black Swan mechanisms in disequilibrium theory (Chen, 2015).

Time-dependent transition probability and regime switching in financial markets

The 2008 financial crisis started with the collapse of the derivative market in the US. We discovered before the crisis that the Black-Scholes model in option pricing is explosive in nature (Chen, 2005, 2010). The base model in finance theory is Brownian motion that is a representative agent model without herd behavior. The better alternative model is the population model of the birth-death process, which is capable of understanding both calm (quasi linear regime) and turbulent (severe non-linear regime) markets including breaking point or market crises.

We developed the stochastic dynamics of changing high moments and regime switch, which can be fully described by a non-linear birth-death process. Its time-dependent transition probability can be estimated from empirical data. We can directly observe the transition probability from the empirical time series by means of the birth-death processes for price dynamics (Tang and Chen, 2015). We found two different market regimes in the recent history of the US financial market that can be seen in Figure 9.1. Clearly, the turbulent regime occurred in the period of liberalization policy. We can estimate when the market broke down by means of the master equation of the birth-death process.

The market tide driven by collective psychology can be visualized as a curve. Its falling segment represents a market tide towards equilibrium while a rising

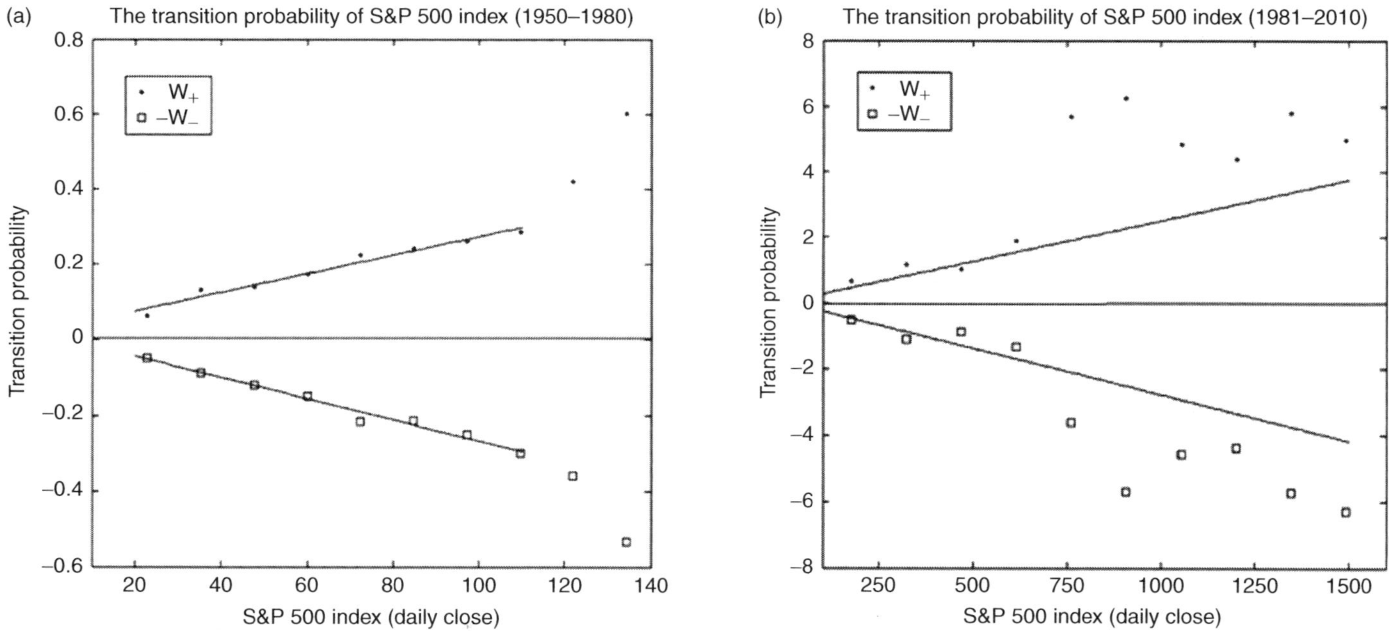

Figure 9.1 The transition probabilities (W_+ and $-W_-$) of the S&P 500 daily close. The horizontal axis is the price level of the S&P 500 daily index. The upper curve W_+ describes the transition probability of the price moving up that signals the strength of the bull camp, while the lower curve W_- describes the transition probability of the price moving down that signals the strength of the bear camp. Market movements were driven by the net effect between the bull and bear camp. (a) The transition probability curve in 1950–80. Its shape is near linear, which is the typical feature of a calm market. (b) The transition probability curve in 1981–2010. Its shape is highly non-linear with two visible humps or dips, which is the typical feature of a turbulent market. The two straight lines here are the extensions of the straight fitting lines in (a)

segment signals a market tide towards disequilibrium. Figure 9.2 shows the numerical results of the net daily change rate, which indicates down-up-down market tides. The up phase describes a collective fad for a market bubble. We assume that the turning point from the up to the down phase may generate a market breakdown or crisis, and therefore a critical point of financial crises. The critical behaviors of crises have also been characterized by diverging high moments and extraordinarily large trading volumes.

From Figure 9.2, the turning point can be estimated from the numerical solution of the non-linear birth-death process. We have quantitative evidence to infer that the stock market breakdown may happen near the 1,229th point. According to historical data, the S&P 500 index closed at 1,209.13 on 25 September 2008, when the Office of Thrift Supervision (OTS) seized Washington Mutual and sold its banking assets to JP Morgan Chase for $1.9 billion. This event was the peak of a chain of events preceding the 2008 financial crisis. Before this event, Fannie Mae and Freddie Mac were nationalized by the US government, Lehman Brothers bankrupted, and AIG experienced a liquidity crisis. Then the stock market went into panic from 26 September 2008. Effectively, our estimation of the historical turning point provides an accurate indicator for the coming crisis in addition to the high moments approach in crisis warning.

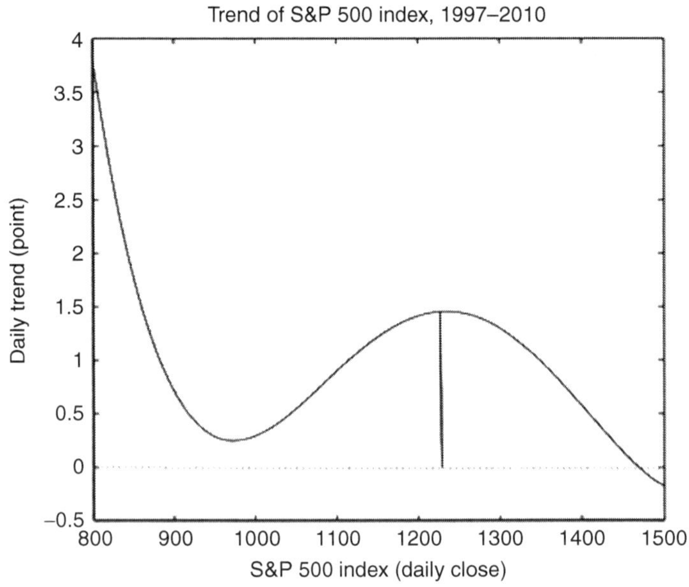

Figure 9.2 The curve of a changing market tide in terms of the net daily change rate (1997–2010). The curve is calculated from the 4th degree polynomial fitted transition probability from 1997–2010. The up segment indicates two hot-speculation periods from 950 to 1,229 in 1997–2000 and 2003–8, and panic in 2008. The vertical line marks the turning (critical) point in market psychology, which is 1,229 in the price level.

Financial deregulation is based on the argument of reducing transaction costs (Coase, 1979). This argument is dubious since deregulation may have increased herd behavior and market volatility. From a complexity perspective, selection mechanism is more relevant for a vital economy with multiple regimes (Chen, 2007).

High moment representation and crisis warning signal

Both transition probability estimation and regression analysis can only be conducted ex post. However, we do have a new tool for monitoring market instability in practice. The rising tide signals an upcoming bubble in the financial market. This is a valuable indicator for an early warning of a crisis.

Neoclassical finance theory mainly considers the first (mean) and second moment (variance) in analyzing financial risk. We find that the high moment representation provides more critical information for diagnosing dynamical instability (Tang and Chen, 2014). High (3rd to 5th) moments would rapidly rise one quarter before and during the crisis. These phenomena indicate a turbulent market, which can be understood by herd behavior induced by interacting agents. High moments are insignificant in a calm market (see Figure 9.3).

Changing high moments (in a range of 100–1,000 times of normal variance) in financial history show that the real market does not follow a stable distribution. Therefore the static picture of the distribution's tails may distort the non-stationary nature of market instability and crisis. The dramatic rising of high moments provides a better signal of market instability than traditional measures, such as the price level changes or fat tails in a static distribution.

Based on the above discussion, we may conclude that the financial crisis was induced by liberalization policy during the last three decades. The turbulent market is characterized by a non-linear regime in transition probability and a coming crisis is signaled by dramatically rising high moments. The mass psychology of herd behavior can be studied by the population model of the birth-death process, which is more powerful than the representative agent model of a random walk or a Brownian motion model. Time-dependent transition probability and high moment representation provide new tools in non-stationary time series analysis, which are useful in crisis diagnosis and monitoring the market.

Policy alternative after the crisis

The second issue in this article is how to deal with financial crises and why country performances varied greatly after the 2008 crisis. We found that the existing tools in mainstream economics were not enough to deal with the crisis. The new perspective of complex evolutionary economics provides new policies with a better understanding of the structural causes of financial crisis and the limits of neoclassical economics.

Limitation of the IS-LM model for monetary policy in dealing with the crisis

One remarkable lesson in this crisis is the limitation of monetary policy during the crisis. Friedman once believed that expansion policy in monetary supply

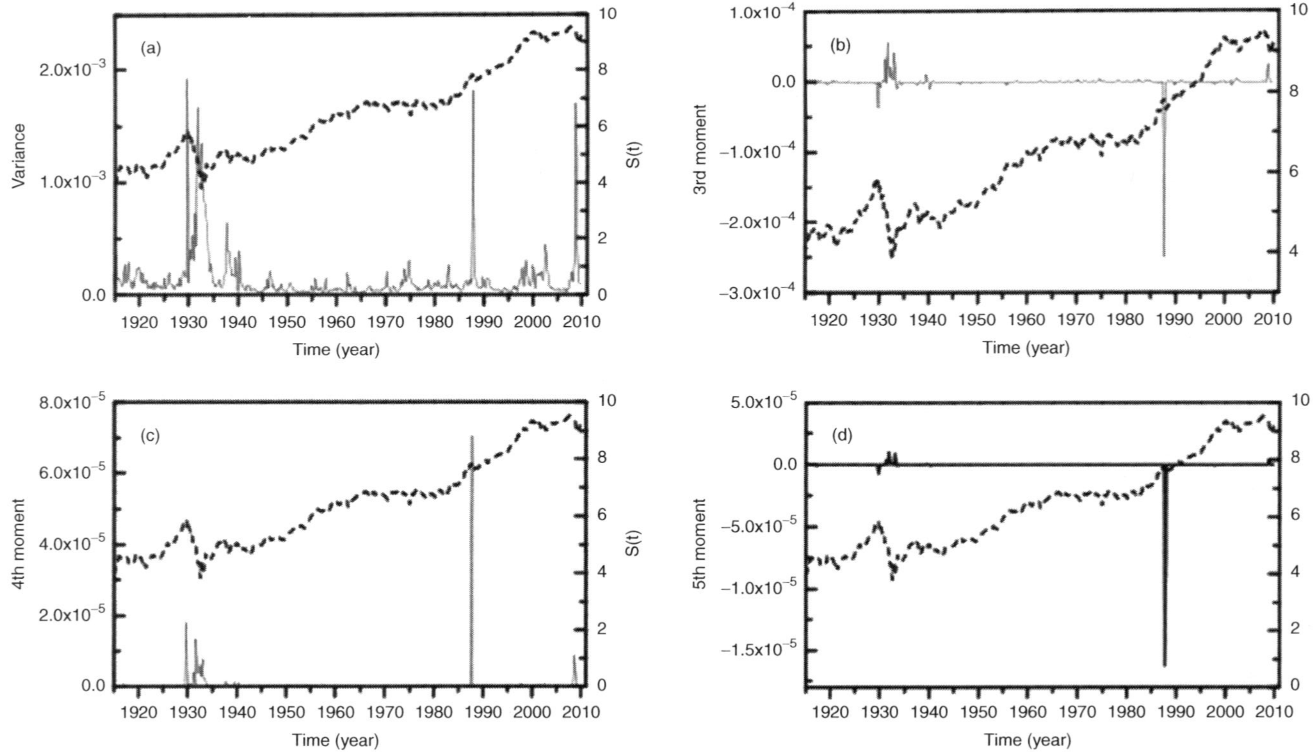

Figure 9.3 The quarterly moments (solid lines) of the Dow-Jones Industrial Average (DJI) index. The original S(t) (dashed lines) is the natural logarithmic daily close price series. Each point in the solid line is calculated with a moving time window; its width is one quarter. Plots (a), (b), (c), and (d) correspond to the 2nd, 3rd, 4th, and 5th moments, respectively. The magnitudes of each moment representation are 10^{-5} for variance, 10^{-8} for the 3rd moment, 10^{-9} for the 4th moment, and 10^{-11} for the 5th moment. The daily data were from 2 January 1900 to 1 September 2010 with 27,724 data points. Here we choose $\sigma_0^2 \sim 10^{-5}$ as the normal level. We would consider high moments when they reach the level of $10^{-1}\sigma_0^2$ or higher

might have prevented the Great Depression (Friedman and Schwartz, 1963). Both the US Federal Reserve and EU Central Bank carried out large-scale quantitative easing, but its effect was limited at best (Bernanke, 2013).

According to the IS model in macroeconomics, lowering the interest rate should increase investment and output. This is a typical case of one-way thinking, which is operational only for the consumer's market in a closed economy without structural changes. In an open economy under global competition, a lower interest rate would lead to three different outcomes: (1) increasing investment if the economy is healthy and competitive; (2) capital flight if other markets (such as emerging markets) have better growth potential; (3) holding cash when uncertainty rules the market. Clearly, the neoclassical model of the IS curve is an oversimplified model for a complex economy. The new global world must understand the multiple possibilities with open competition and regime switch.

There is an old debate between the endogenous and the exogenous schools in money supply (Wicksell, 1898). The discovery of monetary chaos offered strong evidence for endogenous money (Chen, 1988), since the exogenous model is based on random walk or Brownian motion mechanisms (Chen, 1996). The limited effect of the monetary policy during this crisis provided further historical experience that monetary policy is constrained by economic conditions.

Meso-foundation and competition policy

Economic virtualization and the rise of the monetary economy put financial oligarchs in the driving seat in globalization that creates economic polarization and welfare crises in both developed and developing countries (Johnson, 2009). The meso-foundation theory of business cycles reveals the importance of competition policy and anti-trust policy in an international financial order (Chen, 2009).

The counter-Keynesian revolution led by Lucas played a key role in market liberalization over the last three decades. Lucas made a strong claim that business cycles could be explained by an equilibrium (rational expectations) mechanism of workers' choices between work and leisure (Lucas, 1981). His micro-foundations theory is widely discredited by the 2008 crisis. His theoretical flaw was revealed by empirical observations based on the principle of large numbers (Chen, 2002). According to Schrödinger (1944), the founder of quantum mechanics and quantum biology, there is a salient relationship between the number of micro-elements and the variability of aggregate fluctuations.

$$\text{Market variability } (\text{MV}) = \frac{STD(S_N)}{Mean(S_N)} \approx \frac{1}{\sqrt{N}} \tag{9.1}$$

The implication of equation 9.1 is simple. The more micro-elements are involved, the less the aggregate fluctuation will be, because independent fluctuations would cancel out each other. This is the principle of large numbers. This relation can be extended from static aggregation to dynamic growth, such as the population dynamics of the birth-death process (Chen, 2002). Empirically, we can measure

Table 9.1 Market variability and effective cluster number for various aggregate indexes

Item	*MV (%)*	*Nc*
Real personal consumption	0.15	800,00
Real GDP	0.2	500,00
Real private investment	1.2	10,000
Dow Jones Industrial (1928–2009)	1.4	9,000
S&P 500 Index (1947–2009)	1.6	5,000
NASDAQ (1971–2009)	2.0	3,000
Japan–US exchange rate (1971–2009)	6.1	300
US–Euro exchange rate (1999–2009)	4.9	400
Texas crude oil price (1978–2008)	5.3	400

Notes: For non-stationary time series, market variability is measured via the HP filter; the average is estimated from a moving time window in the range of the average length of business cycles, here five years (Chen, 2002).

From this table, we immediately see that there is no evidence for rational expectations and representative agent models in macro-dynamics, since the observed cluster numbers are much larger than 1.

Sources: US aggregate indexes and exchange rates are from the Federal Reserve Bank at St Louis; stock indexes data are from yahoo.finance; the oil price index is from the US Energy Information Administration.

MV from aggregate indexes; we can also infer the effective cluster number N_c, at the micro-level. The empirical results are shown in Table 9.1. The number of households, corporations, and public companies and their implied orders of MV in 1980 are given in Table 9.2.

From Tables 9.1 and 9.2, we can see that household fluctuations contribute only about 5 percent of fluctuations in real gross domestic product (GDP) and less than 1 percent in real investment; small firms can contribute 50 percent of the fluctuations in real GDP or 8 percent in real investment, while public companies can generate about 60 percent of aggregate fluctuations in real investment. Clearly, there are very weak 'micro-foundations' from households or firms but strong evidence of a 'meso-foundation' of financial companies in macroeconomic fluctuations.

One big issue in this financial crisis is how to deal with the financial oligarchs that created the crisis (Johnson, 2009). The US government spent huge amounts of money to save these financial oligarchs on the grounds that they were "too big to fail," since their failure may trigger a chain reaction across the financial industry. From our perspective, these financial giants are "too complex to exist" because

Table 9.2 Numbers of households and firms in the United States (1980)

Micro-agents	*Households*	*Corporations**	*Public companies*
N	80,700,000	2,900,00	20,000
MV (%)	0.01	0.1	0.7

*Only those corporations with more than $100,00 in assets are counted

Source: US Bureau of Census.

they amplify macro-fluctuation. This fallacy of composition misleads equilibrium economists in their representative model of macro-behavior.

More surprisingly, the order of market variability in the oil and currency markets is much higher than real investment and the stock market, which indicates the naked fact of the financial concentration generated by giant financial corporations. This is the real root of this grand crisis.

Dan Gilligan (2009), President of the Petroleum Marketers Association (PMA), has revealed that financial giants such as Morgan Stanley, Goldman Sachs, Barclays and JP Morgan were manipulating the oil price. They put hundreds of billions of dollars in the oil futures market, in addition to money invested by large institutional fund managers such as the California Pension Fund, the Harvard University Endowment, and other institutional investors. They started their speculation in 2000, when the US Congress deregulated the futures market, granting exemptions for complicated derivative investments called oil swaps, as well as electronic trading on private exchanges. Volatility in the price of oil increased dramatically. Later in the decade, within one year, the oil price rose from \$67 a barrel to \$147 a barrel, then collapsed back down to \$45. On one occasion, the oil price jumped \$25 in one day! Surprisingly, changes in oil demand and supply in this period were less than 5 percent, while changes in the price of oil were larger than 100 percent! From the middle of June to the end of November 2008, when a US congressional investigation started, about \$70 billion of speculative capital left the future markets. At that time, demand for oil dropped 5 percent, but the price of oil dropped 76 percent from \$130 to \$30 per barrel. Gilligan estimated that about 60–70 percent of oil contracts in the future markets were controlled by speculative capital at the peak. In the past five years, hedge funds and global banks have poured capital into the oil market. Their 'investment' rose from \$13 billion to \$300 billion.

Clearly, competition policy at the microeconomic level and in financial markets is essential to achieve macro-stability. For stabilizing international financial markets, breaking-up financial oligarchs is more effective than financial regulation. Our research strongly supports the international anti-trust law for preventing the next global crisis.

From the above discussion, we can see that the traditional two-level framework of micro-macro economy is not capable of understanding the mechanism of endogenous business cycles. Our analysis based on the principle of large numbers supports the three-level framework of the micro-meso-macro economy. The meso-level mainly includes financial sector and industrial organizations, while the micro level refers to atomic players such as households and firms. Economic structure at the macro-level can be better understood by using the meso-level. Its importance can be seen from the following discussion.

Structural reform and industrial policy

During this crisis, economic performance varied greatly among developed and emerging countries (see Table 9.3).

Table 9.3 GDP growth rate during the crisis (%)

Country	*US*	*UK*	*Fra*	*Ger*	*Jap*	*Ice*	*Spa*	*Ita*	*Gre*	*Chi*	*Ind*	*Bra*	*Rus*	*World*
2007	1.8	2.6	2.4	3.3	2.2	9.7	3.8	1.5	3.5	14.2	9.8	6.1	8.5	4.0
2008	–0.3	–0.3	0.2	1.1	–1.0	1.1	1.1	–1.0	–0.4	9.6	3.9	5.2	5.2	1.5
2009	–2.8	–4.3	–2.9	–5.6	–5.5	–5.1	–3.6	–5.5	–4.4	9.2	8.5	–0.3	–7.8	–2.0
2010	2.5	1.9	2.0	4.1	4.7	–2.9	0.0	1.7	–5.4	10.4	10.5	7.5	4.5	4.1
2011	1.6	1.6	2.1	3.6	–0.5	2.1	–0.6	0.6	–8.9	9.3	6.4	2.7	4.3	2.8
2012	2.3	0.7	0.3	0.4	1.5	1.1	–2.1	–2.3	–6.6	7.7	4.7	1.0	3.4	2.2
2013	2.2	1.7	0.3	0.1	1.5	3.5	–1.2	–1.9	–3.3	7.7	5.0	2.5	1.3	2.3
AVE(09–13)	1.2	0.3	0.4	0.5	0.3	–0.3	–1.5	–1.5	–5.7	8.9	7.0	2.7	1.1	1.9

The data in the table can be classified into three groups. The first is the major developed countries including the US, the UK, France, Germany, and Japan. The second is the countries in severe crisis including Iceland, Spain, Italy, and Greece. The third is the major developing countries including China, India, Brazil, and Russia; The last column is the World index. The last row is the five-year average growth rate from 2009 to 2013. All data are show in percentage rates.

Source: United Nations Statistics.

From Table 9.3, we found that developed countries suffered more than emerging countries during the 2008 financial crisis, because the financial industry has more weight in developed countries. The role of economic structure is critical for understanding wide differences in economic performance. For example, Greece and Italy have long-term structural problems in balancing the budget and Iceland and Spain experienced great pain from the bursting of the housing bubble. Aging and the debt burden greatly restrict government financial policy in Europe, Japan, and the United States. In contrast, emerging countries are performing much better than developed countries, since their investments are mainly devoted to the real rather than the virtual economy. China made investments in infrastructure, especially the high-speed train, while India's economy is driven by investment in education and infrastructure. In another words, economic structure matters in economic policy performance.

However, Keynesian economics falls short in understanding the structural foundation of insufficient aggregate demand and non-voluntary unemployment. Our theory of metabolic growth pointed out that excess capacity resulted from technology competition (Chen, 2014). A typical growth trajectory for an industry or technology is an S-shaped logistic curve. Its growth ceiling represents resource capacity, market extent, or ecological constraint that is the function of the underlying technology. Under open technology competition, a new technology may replace an old technology or coexist with the existing technology. These results can be seen from Figure 9.4.

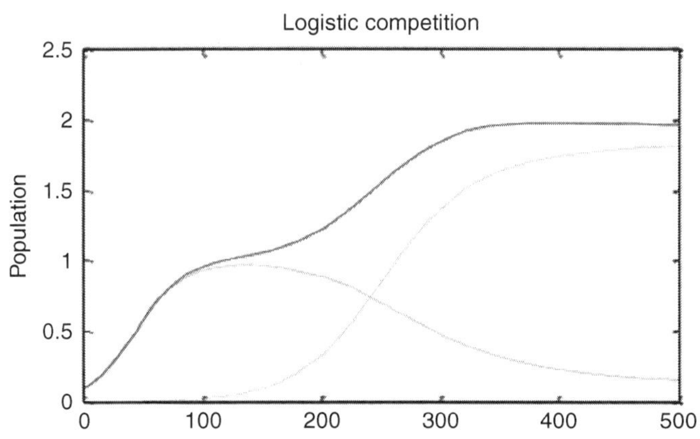

Figure 9.4 Metabolic growth characterized by technology competition. The old technology (lower left line) declines when new technology (lower right line) emerges. The output envelope (upper line) is the sum of their output of all technologies. The units here are arbitrary in computational simulation. Here, $\beta = 0.4$, $C_2 = 2*C_1$. When old and new technologies coexist, both technologies cannot realize their full capacity. The resulting excess capacity is at the root of Schumpeter's "creative destruction"

If C_1 is the full capacity of technology 1, C_2 is the full capacity of technology 2. Technology competition will bring both aggregate growth and creative destruction. We may calculate the costs of revolutionary technology. There are two possible outcomes:

1. When $< \frac{C_2}{C_1} < \frac{1}{\beta}$, here the competition coefficient is $0 < \beta < 1$

Old and new technology will coexist. However, the aggregate outcome is below their full potential:

$$\frac{1}{2}(C_1 + C_2) \le (n_1^* + n_2^*) = \frac{(C_1 + C_2)}{1+\beta} \le (C_1 + C_2) \tag{9.2}$$

Here n_1^* and n_2^* is realized capacity for technology 1 and 2 respectively. We can see from Figure 9.4 that both old and new technology have excess capacity, since neither of them could realize their full potential. This is our new understanding of the origin of insufficient aggregate demand. For a numerical example, $\beta = 0.4$, $C_2 = 2*C_1$, realized output is about 2.143 C_1, that is below the potential output of 3 C_1. The excess capacity is about 0.857 C_1.

2. When $C_2 > C_1/\beta$, where β is the competition coefficient, C_2 will completely wipe out C_1, so that the aggregate output is equal to C_2, while the competition cost is C_1. For a numerical example, when $\beta = 0.4$ and $C_2 > 2.5\ C_1$, C_2 will replace C_1. Even if total output C_2 is more than 2.5 C_1, there is still a sunk cost of full capacity of C_1.

From Figure 9.4, we find out that technology advancement is not an equilibrium mechanism of a diffusion process, but a metabolic dynamics of creative destruction. The rise and fall of technologies can be described by technology wavelets. There is a life-cycle movement in technology competition. This picture is radically different from random walk in real business cycle theory (Kydland and Prescott, 1982), since equilibrium business cycle theory ignores interruptive technology and creative destruction.

Clearly, government policy will be important during technology transition. When a new technology wipes out an old technology, the knowledge and capacity associated with the old technology become sunk costs. Retraining policies for unemployed workers and government assistance for industrial transition will greatly smooth the problems during an industrial transition. When new and old technologies coexist, the government may delay or accelerate technology advancement and structural adjustment. If an interest group associated with obsolete technology is able to block the technology metabolism, laissez-faire policy may delay technology advancement and lost international competition. This is true for both developed and developing countries.

Resource-intensive vs. labor-intensive technology

There is one visible puzzle during this crisis: how did China and India grow much faster than developed countries? We should remember that China and India have much less natural resources than developed countries, such as land on a per capita basis (see Table 9.4).

There is a striking difference between Asia's small grain farms and large Western farms in the corn and cattle agri-business. Neoclassical economics simply ignores the constraints of natural resources and ecological environment, while global warming raises the issue of sustainable development. Our theory of metabolic growth reveals the link between culture and technology (Chen, 1987, 2014).

Generally speaking, an individualist culture is deeply rooted in a resource-intensive and labor-saving technology, while a collectivist culture is associated with resource-scarcity and a population-dense environment. Their economic implication can be explained by the population-resource relation under ecological constraints. In history, we observe that colonialist culture is characterized by risk-taking behavior, while traditional culture is characterized by risk-aversion behavior (see Figure 9.5).

The species competition under ecological constraints can be modified with a different culture factor. Even under the same resource constraint, the equilibrium population size is different for different cultures.

$$n^*_{a<0} < n^*_{a=0} < n^*_{a>0} \tag{9.3}$$

Here, the culture factor a is a measure of risk orientation. If $a > 0$, it is a measure of risk-aversion or collectivism. If $a < 0$, it is a measure of risk-taking or individualism. The case $a = 0$ implies risk neutrality.

According to equation 9.3, the resource utilization rate of the collectivist species ($n^*_{a>0}$) is higher than that of the individualist species ($n^*_{a<0}$). The individualist species needs a larger subsistence space than a collectivist one in order to maintain the

Table 9.4 Cross-country comparison in land resource

Region	*Arable land*[*] *(%)*	*Population (millions)*	*Arable land per capita (ha)*
China	10	1,179	0.08
Europe	28	507	0.26
US	19	239	0.73
fUSSR[**]	10	203	0.79
Japan	12	125	0.04
India	52	899	0.19
Brazil	6	159	0.31
Australia	6	18	2.62
Canada	5	28	1.58

[*] Here, arable land is measured by percentage of the total area.
[**] Former Soviet Union.

Source: Madison (1998).

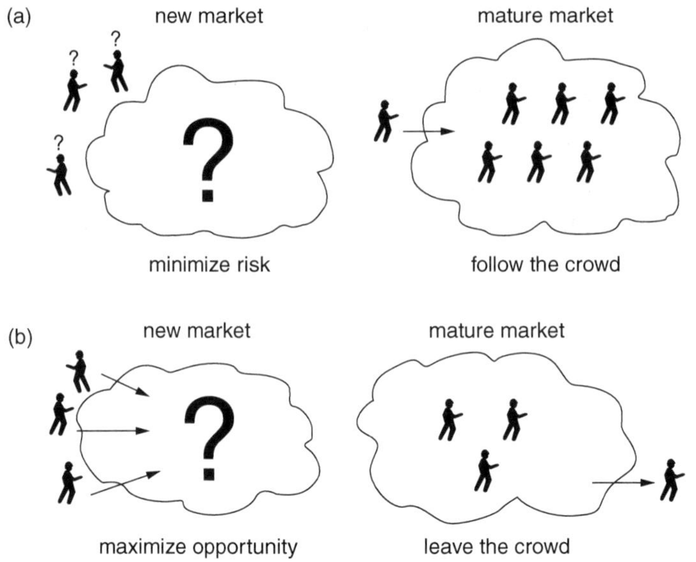

Figure 9.5 Risk-aversion and risk-taking behavior in market-share competition for new resources when technology outlook is uncertain. (a) Risk-aversion behavior (b) Risk-taking behavior

same equilibrium size (n^*). Therefore, individualism is a resource-consuming culture while collectivism is a resource-saving culture (Chen, 1990). This difference is visible between Western individualism and Eastern collectivism. Cultural differences are rooted in economic structures and ecological constraints. Resource expansion is a key to understanding the origin of a capitalist economy and the Industrial Revolution (Pomeranz, 2000).

Wallerstein once observed a historical puzzle that history looked to be irrational (1974). In the Middle Ages, China's population was near twice that of Western Europe while China's arable land was much less. According to the rational choice theory, China should have expanded its space while Europe should have increased in population. But the historical behavior was the opposite!

Culture plays a key role in the technology catch-up game. The Western mode of industrialization has had great success in the past three hundred years when resource utilization was far below ecological constraints. However, the Western mode is facing increasing challenges of ecological crises and global warming. That is why emerging countries are exploring different modes that are compatible with their environment and sustainable in history. If their learning speed is high enough, as with China and India, they may win the technological competition with developed countries. The metabolic growth theory indicates a new scenario in technology development and global competition for market share and sustainable resources.

Now, we have a new perspective in understanding the changing international order. For the exogenous growth theory, the regional development speed will converge towards the population growth rate regardless of their initial conditions. For endogenous growth theory, rich and poor countries will face an increasing gap between them if technological knowledge is accumulative. For metabolic growth theory, the competition outcome for leaders (developed countries) and followers (developing countries) is not certain but depends on innovation and learning speed and the scale of their resources. Therefore, the evolutionary perspective of metabolic growth is richer and more sophisticated than the equilibrium perspective.

Conclusion: new theoretical framework and evolutionary thinking

Economics has more similarity with biology than mechanics (Marshall, 1920). The neoclassical model of the demand-supply equilibrium is a picture for a pre-industrial economy without revolutionary technology advancement and global competition. The 2008 financial crisis reveals the pitfalls of linear equilibrium thinking and limits of monetary and fiscal policy in structural adjustment.

First, methodological advancement in complexity science is changing our way of thinking not only in natural science, but also in economic and social sciences. A non-linear and non-equilibrium framework is essential for understanding living and social systems (Prigogine, 1980; Chen, 2010). Linear and equilibrium models in neoclassical economics simply describe a static market and closed economy, which is far from the modern economy with revolutionary technology, social interaction, and global competition. Endogenous business cycles, regime switching, and financial crises can be explained by the unified theory of population dynamics and market-share competition under ecological constraints. The so-called efficient market is only an extremely simplifying case when non-linear interaction and herd behavior can be ignored. The more complicated situation with non-linear interaction and social psychology can be better understood and monitored by the population model of birth-death processes and high moment representation.

Second, neoclassical and metabolic economics implies different goals and tools in economic policy. Neoclassical economics assumes that the market is self-stabilizing; therefore laissez-faire policy is optimal under any situation. This belief was shattered by this financial crisis. In contrast, metabolic growth theory emphasizes the role of technology competition under resource constraints. Old technology is constantly replaced by new technology that is the very foundation of economic complexity and non-equilibrium dynamics. Economies are more like living organisms rather than calculating machines. Organisms may be healthy or sick, which depends on environmental impact and development stage. Government policy plays different roles at different stages and situations in technology life cycles. For example, public support for R&D is essential at the infant stage of technology, industrial policy is crucial at the growth stage, competition policy is important at the mature stage, and social policy is much needed in the case of declining industries. The mixed economy with diversified industries is vital for a sustainable economy. Economic players have to adapt to their specific environment and historical conditions. There is no standard economic recipe for all problems. This is a common understanding in a changing world, since economic complexity implies social diversity.

Third, structural analysis in a biological perspective is more useful than equilibrium analysis of demand and supply in dealing with technology transition and economic crisis. Economic structure can be better studied by the three-level framework of micro-meso-macro economy. The principle of large numbers indicates the clear link between competition policy and macro-stability. The liberal policy for the last three decades in the States led to the financial concentration that was at the structural root of the 2008 financial crisis.

Fourth, human nature is to be a social animal with physical and ecological constraints. There is a trade-off between system complexity and structural stability (Chen, 1987, 2014). The Western mode of division of labor is based on labor-saving and resource-intensive technology that is facing increasing stress under ecological crisis and global warming. The development of green technology will change the current mode of production and consumption as well as economic institution. The equilibrium paradigm implies a convergent process in social evolution, while non-linear and non-equilibrium dynamics indicate a two-way evolution towards biodiversity and economic vitality. We are at a historical turning point for a new world of sustainable economy and diversified civilizations.

Finally, the new science of complexity and non-equilibrium physics provides new tools for integrating economic insights from Smith, Malthus, Darwin, and Marx, to Schumpeter, Hayek, Keynes, and Minsky. We are developing a unified theory of complex evolutionary economics.

Acknowledgments

The author thanks Peter Allen, Wolfgang Weidlich, Edmond Phelps, Joseph Stiglitz, James Galbraith, Ulrich Witt, Justin Lin, Wolfram Elsner, Andreas Pyka, Edward Fullbrook, Steve Keen, Zhengfu Shi, Yinan Tang, Huajun Li, and Jie Meng for their stimulating discussions.

References

Bernanke, Ben, Gertler, Mark, and Gilchrist, Simon (1996) "The financial accelerator and flight to quality," *Review of Economics and Statistics*, 78: 1–15.

Bernanke, Ben S. (2013). *The Federal Reserve and the Financial Crisis*, Princeton: Princeton University Press.

Chen, Ping (1987) "Origin of the division of labor and a stochastic mechanism of differentiation," *European Journal of Operational Research*, 30: 246–50. Reprinted in P. Chen (2010) *Economic Complexity and Equilibrium Illusion: Essays on Market Instability and Macro Vitality*. London: Routledge, Chapter 8. Hereafter Chen (2010).

Chen, Ping (1988) "Empirical and theoretical evidence of monetary chaos," *System Dynamics Review*, 4: 81–108. Reprinted in Chen (2010: Chapter 4).

Chen, Ping (1990) "Needham's question and China's evolution – cases of nonequilibrium social transition," in George Scott (ed.), *Time, Rhythms and Chaos in the New Dialogue with Nature*. Ames, IA: Iowa State University Press, Chapter 11, pp. 177–98. Reprinted in Chen (2010: Chapter 10).

Chen, Ping (1996) "A random walk or color chaos on the stock market? Time-frequency analysis of S&P indexes," *Studies in Nonlinear Dynamics and Econometrics*, 1 (2): 87–103. Reprinted in Chen (2010: Chapter 6).

Chen, Ping (2002) "Microfoundations of macroeconomic fluctuations and the laws of probability theory: the principle of large numbers vs. rational expectations arbitrage," *Journal of Economic Behavior and Organization*, 49: 327–44. Reprinted in Chen (2010: Chapter 13).

Chen, Ping (2005) "Evolutionary economic dynamics: persistent business cycles, disruptive technology, and the trade-off between stability and complexity," in Kurt Dopfer (ed.), *The Evolutionary Foundations of Economics*. Cambridge: Cambridge University Press, Chapter 15, pp. 472–505. Reprinted in Chen (2010: Chapter 3).

Chen, Ping (2007) "Complexity of transaction costs and evolution of corporate governance," *Kyoto Economic Review*, 76 (2): 139–53. Reprinted in Chen (2010: Chapter 14).

Chen, Ping (2008) "Equilibrium illusion, economic complexity, and evolutionary foundation of economic analysis," *Evolutionary and Institutional Economics Review*, 5 (1): 81–127. Reprinted in Chen (2010: Chapter 2).

Chen, Ping (2009) "From an efficient market to a viable market: new thinking on reforming the international financial market," in R. Garnaut, L. Song, and W. T. Woo (eds), *China's New Place in a World in Crisis: Economic, Geopolitical and the Environmental Dimensions*. Canberra: Australian National University E-Press and Brookings Institution Press, Chapter 3, pp. 33–58. Reprinted in Chen (2010: Chapter 16).

Chen, Ping (2010) *Economic Complexity and Equilibrium Illusion: Essays on Market Instability and Macro Vitality*. London: Routledge.

Chen, Ping (2014) "Metabolic growth theory: market-share competition, learning uncertainty, and technology wavelets," *Journal of Evolutionary Economics*, 24 (2): 239–62.

Chen, Ping (2016) "Mathematical representation in economics and finance: philosophical preference, mathematical simplicity, and empirical relevance," in Emiliano Ippoliti and Ping Chen (Eds), *Proceedings of the Workshop on Finance, Mathematics, and Philosophy* in *Rome on June 12–13, 2014*. Berlin: Springer.

Coase, Ronald H. (1979) "Payola in radio and television broadcasting,' *Journal of Law and Economics*, 22 (2): 269–328.

Dopfer, Kurt (ed.) (2005) *The Evolutionary Foundations of Economics*. Cambridge: Cambridge University Press.

Elsner, Wolfram (2012) *Microeconomics of Interactive Economies: Evolutionary, Institutional, and Complexity Perspective*. Cheltenham: Edward Elgar.

Friedman, Milton and Schwartz, Anna J. (1963) *Monetary History of United States, 1867–1960*. Princeton, NJ: Princeton University Press.

Frisch, Ragnar (1933) "Propagation problems and impulse problems in dynamic economics," in *Economic Essays in Honour of Gustav Cassel*. London: George Allen & Unwin.

Gilligan, Dan (President of the Petroleum Marketers Association) (2009) "Speculation Affected Oil Price Swings More Than Supply and Demand," interviewed by Steve Kroft, CBSNews, *60 Minutes*, 8 January.

Johnson, Simon (2009) "The quiet coup," *Atlantic*, 303 (4): 46–56.

Kydland, Finn E. and Prescott, Edward C. (1982) "Time to build and aggregate fluctuations," *Econometrica*, 50 (6): 1345–70.

Lucas, Robert E. Jr (1981) *Studies in Business-Cycle Theory*. Cambridge, MA: MIT Press.

Mandelbrot, Benoît B. (1997) *Fractals and Scaling in Finance: Discontinuity, Concentration, Risk*. New York: Springer.

Mantegna, Rosario N. and Stanley, H. Eugene (2000) *An Introduction to Econophysics: Correlations and Complexity in Finance*. Cambridge: Cambridge University Press.

Marshall, Alfred (1920) *Principles of Economics*, 8th edn. London: Macmillan Press.

Pomeranz, Kenneth (2000) *The Great Divergence: China, Europe, and the Making of the Modern World Economy*. Princeton, NJ: Princeton University Press.

Prigogine, Ilya (1980) *From Being to Becoming: Time and Complexity in the Physical Sciences*. San Francisco: Freeman.

Schumpeter, Joseph A. (1934) *The Theory of Economic Development*. Cambridge, MA: Harvard University Press.

Schumpeter, Joseph A. (1950) *Capitalism, Socialism and Democracy*, 3rd edn. New York: Harper.

Schrödinger, Enwin (1948) *What Is Life?* Cambridge: Cambridge University Press.

Tang, Yinan and Chen, Ping (2014) "Time varying moments, regime switch, and crisis warning: the birth-death process with changing transition probability," *Physica A*, 404: 56–64.

Tang, Yinan and Chen, Ping (2015) "Transition probability, dynamic regimes, and the critical point of financial crisis," *Physica A*, 430: 11–20).

Wallerstein, Immanuel (1974) *The Modern World System I: Capitalist Agriculture and the Origin of the European World-Economy in the Sixteenth Century*. New York: Academic Press.

Wicksell, Knut ([1898] 2014) *Interest and Prices: A Study of the Causes Regulating the Value of Money*. Charleston, SC: Nabu Press, paperback reprint.

10 On crises and changes of growth regimes after the 2008 financial crisis

A regulationist perspective

Pascal Petit

In the early aftermath of the 2008 financial crisis, drastic reforms of the financial system seemed very likely. This trend of reforms rapidly petered out with the opening of the debt crisis in the Eurozone. The question of whether the reforms will come or is such drastic change definitively over has been constantly raised. Are we still in a transition period between two growth regimes? Is such transition longer than experienced earlier in modern history? Will the changes that we can foresee represent major changes of regimes or mere adjustments of past ones? The question is not restricted to specific fields like finance but concerns the whole system of development, e.g. the patterns of regulations and institutions as well as the economic relations they support. History gives us many examples of long transition periods. The present crisis has unprecedented international dimensions. We argue that changes to new growth regimes are much influenced by the challenges that countries are facing. The traumas of World War II and the existence of a communist alternative played their parts in the shift towards the "modern capitalism" of the 1960s. The challenge that may today force such a radical change of regime is likely to be the environmental one. This paper tries to assess some of the major issues that such great transformation raises. By growth regime we refer to the specific interplay between supply and demand factors that tends to reproduce itself over some time period in a given institutional context. Five structural forms are retained to describe this institutional context. The relative hierarchy presiding among these forms helps to qualify the growth regime.[1] A major question raised in this contribution is thus whether the prevalence of finance observed in a recent period is a lasting characteristic or a transitory feature leading to new growth regimes to be identified with their requisite conditions of emergence. The first section recalls the vicissitudes of the last decade where finance played a major role. The second section stresses the contrasts with the Fordist period experienced in the three post-World War II decades. the third section questions the nature and consequences of the democratic deficit tied in with financialized growth regimes. The fourth section concludes with the changes that the environmental challenge can channel.

Will the global financial crisis of 2008 put an end to thirty years of pitiful economic neoliberalism?

The balance sheet of the thirty years of neoliberalism that followed the thirty "golden years" of post-World War II modern capitalism[2] has been pitiful for most developed economies. The development phase that replaced the Fordist regime at the turn of the 1980s has indeed been associated in many countries with low GDP growth, rising income inequalities, and the dominance of short-term financial criteria in big business activities. The contrast between the two periods was quite obvious even before the 2008 crisis.[3] Beyond the diversity of the developed economies under review, these poor achievements appear as a common feature of them all. However, the neoliberal turn that all developed economies experienced after the early 1980s did not seem to encompass such a deep break with the Fordist period. It had been initiated by the populist governments of Reagan and Thatcher and was not expected to be so detrimental for the lower middle classes as it turned out to be. The process that was launched in the 1980s and developed afterwards under right or left governments must have had cumulative impacts that progressively harmed a majority of citizens. Such a contention can be based on various indicators: the widespread rise in income inequality within OECD countries or the widespread reduction in social protection, all of which accompanied a marked departure between the slowly continuing rise in GDP and a much lower trend in various well-being indicators.[4] Either no credible alternative was proposed or the alternatives were credited with even worse outcomes. It can also be the case that step by step the expectations of the neoliberal turn have been wronged. It seems thus that the advantage that will take the financial sector in this broad wave of liberalization may well have been underestimated … but one may conversely have overestimated the impact of liberalization on manufacturing industries and their capacities to boost productivity gains in developed economies. It is also surprising that the same fate occurred in all developed economies despite their diversity. In that sense there is no model, no winners and losers, especially in Europe where one is used to singling out models. The only ones exhibited by the OECD and other big international institutions have been at the turn of the 2000s: Spain and Ireland (if not Iceland) where speculative bubbles were dangerously boosting the building sector – and the banking sector as in the US – leading finally, thanks to the interconnections between liberalized banking sectors, to a fully global financial crisis in 2007–8.

By all means the economic crisis launched by the global financial crisis of 2008 outlines the general failure of the neoliberal turn and raises questions over how has it been politically successful for so long and conversely how to get out of the process that led to such a disastrous situation.

In effect this last question, referring to the resilience of neoliberalism,[5] remains open in the aftermath of the 2008 crisis as few business rules have been changed, though some reforms are painfully taking place (see for instance the Dodd-Franck reform in the US[6]) in business activities and international affairs in the developed world.

This resilience is all the more surprising since, before and after the global financial crisis, drastic criticisms of liberalized finance, a major driver of the whole liberalization process, have been voiced from all sides.

In the early 1980s, a majority of economists did think that liberalized finance could help to steer economic growth in stimulating innovations. This belief lasted for two decades, time for the liberalization motto to diffuse worldwide. But at the turn of the twenty-first century, after the East Asian crisis of 1997 and the fall of the LCTM hedge fund in 1998, soon followed by the dot.com crisis on financial markets in 2001, opinions started largely to reverse (Bidhe, 2009). The finance of the 2000s was clearly seen as speculative and largely fraudulent. After all, Shiller's bestselling book *Irrational Exuberance* (2000) followed Bernanke's remark on the explosive behavior of the stock market of the 1990s and predicted the collapse of the tech stock bubble which happened in 2001. In the 2005 second edition, Shiller simply added real estate into his analysis of market volatility that was bound to lead to a major global financial crisis, as occurred in 2008. Indeed this dangerousness seems to have been perceived by a lot of professionals in the financial sector. It is clearly stressed in the report of the Financial Crisis Inquiry Commission (FCIC) that the US government set up to investigate the causes of the financial crisis. The first public hearing of the Commission was held on 13 January 2010, with the presentation of testimony from various banking officials. Hearings continued during 2010 with "hundreds" of other persons in business, academia, and government testifying. The conclusions released in January 2011 were especially severe (see the nine major conclusions listed in Table 10.1).

These conclusions were more than critical of all actors and structures in the finance industry, and it applied to all the liberalized finance industries across the world.[7] No wonder then that in echo to the conclusions of the FDIC many professionals and politicians acknowledge the mistrust of the public. Let us just quote António Horta-Osório, the CEO of Lloyds Bank in a speech at the annual CBI dinner in Scotland, September 2012: "The banking industry has done itself

Table 10.1 Concluding points of the FDIC set up by the US government (January 2011)

1. This financial crisis was avoidable.
2. Widespread failures in financial regulation and supervision proved devastating to the stability of the nation's financial markets.
3. Dramatic failures of corporate governance and risk management at many systemically important financial institutions were a key cause of this crisis.
4. A combination of excessive borrowing, risky investments, and lack of transparency put the financial system on a collision course with crisis.
5. The government was ill prepared for the crisis, and its inconsistent response added to the uncertainty and panic in the financial markets.
6. There was a systemic breakdown in accountability and ethics.
7. Collapsing mortgage-lending standards and the mortgage securitization pipeline lit and spread the flame of contagion and crisis.
8. Over-the-counter derivatives contributed significantly to this crisis.
9. The failures of credit rating agencies were essential cogs in the wheel of financial destruction.

no favors. Issue by issue and scandal by scandal, the faith and trust in our industry has been eroded." To restore trust, "the industry must, should be boring."[8] François Hollande gives us another example, saying in a large broadcasted meeting, during his campaign in 2012 to become President of France, "Finance is my enemy." Why then has so little been done some six years after to reform a system so widely condemned?

There was clearly a turn in 2012, with the general rise in public debts which among other effects fueled a Eurozone crisis. Public debts rose sharply in most developed economies following the financial crisis: the States had to bail out in emergency some of their financial institutions. Then they had to face the rise in welfare costs provoked by the economic crisis that followed the financial shock. As states did not organize any broad international solidarity scheme to help Eurozone members in difficulties, these countries had to find how to finance their own deficits directly on the stock markets. The more vulnerable states were thus forced to accept drastically expensive conditions of refinancing, all of which put the Eurozone in a difficult situation while alleviating the pressures on banks given more consideration as financers of public deficits. Quantitative easing of the European Central Bank, in facilitating cheap borrowing to states in difficulties, was one way to help to bypass the market power of the banks, a means more rapidly put to use in the US and the UK than in the EU.

Still this reinforced dependence on financial markets did not lead to a complete reversal of opinions on the financial sector. The fraudulent behaviors of the big banks were still being investigated by courts and their misconducts were progressively being fined. Between 2008 and 2012 the fines came to amount to some 150 billion GBP (according to the record of the Conduct Cost project of the London School of Economics), one third of which concerned some European banks.[9]

Court actions were not the only attempt to domesticate finance. New prudential rules have been introduced with Solvency II and Basel III, though still falling short of facing the systemic risks at work, as experienced at the beginning and at the end of the 2000s.[10] The project of banking union has a more systemic dimension, rallying EU member countries to set up a single supervision body (in that case the ECB – the European Central Bank) to supervise the banks and organize the resolution in case of bankruptcy, all of which would become effective in January 2016. One could see as a further step of this domestication of finance the development of a bond bubble by which governments are issuing bonds in large numbers, while the monetary authorities are asking financial institutions (e.g. banks, pension funds, and insurance companies) to maintain high ratios of bonds in their portfolios "for safety reasons,"[11] all of which contributes to keeping the bond rates very low by historical standards. Such low rates on bonds are also putting pressure on pension funds which have defined benefits to pay. Definitely this specific "bond bubble" is weakening the position of financial institutions, which should therefore be more open to new compromises. Let us notice also that the slow growth limits the possibility of speculative runs on non-renewable resources, all of which occurred during the 2000s.

How are we to interpret the above? Are we going back to the "boring finance" that Bidhe (2009) was referring to and which prevailed during the Fordist period (of the three decades after World War II)? Or are we witnessing in all the developed world an adjustment of the globalized finance that developed at the turn of the twenty-first century? In both cases are we heading towards a new "growth regime" or adjusting to a more domesticated financialized growth regime, less prone to speculative bubbles? It is difficult to sort out whether all the developed economies under review are in transition from one growth regime to another or fine-tuning a still financialized growth regime (e.g. where finance is the prevailing structural form), which has been developing rapidly over the last two decades in the wave of a widely diffused motto of economic liberalism. It may be useful to make such assessment to refer to the institutional and political framework that helped to describe the cumulative dynamics at work in the Fordist growth regime. Meanwhile let us add in passing that the period under view is one of slow growth in most developed economies and of rising (income) inequalities within countries, all of which questions the kind of political support that such a financial growth regime could gather to perpetuate itself.

Comparison with the growth regime of the Fordist period

Let us go back to the construction of the Fordist growth regime of the aftermath of World War II, just to recall rapidly its key institutional elements and the kind of political conventions that installed it as a true growth regime.[12] Keynes had clearly won over Hayek at the end of World War II and state interventionism was fully legitimized. The active role states played in the reconstruction period made it clear but more specifically it is the commitment of nation states to develop various kinds of welfare states which fostered the rise of Fordist growth regimes. Full employment conventions played a key role in this respect, ensuring by various means some welfare progress to the workers in due proportion with the overall productivity improvement that the negotiated work organization allowed. This project balanced the diffusion of new forms of work organization with the increasing access of wage earners to much "advertised" patterns of consumption.[13] This dynamic implied a relative compression of profits … a situation that the existing "boring" finance did not try to change.[14] Figure 10.1 illustrates the cumulative mechanism at work in this "Fordist" accumulation regime.

The cumulative causation of the underlying growth process is basic: the extension of markets is allowing economies of scale and structural adjustments leading to productivity gains which are benefitting wages and employment which in turn lead to increases in domestic demand, e.g. in the extension of internal markets. But such a cumulative causation mechanism needs work to be supported by a certain institutional context. The regulation theory has distinguished five structural forms featuring this supportive institutional context (qualified mode of regulation). These five forms are not specific to a growth regime.[15] What is specific to a regime is the interrelationships of these five structural forms in a historical phase. There are also some national specificities in these articulations of structural forms which will account for the variety of capitalism that one meets in a given period.

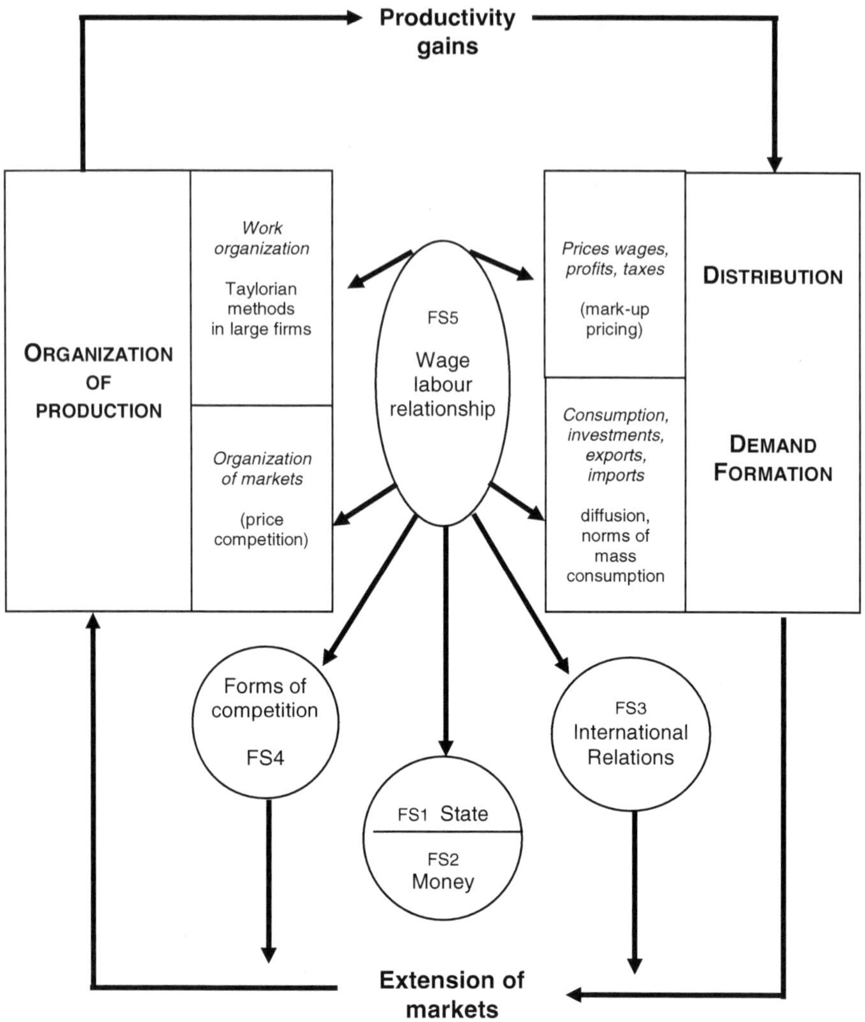

Figure 10.1 The Fordist growth regime and its structural forms: the prevailing role of the wage relationship

Let us first recall what these structural forms are. Considering them in order of appearance in a long historic perspective, we first have the three regalian functions of (1) the state, e.g. the public administration, including justice and police; (2) money as a distinct institution, tying a community into some trust in a common future; and (3) international relations, a set of accords shaping trade flows, traveling rights, and defense issues. These three structural forms can be found in many kinds of antique societies. More contemporary of modern post-industrialization times are the two other structural forms. These are (4) the forms of competition which appear as the set of rules governing market exchanges, e.g. the rules of pricing, the norms and standards of product quality, as well as the relative power allowed for market agents; and finally (5) is the wage labor relationship which progressively between the mid nineteenth and mid twentieth centuries acquired its full specificity. Figure 10.1 gives a first illustration of the main impact of these structural forms on the various phases of the cumulative causation scheme. FS5, the wage labor relationship, plays a key role in this supportive action. New rights and codes are developing, either following struggles between workers and employers' organizations or varying the forms of sharing and redistributing productivity gains. States are playing a complementary role in these constructions, be it in arbitraging conflicts or in initiating some "social progress" as part of political mandates. By comparison the other structural forms are much less continuously evolving, having been shaped in the early part of the regime, in the aftermath of World War II, be it in the new postwar constitutions or in the new international institutions such as set in Bretton Woods (with the gold exchange standard and the hegemony of the US as key elements of this international system), fixing at the same time the set of countries to which the above applied, e.g. the Western world).

Having explained the institutional background of an accumulation process, one can more easily define what we may consider as a growth regime.

As a canonical description of the working of a system the term "regime" hints at a generic property of the scheme that could fit a variety of situations. As defined in Böhm and Punzo (2001) "a regime is a class of 'dynamic' behaviors which are sufficiently similar from a qualitative point of view so that they can be considered (as being generated) by variants of the same basic model." It implies that within a regime of accumulation underlying changes are occurring that may over time lead to major breakdowns and changes of regimes, but which are at a point in time in the continuation of the prevailing logic in which the system (or mode of regulation) is functioning. This evolutionary perspective raises right away the question of the long-term sustainability of the regime under review.

Clearly the fixed exchange rates regime that prevailed in the Fordist regimes could not accommodate indefinitely differences in national inflation rates (partly fueled by differences in the extension of wage costs and welfare) and external deficits with the rest of the world (which provoked the collapse of the gold exchange standard system in 1973, once the US dollar was no longer convertible to gold).

This kind of threat to the economic sustainability of the accumulation regime has long been since before 1973 at the heart of the discussions within international institutions and international arenas. But interestingly another major threat on this sustainability did not receive any attention until the turn of the 1970s, e.g. the environmental unsustainability which the Meadows *et al.* Report (1972) to the Club of Rome stressed. The notion of sustainable development was finally specified and widely diffused in the Bruntland Report (see United Nations, 1987) which grounded it on three pillars: economic, political, and environmental.

We understand straightforwardly what is the economic condition of sustainability. The crisis of the (variety of) Fordist regimes in the 1970s made it clear. The contemporary debates on the environmental threat clarify this source of unsustainability. Finally the third pillar, e.g. that of political sustainability, is left as the one largely under question.

The only "broad convention" that could have claimed to give such frame of political sustainability to the early time of post-Fordism, e.g. in the 1980s, was the ideology of economic liberalism (a neo-lib convention afterwards).

A regime of flexible exchange rates, a focus on entrepreneurial initiatives and on the virtues of competition and policies of privatization, all led to conclude that the forms of competition had become in the new mode of regulation the prevailing structural form and that all the institutional adjustments were to be centered in accordance with this primacy. But how can such orientation be fully compatible with a political sustainability in democratic countries where this orientation has to rally the majority of voters? It is all the more puzzling when such "neo-lib" moves are initiated and backed by populist politicians such as Reagan and Thatcher. Some major structural changes had in the meantime changed the scene of post-Fordism (e.g. the growth regimes that could emerge after the end of Fordism, implying a transition phase that has to be taken into account).

The collapse of the socialist alternative (within a decade of the liberal turn of the 1980s) is one of them. A trade liberalization gaining some momentum and opening progressively to an internationalization of production processes (global value chains) is a second major structural change. Consumers of the old "Fordist" developed economies have certainly been attracted by this extension of free trade, if only because of the sizeable consumer surplus they gain from it, with lower prices and more innovative products, an advantage largely claimed in political discourses on the neo-lib convention stressing its Schumpeterian perspective. But on the other side of the coin, developed economies had to compete in certain sectors with low-wage countries, all the more so than these developing countries were rapidly catching up in terms of technological know-how, if only because production processes rapidly started to be extensively internationalized (thanks to the liberalization of finance). In this new context the old Fordist developed economies could only grow slowly while the rest of the world, and especially East Asia, experienced a rapid growth, all of which redistributed around the world the economic power, previously centered in the old developed economies. In such a global context the slow growth of the old welfare states was bound to strongly reduce their ability to create employment. All the backlash of this structural adjustment hit the wage labor relationships. The call for labor market flexibility became widespread and supported by most international institutions. The attempt to develop flexicurity as a mean to increase labor mobility while maintaining social protection and advantages between jobs and even out of employment was rather short lived (even in Nordic countries where such a model emerged). Meanwhile the financial sector has strongly taken advantage of its liberalization, becoming a major actor in the internationalization of production processes (by means of foreign direct investments and mergers and acquisitions) as well as in the development of speculative bubbles in housing at the root of the financial crisis of 2008.

Clearly after two decades of the diffusion of economic liberalism of the 1980s and 1990s, it was straightforward to identify as successors of the past Fordist regimes financialized growth regimes. Many economists, either post-Keynesian (Godley and Lavoie, 2007; Le Heron and Mouakil, 2008) or regulationist (Boyer, 2000; Aglietta, 2000) thus specified the mechanisms of such finance-led regimes of accumulation. They indeed all stressed the instability of such regimes, prone to crises in their search for speculative bubbles.

Still, can we speak of finance-led regimes for such phases of capitalist development lacking of an obvious political support? The question is open. In a long-term perspective one will most likely see these three decades that preceded 2008 as part of a long period of transition. We tend to agree with Susan Strange (1986) who points at the political unsustainability of the new mode of casino capitalism. This position is in accordance with the bashing of the role of finance, before and after 2008, that we recalled in the first section.

It is also putting in another context our questioning of what is likely to happen in the next decade in the group of Western economies under review. Will a finance-led regime emerge that is fully sustainable, having constructed some political support? Will the domestication of finance be so full that another regime can develop, grounding its sustainability in its capacity to meet the main challenges that the three pillars present at a global level? Another (grim) alternative is that the condition of political sustainability could be dropped altogether, in that it assumes persistent democracy when some authors outline that this political sustainability is no longer an issue in societies which have already turned to a post-democracy phase.

On the sustainability of future growth regimes and democracy

Looking at the effectiveness of democracy is a sound precondition to clarifying the growth regimes likely to emerge from the present "transition" period. One is too often led to think that more international transactions between countries with widely different political regimes will lead in the end to the diffusion of democratic models. Despite the wide diffusion of information and knowledge, this may not be the case. Economic success is not clearly bringing such outcome. Comparative studies on the respective economic performances of democracies versus dictatorships have so far been unable to conclude on the superiority of democracies (see Przeworski and Lemongi, 1993). Hence lessons may well go the other way round and democracies, challenged by this far-ranging internationalization, may tend to turn to more authoritarian government as found in China or Singapore for instance, and more generally in rentier economies based on non-renewable resources as oil in some Arabian countries.[16]

This decay of democracy may have many origins. Some are claiming that representative democracy has been eroded from the inside so to speak, following an excess of mediations (see the post-democracy thesis of Crouch (2004) stating that the political energy has gone out of the formal institutions of democracy, blaming in the first place the manipulation of the usual democratic procedures by the media).

Others refer to more external causes such as Streeck (2014) for whom the capitalists have deliberately broken the political compromise, and are asking to reduce their tax rates. This position clearly departs from that of the public choice theorists such as James Buchanan and Gordon Tullock, who claimed that the break-up would come from the excessive claims of democrats willing to develop welfare states further. We suggest a different reading of this turn against fiscal levies. The liberalization of capital mobility that was part of the neoliberal convention gave to capital owners opportunities to escape taxes. It fueled a fiscal competition (that extended to fiscal havens) and clearly discriminated between sources of income, whether it was coming from capital or from labor. Reducing the high tax rates on income localized in one's country was then a way to reduce this disparity between sources of income. Liberalization of capital mobility was indeed a claim of the capitalists. The consequences on the tax rates of high wages was, in a way, a collateral damage. It did create a situation of rising income inequality that has been more and more denounced, from Obama criticizing "obscene wages" during his first campaign[17] to the worldwide success of Piketty's book (2013) on capital, denouncing the rise in income inequality between the top 1 percent and the rest, a success that can only be explained by the bitterness with which the middle and upper middle classes[18] have seen the diffusion of these obscene wages to a very small group of international managers to keep these wage earners up with the real capitalist owners of ever growing fortunes.[19] The G20 has also denounced such high wages, in particular in financial sectors just saved by massive bailouts. Professional codes of conduct made similar recommendations of moderation in many countries such as France, the UK or the US, with little effect so far, not to mention the name-and-shame strategy of many CSOs (civil society organizations) which are more and more active in pushing shareholders meetings to counter practices of obscene wages for CEOs. So this issue is clearly not over and the situation created by the bond bubble, for instance, may force weakened financial institutions to comply and take stricter actions.

Let us also mention in passing that the rise of extreme right movements does not constitute political blocks that could back such a "voluntarist retreat" of capitalists from the modern capitalism compromise as most of these movements are strongly opposed to capitalists who are seen as too internationalized, a situation clearly different from that experienced in the 1930s.

Taking another perspective, skirmishes on fiscal issues have always been part of the political debate in any regime. One needs to be more specific to detect a real break, putting an end to a development regime. Even the once well known Laffer curve, invented in 1974,[20] had some success in helping Ronald Reagan to pass Proposition 13 in 1978 constraining California to vote a balanced budget, finally ended as a political anecdote illustrating the lack of seriousness of a large part of the economic profession in supporting this pseudo law. Somehow, like the denial by some scientists of the human origin of climate change, such fake assertions finally peter out.[21]

A basic conception of a representative democracy as conceived in our Western world combines three dimensions:

- some general values (on equality, liberty, on the legitimacy of the will of the citizens to have their say in the running of the state);
- a set of procedures to express votes and opinions in a peaceful context;
- institutions warranting the separation between legislative, executive, and judicial powers.

But all these formal arrangements have to enable the society under review to face the basic challenges that the society in question considers as essential at a given time in history. It has been successively to feed the population, to secure housing, to reconstruct the country after a war. Post-World War II conventions on employment clearly prioritized employment and welfare as a central objective shared by many countries so that it would also ensure peace. In the post-Fordist era the political compromise did not seem to deliver these objectives any longer. Welfare states have been eroding in slow growth environments and, in the period which followed the demise of the socialist bloc, even peace seemed again at stake in Yugoslavia, then in Ukraine, while the Middle East saw conflicts expanding on the very borders of the EU. Financialization only brought in that respect a permanent fear of irrational crises and rising income inequality within countries. Clearly even if post-democratic times have not clearly started, a real disenchantment has weakened the strength and consistency of the combination of the three dimensions of representative democracy. Indeed new forms of expression have concomitantly been developing with the diffusion of the Internet and of sets of non-governmental organizations (NGOs). One still cannot contend that these evolutions have constituted a new form of democracy that can be substituted for the decaying representative democracy of nation states. Most would like them to be complementary. If it is not the case (as the post-democracy thesis assumes) then one is led to look for alternative sources of democracy. Much was expected from the European Union but so far it has failed to deliver in terms of securing welfare states or on defense issues. On one side the EU is still struggling to establish itself as a global player that could efficiently contribute to domesticate the world of globalized finance which contributed to the erosion of the welfare state. On the other hand the EU is still more dependent on major member states than on the parliament when confronted with major choices. But new balances can emerge if the EU is confronted by radically new situations.

Looking ahead a major challenge that our societies will have to face is the environmental one. As this challenge is by essence global, the EU as a global player has an opportunity to rally member states and revive a democratic base in cooperation with its member states. Indeed the EU has tried to adopt such a role in taking the initiative with the Kyoto Protocol (1997) in order to extend the 1992 United Nations Framework Convention on Climate Change (UNFCCC). The Kyoto

Protocol asked countries to commit themselves to reduce greenhouse gas emissions, taking into account their development level (hence their past contribution to the stock of greenhouse gas).[22] The first round started in 2008 and ended in 2012. In the second round many of the 192 countries withdrew, leaving only 37 with binding targets. It did acknowledge the EU as a "soft" global player. Its success has been weak despite the many efforts, starting with failed attempts to monitor the energy policy of member states, after which the EU tried also unsuccessfully to introduce an ecotax (1985–97). Finally it put all its efforts into developing an adaptation strategy (see the Green Growth Strategy in its EU2020 Agenda that followed the 2000 Lisbon Agenda). The strategy of the reduction of greenhouse gas emissions was de facto largely left to each member states to decide (according to the subsidiarity principle), the EU playing a role of facilitator. Having nevertheless established itself as a global player with some capacity to impose changes, the EU is in position to steer a revival of a democratic space around environmental issues in all its member states.

As these member states already share most of the values listed in the first dimension of what a democracy is, the revival that the EU will have to govern will come to bear mainly on (a) the procedures of political expression and (b) on the background of institutions that support this political life.

As far as the expressions of democratic dialogue are concerned, building up strong interfaces with the civil society organizations (CSOs), which are bound to be more and more important on environmental issues, seems a key condition of success. Regarding the context of institutions that are required to support such a political revival, it will have to match the institutional initiatives that international bodies like the United Nations will be developing to channel similar environmental policies around the world. The whole process is complex and may take a long time. The expectations of NGOs have been disappointed in Copenhagen (2009), a conference where some major countries refused to make any commitment to reductions so that no result was achieved. CSOs are by now convinced that the modest results obtained at the December 2015 climate conference in Paris still require a strong and lasting mobilization of their constituencies to put the globe on a sustainable trajectory. Dramatic events may speed up this process. In a more positive way, the European institutions can also encourage a wide mobilization of citizens across Europe on such political issues, which seems to be a necessary condition for any sustainable regime to take place. Until our democracies find a proper way to address in a credible manner the environmental threat, one cannot expect to get beyond the present transitional state, open to fears and crises. The EU, as a global soft player rallying member states with similar values, can definitely play a role of coordination on the road towards a truly sustainable mode of development.

Towards a second great transformation

We seem to have entered into the twenty-first century in a long process of transitions. We thought first that the developed world was turning in the 1980s towards a consumer-led growth regime where the free market economics promoted by Reagan and Thatcher would lead to increased consumer surpluses. We then observe in the 1990s that financial operations were the main beneficiaries and agents of changes. The obvious failure of any financialized regime in the 2000s and the rising concern over the broad environmental threat have led the world on an irreversible path. And all the more so that the issues raised are definitively global, e.g. beyond all what we previously experienced in terms of number of countries, surface of lands and size of populations concerned. We have to go back to the perspective taken by Polanyi (1944) when studying the great transformation of our modern societies into market societies, e.g. societies in which all organizations had to be consistent with the market mechanisms that were more and more governing the production and demand sides. In this embeddedness our natural environment was omitted and its importance denied. We cannot really pull back, the path taken is irreversible but amendable with a tension between its economic sustainability which requires some soft landing and its environmental sustainability which is calling for rapid actions in order to meet definite targets (such as the 2°C maximum of global warming by 2050). The balance has to be struck by the politics. There is no technological escape from this dilemma. And politics can only be democratic in the sense that the changes in behaviors that are implied by environmental policies in the long run are so important that they cannot be imposed and have to be democratically decided and accepted. Social acceptability of the changes that could meet the challenges of the environmental threat is clearly a central issue. States are constrained by two opposing imperatives to take actions: (1) to protect/restore the environment and (2) to take into account the limited capacity of agents to change at each step. Authoritarian political regimes would rapidly collapse under social unrest and economic crises. In this long-term perspective of a second great transformation, one can still try to identify intermediate phases where different zones of the world adjust step by step to the new global context. China and the US give clear examples of the difficulties encountered in meeting the environmental challenge. In the great transformation that is underway they will not converge towards similar growth regimes. Neither will Europe – still in the step-by-step process in which it seems to be stuck the imperative of meeting the environmental threat is bound to become the main driver of changes. It is worth studying these different "intermediary" regimes and how they reach an accommodation, if only to adjust international policies, check whether they will succeed in meeting the environmental challenge, and consider how long it will take. Such global transformation if the world is to reach a sustainable trajectory is of a much bigger order of magnitude than the transition of growth regimes we could foresee from the long battle of the respective roles of labor and capital in our industrialized economies. It implies among other things a deep rethinking of economics to be able to take into account the diversity of economies at the world level. Relying on the idea that single markets mechanisms, be it a CO_2 market, can overcome this diversity would be a fatal mistake. Attractive visions of alternative "growth" patterns will have to be developed, embedding new views on welfare, enhancing social cohesion, and reducing individualistic behaviors to be consistent with the expected rising attachment to the global common good that a sustainable environment represents. It may seem a long way to go. Environmental disasters may hasten the process. More optimistically, the recent rally around universal sustainable development goals (SDGs) sponsored by the United Nations Environmental Program (UNEP) in September 2015 in New York may also look to be a first step on the bumpy road towards a global compromise that could lead the world governance on a sustainable path and serve as an effective framework for various regional growth regimes.

Notes

1 Let us note in passing that the notion of "growth regime" should be taken in a broad sense to include eventually cases of stagnation or of "de-growth" if they are set in a self reproductive pattern.
2 To echo the qualification given to the period by Marglin and Shor (1992) on one side and Shonfield (1968) on the other side.
3 See for France, for instance, Baverez (2004).
4 Indeed this may not apply to some countries which underwent specific "transition" over the period as did the countries of Eastern Europe.
5 See among others participants to the debate over the resilience of neoliberalism the recent book by Colin Crouch (2011).
6 The Act undertaken to enhance the integrity, efficiency, competitiveness, and stability of United States financial markets, promote market discipline and maintain investor confidence … the Act was presented by the White House to the Congress in July 2009 and six years later a lot of provisions have still to be passed and most provisions remain contested in courts.
7 Actually a bit less to East Asian countries which were more cautious in the 2000s, after the damage experienced with the East Asian financial crisis of the late 1990s.
8 http://www.telegraph.co.uk/finance/financialcrisis/9526609/Banks-need-to-be-boring-says-Lloyds-chief.html#
9 See for a review of conduct costs http://blogs.lse.ac.uk/conductcosts/2013/12/11/a-review-of-conduct-costs/.
10 A systemic dimension that stressed the FDIC report (see Table 10.1).
11 Last in a row Mario Draghi, Director of the ECB, announced in March 2015 that the ECB would injects some 1.2 trillion euros between March 2015 and September 2016 (i.e. some 60 billion per month over the period).
12 For a comprehensive exposition of the regulation theory approaches see Boyer and Saillard (2002).
13 Often referred to in Europe as the American way of life.
14 A quote from the US President Thomas Jefferson gives an idea of the view of finance that inspired decades afterwards the US reforms of banking following the 1929 crisis: "I believe that banking institutions are more dangerous to our liberties than standing armies. If the American people ever allow private banks to control the issue of their currency, first by inflation, then by deflation, the banks and corporations that will grow up around [the banks] will deprive the people of all property until their children wake-up homeless on the continent their fathers conquered. The issuing power should be taken from the banks and restored to the people, to whom it properly belongs" (http://www.quotationspage.com/quotes/Thomas_Jefferson/).
15 A detailed account of the interrelations between structural forms in a regulation theory approach can be found in Petit (1999).

16 Acemoglou and Robinson (2012) rightly oppose institutional contexts which are "inclusive" to those which are "extractive" referring to these rentier economies where the gains drawn from the extraction of non-renewable resources are confiscated by a closed ruling minority.

17 See Steiner (2011).

18 For example, the technocracy of the old industrial state the importance of which Galbraith (1967) stressed.

19 A recent survey in the UK showed that the 100 biggest fortunes domiciled in the UK had doubled their capital since 2008 ... a very telling result even if the names in the list have changed somewhat over the period.

20 A "law" written on the back of an envelope by a young economist professor Artur Laffer at a diner with students in Los Angeles in 1974, postulating that, beyond a certain rate, the fiscal pressure had a strong disincentive effect on individual activities, an assessment that no study ever grounded. See http://rationalwiki.org/wiki/Laffer_curve.

21 Even if the phenomenon may return on other close topics as was the case with the negative effect of public debt on the capacities of countries to get out of crises in a longer run. (See the controversy over Rheinhard and Rogoff's (2009) claim that over a 90 percent ratio of public debt to GDP, countries' economic growth was historically significantly reduced, which Herndon *et al.* (2013) found to be based on statistical mistakes.)

22 On the long and complex story of climate governance see the work by Aykut and Dahan (2014).

References

Acemoglu, Daron and Robinson, James (2012) *Why Nations Fail*. New York: Crown Business.

Aglietta, Michel (1998) "Le capitalisme de demain," *Note de la fondation Saint Simon*. Paris: Fondation Saint Simon.

Aglietta, Michel (2000) "Shareholder value and corporate governance: some tricky questions," *Economy and Society*, 29 (1): 146–59.

Aglietta, Michel and Hourcade, Jean Charles (2012) "Can indebted Europe afford climate policy? Can it bail out its debt?" *Intereconomics*, 47 (3): 140–64.

Aykut, Stefan C. and Dahan, Amy (2014) *Gouverner le climat?*" Paris: Presses de Sciences Politiques.

Baverez, Nicolas (1998) *Les trente piteuses*. Paris: Flammarion, coll. « Essais ».

Bidhe, Amar (2009) "In praise of primitive finance," *Economists' Voice*, February.

Böhm, B. and Punzo, L. F. (2001) "Productivity-investment fluctuations and structural change," in L. F. Punzo (ed.), *Cycles, Growth and Structural Change*. London and New York: Routledge, Chapter 3.

Boyer, Robert (2000) "Is a finance-led growth regime a viable alternative to Fordism? A preliminary analysis," *Economy and Society*, 29 (1): 111–45.

Boyer, Robert and Saillard, Yves (2002) *Regulation Theory. The State of the Art*. London and New York: Routledge.

Crouch, Colin (2004) *Post Democracy*. Cambridge: Polity Press.

Crouch, Colin (2011) *The Strange Non-Death of Neo-liberalism*. Cambridge: Polity Press.

Galbraith, John Kenneth (1967) *The New Industrial State*. Princeton, NJ: Princeton University Press.

Godley, Wynne and Lavoie, Marc (2007) *Monetary Economics: An Integrated Approach to Credit, Money Income, Production and Wealth*. London: Palgrave Macmillan.

Herndon, Thomas, Ash, Michael, and Pollin, Robert (2013) *Does High Public Debt Consistently Stifle Economic Growth? A Critique of Reinhart and Rogoff*, Massachussets University, PERI Working Paper, April.

Le Heron, Edwin and Mouakil, Tariq (2008) "A post-Keynesian stock-flow consistent model for the dynamic analysis of monetary policy shock on banking behaviour," *Metroeconomica*, 59 (3): 405–40.

Marglin, Steve A. and Shor, Juliet B. (1992) *The Golden Age of Capitalism: Reinterpreting the Post War Experience*. Oxford: Clarendon Press.

Meadows, Denis, Meadows, Donella, Randers, Jorgen, and Behrens, William (1972) *The Limits to Growth: A Report for the Club of Rome's Project on the Predicament of Mankind*. New York: Universe Books.

Petit, Pascal (1999) "Structural forms and growth regimes of the post Fordist era," *Review of Social Economy*, 57 (2): 220–43.

Piketty, Thomas (2013) *Le capital au XXIème siècle*. Paris: Le Seuil.

Polanyi, Karl (1944) *La Grande Transformation: Aux origines politiques et économiques de notre temps*. Paris: Gallimard.

Przeworski, Adam and Lemongi, Fernando (1993) "Political regimes and economic growth," *Journal of Economic Perspectives*, 7 (7): 51–61.

Reinhart, Carmen M. and Rogoff, Kenneth S. (2009) *This Time Is Different – Eight Centuries of Financial Folly*. Princeton, NJ: Princeton University Press.

Shiller, Robert J. (2000) *Irrational Exuberance*. New York: Crown Business.

Shonfield, Andrew (1968) *Modern Capitalism*. Oxford: Oxford University Press.

Steiner, Philippe (2011) *Les rémunérations obscènes. Le scandale des hauts revenus en France*. Paris: Zones.

Strange, Susan (1986) *Casino Capitalism*. Manchester: Manchester University Press.

Streeck, Wolfgang (2014) *Du temps acheté. La crise sans cesse ajournée du capitalisme démocratique* (trans. from German 2013). Paris: Gallimard.

United Nations (1987) *Report of the World Commission on Environment and Development*, General Assembly Resolution 42/187, 11 December (retrieved 14 November 2007).

11 Innovation and national systems of innovation policies

A network approach

Shuanping Dai

Introduction

Innovation is complex. In a strict Schumpeterian view, innovation is the commercial introduction of new technologies, production processes, management, products, and so on. Innovation is "creative destruction" (Schumpeter, 1942), which leads to the dynamic changes in employment and market competiveness in firms. Hence, the impact of innovation on firms and growth is full of uncertainties. Normally, innovators should get acceptable profits and survive in the market, but because of business failure this is not always the case. Schumpeter defined innovators as the group of entrepreneurs who are pioneers and "act with confidence beyond the range of familiar beacons" and precisely break up old, and create new, traditions. Innovation, in this regard, is a typical entrepreneurial endeavour and a way of obtaining comparative advantages in the market for firms. In fact, not all entrepreneurs can fully meet the requirements of innovation, and also cannot foresee the outcomes properly. Even if the entrepreneurs are well able to deal with technology issues they must still face the challenges from the consumers and market competitors. Hence, innovation is not a simple matter of success or failure, of technology or capital, but rather of how individuals interact in the process.

As an interactive process, innovation emerges from social interactions among firms, individuals, and research units, etc., and is rooted in searching and learning. Interaction takes place at least at three different levels, namely: (1) interaction between different steps, such as research, production, market exploration, etc., of the innovation process; (2) interaction between organizations; and (3) interaction between different departments and individuals of the same organization (Lundvall and Borras, 1998). Hence, understanding innovation must depart from a simple investment-output framework, and must take the specific attributes of involving agents (firms, investors, innovators, etc.) and investigated projects into account. Interactive searching and learning is socially embedded and there is thus no 'economic sphere' that can be strictly isolated from the social sphere (Lundvall and Borras, 1998). Innovation is not necessarily to be defined as technology-based knowledge creation; rather it takes place in every social, economic, and political domain, and under most situations, it is technologically irrelevant. But there is no doubt that knowledge accumulation and creation is the crucial point. In turn, agents in the interactive creation and production process may learn and search, and work an innovative project out. So, innovation can be defined as a perfection, such as moving from an ineffective equilibrium to an effective one, in the interaction process.

This chapter assumes a point of view of the innovation process as interdependent and aggregative, in order to reflect the complexity of innovation, since "for today's economies ... the strengthening of innovation systems has to be based on strengthening and improving structures that allow agents to interact and exchange knowledge" (Elsner *et al.*, 2015: 486). Hence, how to structure agents to interact and to be innovative becomes a crucial question. We define in this chapter that innovation emerges in a coordination interaction, for example if agents can move from a risk dominant equilibrium to a payoff dominant equilibrium, we would say it is an innovation. Innovation is risky but profitable and worthwhile. It has been evidenced widely that people are usually locked into a specific technological or institutional situation, some have even tried to break out but, due to the problem of coordination failures, eventually such inefficient equilibria are persistent (Arthur, 1989; Khalil, 2013). The reasons are various. This chapter will provide a network angle to understand why people are locked in and how to break out.

Another concern of the present chapter is to provide a systemic perspective for designing innovation policy, after we have understood the network origins of innovations. The systemic approach of innovation has received extensive attention from scholars in innovation studies, yet the policies for promoting innovation are still not investigated well in a systemic way. Edquist (2002) offers an illuminating framework for designing the innovation policy from the perspective of systems of innovation (SI). He points out that innovation policies should reflect the differences in the existing systems historically and/or geographically, so that concrete empirical and comparative analyses are the ways to identify problems and design policies. Here, this chapter may launch another view of systemic innovation policy, that is how to design a system where all innovation policies are interacting with each other. Thanks to the expansion of communication scale and the increasing interdependences of the global markets, the construction and functioning of innovation policies should reflect this inherent fact. Conventionally, the dominating paradigm for innovation policy formulation is to focus on the correction of "market failure" (*Policies I and II* in the proposed framework in this chapter, see the third section below); however, it fails to capture the systemic and interactive features of the innovation process. A better pursuit of innovation policies naturally should reveal the interactive property among policies in the process of innovation, which is our main attempt in this chapter. We propose that, besides the conventional, innovation policy also includes helping agents to form common understandings of conventional policies and to coordinate their innovative actions, that is to say a comprehensive innovation framework needs another policy perspective (*Policy III*) and may reflects the national specialization in innovation systems (Lundvall *et al.*, 2011).

The remainder of this chapter is structured as follows. Firstly, we will give a model of the emergence of innovation from an innovator's interaction perspective. Then, given the significance of networks in innovation, we propose a policy framework that is based on the interactive feature of innovation. Finally, we conclude.

Coordination and innovations

A coordination game of innovators

A coordination game is a proper setting for investigating the emergence of technological innovations (see, for example, Young (2011) and Shi (2014)). Consider a case of two innovators (e.g. entrepreneurs, investors, inventors, firms, etc.) who are going to make efforts to purse innovations and make profits in the market at same time. We assume that they may have new ideas or projects, of which some will be similar as the innovators have homogenous beliefs about the market. And suppose that they have different capacities in terms of market accessibility, knowledge, business talent, etc. Hence, we will observe that sometimes they can take the same actions and sometimes different ones, but can coordinate properly (i.e. coordination and anti-coordination).

Consider $N = \{1, 2, 3, \ldots, n\}$ potential innovators (agents) on a network G, which is represented by a matrix $g \in \{0,1\}^{n \times n}$. Formally, let $l_{ij} = \{ij | i, j \in N, and\, i \neq j\}$ be the link between the agent i and j, and let the links represent the interactions (directly or indirectly) among the innovators. This connection can be understood as the innovators enter the same market at the same time and they must deal with the relationship (coordination in this model) to each other. We suppose that $l_{ij} = \{0,1\}$, and if $l_{ij} = 1$ say that the agent i has a direct innovation involving connection with agent j; conventionally, one agent cannot connect with himself, say $l_{ii} \notin g$ and $l_{ii} = 0$. The set of neighbors of agent i is denoted by $N_i(g) = \{j \in N | ij \in g\} = k_i(g)$. In addition, the degree ($d_i(g)$) of an agent i is presented by the number of its neighbors, say $d_i(g) = N_i(g) = k$.

Each innovator i will take an action $x_i \in X$, say they can choose technologies or innovative projects from the whole available technologic pool. The payoff of innovator i is a function of his own action and the actions $x_{-i} \in X_{j \in N_i(g)}$ of his neighbors ($N_i(g)$). Hence, it can be formalized as: $\pi(x_i, x_{-i})$ which can be understood as that the payoff to one technology taken will depend on the technologies taken by neighbors and himself. For simplicity, we denote the actions of neighbors as x_{-i} from now on. The agents, who have the same degree and neighbors, will gain the same payoff, as they are taking the same strategies. That is, the payoff is independent of personal profile, given the network structure and network endowments.

Considering the attributes of actions, at least two scenarios will be our concern, strategic complementarity and strategic substitutability. As the innovators enter the same market using the same technology at the initial state, if one agent (i) decides to adopt a better technology x_i (note, $x_i \geq x_i'$), it will lead to relatively higher payoffs (increasing differences) when the others follow the first mover (i), compared to the situation where the others stay with the lower technology. This is so-called strategic complementarity and can be given by:

$$\pi_i(x_i, x_{-i}) - \pi_i(x_i', x_{-i}) \geq \pi_i(x_i, x_{-i}') - \pi_i(x_i', x_{-i}')$$
$$\text{for all } x_i \geq x_i' \text{ and } x_{-i} \geq x_{-i}'$$

The kinds of coordination games are the canonical examples of strategic complementarity. The basic 2 × 2 coordination game (see Table 11.1) has two Nash equilibria, which are (A, A) and (B, B).

If $a > b$ and $a - d < b - c$, such situation can be termed as a Stag Hunt game. In this case, (A, A) is Pareto efficient and payoff dominant, (B, B) is risk dominant in the terminology of Harsanyi and Selten (1988). Hence, if agents want to improve the payoffs, for example, moving from risk dominant equilibrium to the payoff dominant equilibrium, they must update their actions at the same time, otherwise coordination failure will emerge (Cooper and John, 1988).

Let us consider two innovators who are working on two independent projects (A and/or B in Table 11.1) which can contribute to each other (a public good for both). An innovation can be a public good for anyone who can benefit from it; even the benefits and inputs are asymmetric. That is, if these two innovators can maximize the effort level, then a public good will be produced much faster and more effectively. Let us say, if $a > b$, as the innovators move from an equilibrium (B, B) to (A, A), they have already improved the existing situations, for example, of technologies, products, etc. Hence, we define innovation as a perfection of strategies in a coordination situation here, or simply say that, when agents can upgrade their profiles, which can be reflected by the technologies adopted, management system taken, market explored etc., it can then be defined as an innovation.

The remaining question is how much effort they can make and how to coordinate doing so, that is which equilibrium states can be achieved. Normally, everyone desires to invest in the more advanced technology, and in the terms of games, to play the payoff dominant strategy. But we cannot in a static game figure out which equilibrium can be stable in the long run. Hence, we do not know much about whether human beings try their best to pursue a better solution. Nevertheless, taking the other factors, for example, the interaction structure of agents (innovators), can provide some hints to tell which kinds of equilibrium (technology for instance) we can have eventually.

Table 11.1 A coordination game

		Agent 2	
		A	*B*
Agent 1	*A*	a, a	c, d
	B	d, c	b, b

The other possibility is that if an effort made by one agent affects the payoffs (outputs of investment) of the others negatively, we say that their strategies are substitutable. This can be given by:

$$\pi(x_i, x_{-i}) - \pi(x_i', x_{-i}) \leq \pi(x_i, x_{-i}') - \pi(x_i', x_{-i}')$$

for all $x_i \geq x_i'$ and $x_{-i} \geq x_{-i}'$

In contrast to the situation of strategic complementarity, agents in the equilibrium of strategic substitution play different strategies in an anti-coordination way in order to avoid a big loss. Given the existence of such substitution effects, for example when experimenting with a new technology, agents will tend to be a free riders and wait more for their neighbor's experiment (Foster and Rosenzweig, 1995). Also, even in a case of investing in new technology, if too many firms are involved in the same project, it will lead to overcapacity or excessive competition in the market. Hence, rational agents should take different strategic paths and share the market by integrating their unique resources as well as innovative opportunities. When some agents are investing in a new technology, others should be working with them, for instance providing services.

Hence, our model covers two reflections of innovation creating behavior. It includes, firstly, a coordination scenario that models the innovation outputs as agents are intending to cooperate and work in the same way, and secondly, an anti-coordination scenario where agents choose different strategies and cooperate.

Behavioral rule

Now, the question is how the agents can coordinate on one innovation. We assume that agents in every round of the game (an innovation project) can adjust their strategies (different innovation strategies) based on a myopic best reply rule to the state: in every period an agent chooses a best reply to the actions the others took in the last period. Formally, we have the behavioral rule as follows:

In a population state N for both strategies A and B:

(1) *An agent playing strategy A switches strategy when* $\Pi(A|n) < \Pi(B|n-1)$, *analogously,*
(2) *An agent playing strategy B switches strategy when* $\Pi(B|n) < \Pi(A|n-1)$.

This implies that when the current payoff from games is lower than the potential payoff after switching strategies, the agents will change their strategies. When n of N agents (including the objective agent himself) are playing A, if the payoff to the objective agent is less than the payoff he would obtain if he were switch to B, when $n-1$ agents (excluding himself) still play the strategy A, then he should also change to play B. Alternatively, we may simply say the agent only needs to compare her current payoff to the expected immediate payoff, because they cannot have sufficient knowledge and computing abilities to have the payoff expectation of the very far future. That is, once agents realize that a different technology brings better outcomes, they should, if they can, immediately adopt the same technology rather than stick with the old one. This adjustment does not necessarily require a real improvement in technology itself, but rather results from the changes in the technological environment.

The stochastic stable equilibrium

We describe the evolutionary behavior of agents via a discrete-time, irreducible, recurrent, aperiodic Markov chain $\left\{\theta_i^{N,\varepsilon}\right\}_{i=0}^{\infty}$ on the state space θ^N, where $\varepsilon > 0$ represents the noises or mutations, or, say, some agents have an independent probability to drop the previous strategies and simply switch to a new one without any appropriate reason or by mistake in the gaming process. The state space θ is typically presented by the numbers of agents playing certain strategies. For given $\varepsilon > 0$, let $P(\varepsilon)$ denote the transition matrix of states in the perturbed process and μ denote the limit invariant distribution of P, then we have $\mu = \mu P(\varepsilon)$ which gives the long-run trend of the Markov chain. The notion of SSE can be defined as follows:

> *The population state ($\theta \in \theta^N$) is stochastically stable if it has positive weight in the limit invariant distributions ($\mu^{N,\varepsilon}$) of Markov chains, i.e.* $\mu_t(i) = \mathrm{P}(\theta_t = i)$, *when the mutation ε goes arbitrarily small or zero*:
>
> $$\lim_{\varepsilon \to 0} \mu^{N,\varepsilon}(\theta) > 0$$

This implies that all states could be stable, as long as they can be reached with positive probability in the long run when $\varepsilon \to 0$. The main idea of SSE is that the vanishing mutation rate is a selection mechanism which chooses the comparative stable absorbing states of the multiple equilibria, since the number of mutations (or the cost of switching, or the length of path) determines the final states achieved, that is the states can be achieved through minimum mutations. For several algorithm examples, refer to, for example, Young (1993), Kandori *et al.* (1993), and Ellison (1993, 2000). This approach refines the multiple equilibrium selection.

For example, in a 2×2 coordination game, as Table 11.1 above shows, there are two stable states, i.e. all the population are playing either of two strategies *A* or *B*. However, we could not, before the SSE approach, tell which state is stable in the long run. In order to have a specific understanding of SSE, let us take the algorithm developed in Kandori *et al.* (1993) as an example. Formally, there are two basins of attraction: agents play A or B with a boundary of $q^* = \frac{n(b-d)+a-d}{a+b-c-d} \neq \frac{n}{2}$, as there are *n* agents playing this game. Then, if $q^* < \frac{n}{2}$, the limit invariant distribution will put probability one on *n*; and if $q^* > \frac{n}{2}$, it puts probability one on 0. That is the equilibrium with the larger basin of attraction will be selected in the long run because it needs less simultaneous mutations and lower convergence cost to reach.

The emerging innovations

A coordination scenario

In our model, we will adapt the approach developed in Kandori *et al.* (1993) as a benchmark, and find out the influence of linkage dynamics, which indicates the structural property of innovators on the equilibrium selection. In the standard model of Kandori *et al.* (1993), agents are playing a game with the whole population and cannot choose the interacting partners. Once they are in the game, the only thing they can do is to adjust their strategies. However, in reality, besides adjusting strategies, agents should be free to choose interacting partners, to enter or leave from interactions, and to decide the scope of interaction. Hence, severing or establishing links with neighbors might be a mechanism for equilibrium selection. In a coordination scenario, we propose that innovation emerges as agents move to a payoff dominant equilibrium and take risk.

As agents are involving an attempt to innovate and trying to coordinate with others, they must link with each other, for example by cooperating in technology adoption. In this case, linkages reflect the fact that they cooperate, communicate, and share information, etc. Of course, we suppose that any linkage is costly, which includes the cost of establishing links (K_e), the cost of maintaining links (K_m), and therefore the marginal cost of link adjustments ($K_e - K_m$). We assume that, at each round, the agents will be informed of or can observe the payoffs and the distribution of strategies (the adoption of technology for instance), and will then decide to change the strategies, or to sever links with those who play the opposite strategy, or to adjust links and strategies simultaneously.

For the first case, when agents are facing strong linkage cost constraints, $a > k_e > k_m > b > d > c$, it is relatively straightforward to establish and maintain their connections. Due to the high linkage cost, agents have no choice but to play strategy B, and have to remain the dominant-payoff strategy for a positive payoff. Indeed, any kind of coordination (or, in other words, for example, cooperation, coalition, or joint venture) of technology may endanger the independence of individual firms, and may hamper market freedom or market monopoly. Hence, firms must invest much efforts to operate this kind of linkage, and must pursue the best profitable technology to cover the cost. Furthermore, the adjustment process is not dependent on the network structure. When the innovators form links, whether unilaterally or bilaterally, including establishing a link or severing one, they make strategic decisions on removing or adding links based on the computation of the payoff following the assumption of the myopic best reply rule. Given a state where N agents are complete connected playing strategy B, all of them will lose at least $k_m - b > 0$ at each stage. In such a situation, the innovators, in one option, can keep the complete network disconnected to avoid losses, that is they must leave the market and avoid of any kind of business contact with others; in the other option, that is maintaining the networks and keeping all connections profitable, the agents have to adjust the strategy to the payoff-dominant one (strategy A). Hence, intuitively, in a situation with higher costs to keep the interactions, the innovators will be forced to find the only profitable innovation; otherwise, they will face more uncertainties as in the case of isolation. Conversely, in a situation where all agents are playing strategy A, no agent would change strategy. Some agents might adjust strategy mistakenly, but he or she will revert immediately. However, when the linkage adjustment depends on the mutual agreement of agents, then the agents cannot freely make the linkage decisions based on personal payoff in each period the process of strategic adjustment is based on the mechanism of linkage formation. Nevertheless, if they face very strong cost constraints on the link adjustments as above, the network formation will be obviously at the payoff-dominant state and all innovators will pursue more efficient technologies, because no agents have the incentive to leave the profitable state.

When linkage cost constraints are not significant and agents do not invest too much in forming a group which cooperates, the cost of maintaining and establishing the links cannot determine the selection of multiple equilibria. If the market is competitive fully, firms will are under no pressure to establish business contacts with a higher cost, hence a low specific cost in the linkage formation would be a normal situation. When the links are unilateral, mis-coordination will be avoided due to the weak cost constraints; we thus only need to address the question of the selection of multiple equilibria. Now, the agents will have three options to adust their strategies and linkages. First of all, if they can switch between strategies but do not change the linkages, the strategy taken will be determined by the benefits of the strategies and the network size of agents. In addition, the network structure also matter for the equilibrium selection. (For a detailed explanation, see the static selection model in Chapter 3 of Dai (2015).) Secondly, the agents can extend the cooperation size without any change in strategy. Thus the formation of the network will be continuously changed as the strategies are adjusted. To see this, suppose all agents are initially playing strategy A and are completely connected with each other. Some agents unintentionally switch to playing strategy B, so the agents playing A would be likely to sever links with those agents at once to avoid more losses. Hence, the agents playing B are isolated and the former network collapses, and two clusters of agents playing strategy A and B will appear. In other words, as long as the mistakes cannot be avoided, the formation of networks will converge to two stable states rapidly; however, the stable states are not easily kept because of the relatively lower cost of link adjustments. Furthermore, it is assumed that the agents cannot change their strategies, hence there are no issues of equilibrium selection, and the structure of distribution of strategies is highly dependent on the initial states of the strategies. In other words, as long as firms can easily establish or end cooperation, the adoption of technology will be diversified. That could be one reason for the persistence of inefficient technologies. Nevertheless, the market cannot be easily separated, so not all the clusters of technologies can survive as the model shows.

However, if the links are bilateral, we may have to consider the possibilities of mis-coordination, because the overall payoff of an agent is based on the interacting partners. Once an agent has changed his strategy in order to adapt to some other partners, the remaining partners will be trapped in mis-coordination. For example, suppose an agent playing strategy A switches his strategy to B in order to react to his increasingly interactive partners who are playing B; his neighbors playing A will be exploited by him, but cannot sever links with him without his permission. We will not discuss the situation, in the case of unilateral link formation, where agents can only adjust their strategies, because of the tiny linkage cost. Intuitively, if the benefit of links is zero or negative for both, this link can be severed. We start from a situation where all agents (n of N) are playing strategy A, and some of them (denoted by l_ε^{AB}) switch from A to B by mistake; if the other agents ($n - l_\varepsilon^{AB}$) do not adjust their strategy, the l_ε^{AB} agents have no incentive to sever these links because they can exploit the other agents playing the opposite strategy. Similarly, if we start from a situation where all are playing B, the remaining ($n - l_\varepsilon^{BA}$) will benefit from the trembles of l_ε^{BA} and prefer to stay in such a state. In words, the networks will be at two stable states if the agents cannot adjust strategies.

Thirdly, still under the conditions of weak linkage adjustment costs, the agents can adjust the links and strategy simultaneously, and the network therefore is formed endogenously. Suppose that any agent can adjust their strategies and connections as they are under the situation of mis-coordination. Thus, the expected payoff function will be dependent on the individual strategy. The probability of meeting the specific strategic species (with probability $\rho_{ij} > 0$ we assumed the fraction of new linked agents playing same strategy is ρ_{ij} after the strategy adjustment). We start from the condition of all agents playing strategy A, and l_ε^{AB} agents make mistakes. Thus we have the expectation payoff function:

$$\Pi_{iA} = \left(n - 1 - l_\varepsilon^{AB}\right)a + l_\varepsilon^{AB}c$$
$$\Pi_{iB} = (1 - \rho_{ij})l_\varepsilon^{AB}d + \rho_{ij}l_\varepsilon^{AB}b + \left(n - 1 - l_\varepsilon^{AB}\right)b$$

The agents may adjust the strategy, if $\Pi_{iB} > \Pi_{iA}$, then:

$$l_\varepsilon^{AB} > \frac{(n-1)(a-b)}{\left[a + d - b - c + \rho_{ij}(b-d)\right]} = l_\varepsilon^{AB*}$$

Suppose that there are N agents playing strategy B at the initial state:

$$\Pi_{iB} = \left(n - 1 - l_\varepsilon^{BA}\right)b + l_\varepsilon^{BA}d$$
$$\Pi_{iA} = \left(1 - \rho_{ij}\right)l_\varepsilon^{BA}c + \rho_{ij}l_\varepsilon^{BA}a + \left(n - 1 - l_\varepsilon^{BA}\right)a$$

The agents may adjust the strategy, if, $\Pi_{iA} > \Pi_{iB}$, then:

$$l_{\varepsilon}^{BA} < \frac{(n-1)(a-b)}{\left[a+d-b-c-\rho_{ij}(a-c)\right]} = l_{\varepsilon}^{BA*}$$

In order to compare the relative cost of strategic adjustment, we should compare the value of l_{ε}^{AB*} and l_{ε}^{BA*} first. Then, we have:

$$l_{\varepsilon}^{AB*} - l_{\varepsilon}^{BA*} = \frac{\rho_{ij}(n-1)(b-a)(a+b-c-d)}{\left[a+d-b-c+\rho_{ij}(b-d)\right]\left[a+d-b-c-\rho_{ij}(a-c)\right]} < 0$$

that is $l_{\varepsilon}^{AB*} < l_{\varepsilon}^{BA*}$. The space will be divided into three domains by l_{ε}^{AB*} and l_{ε}^{BA*}. Thus we face three possibilities in discussing the stable states:

- I: if $l_{\varepsilon}^{AB} > l_{\varepsilon}^{BA*}$, it converges to the payoff dominant one in the long run, since $l_{\varepsilon}^{AB} > l_{\varepsilon}^{BA}$;
- II: if $l_{\varepsilon}^{BA} < l_{\varepsilon}^{AB*}$, it converges to the payoff dominant one in the long run too, since $l_{\varepsilon}^{AB} > l_{\varepsilon}^{BA}$;
- III: if $l_{\varepsilon}^{AB*} < l_{\varepsilon}^{AB} \lesseqgtr l_{\varepsilon}^{BA} < l_{\varepsilon}^{BA*}$, in this sub-domain, the comparison between the relative costs is ambiguous. Therefore, both states are possible.

Now, the issue of the value of trembling becomes crucial. Obviously, if the values of l_{ε}^{AB*} and l_{ε}^{BA*} are closer, the possibility of $l_{\varepsilon}^{AB} > l_{\varepsilon}^{BA}$ will be higher. That is to say, as the cost of adjusting from B to A is smaller, or the cost of from A to B is larger, the higher will be the possibility of converging to the payoff dominant strategy. Let $l_{\varepsilon}^{AB*} = l_{\varepsilon}^{BA*}$; we will then have $b - d = a - c$, that is the risk of strategy adjustment is the same for both sides. In general, in Stag Hunt games, such ambiguous situations will not disappear. However, the population size and probability of meeting the same strategy have a strong impact on the achievement of the payoff dominant strategy. As the population size is increasing, the probability of meeting the same strategy agents is decreasing; accordingly, the critical mass for the payoff dominant strategy will be increasing. Hence, if firms are trying to enlarge the interaction scope, for example by extending the adoption of certain technologies, it may make innovation more difficult, because any innovative attempts require more simultaneous actions to leave than the inefficient one.

When the links are bilateral and the link adjustment is based on mutual agreements, the requirements for adjusting the links and strategy simultaneously therefore cannot be satisfied, since the exploiters do not have incentives to sever links, as the links are unilateral as shown before. The exploiters will not disappear until all agents are playing strategy B. Hence, as the mutation rate goes to zero, the network will be stable at the risk dominant strategy in the long run.

An anti-coordination scenario

When agents switch from one equilibrium to another where there is no improvement in overall payoffs, it still has significance for innovation. Think about one firm exploring a new product. Normally, it needs to take it market and maximize profits, which is a necessity for any innovative action. In contrast to the coordination of innovations, the firm at this moment hopes to protect the property rights of this product and monopolize the whole market. Under most situations, this indeed works. But if several firms realize this opportunity, in turn they will compete fiercely and get less profits. At the same time, the firms also need to invest in products supporting the main product. That is to say, a computer producer needs to produce all the components itself, or – in the terms of our game – agents will play strategies A and B in an anti-coordination situation at the same time. It is not a game anymore of course. Hence, the basic point is that, in order to promote innovation effectively, firms should provide different products in order to build firm specific market competencies (Nooteboom, 1999).

Straightforwardly, if the agents cannot diversify their strategies completely (i.e. the number of available strategies is smaller than the number of agents), two of them at least will be locked in competition and cannot coordinate to produce different products. But, if we assume agents are not in a complete network or they interact with a certain path, then a pure anti-coordination game is possible. Thus coordination is possible on any network, but anti-coordination is not. From a resource-based perspective, Stieglitz and Klause (2007) argue that firms which have complementary assets need to actively manage the complementarities between them in order to stimulate internal innovation. Unfortunately, an appropriate coordination and cooperation mechanism is rarely analysed.

In the anti-coordination setting, i.e. $d > c > a > b$ in the matrix above, the Nash equilibria are (A, B) and (B, A). The agents play different strategies in order to maximize the total payoff. As in the coordination situation, it is assumed that agents are linked on networks and make linkage and strategy decisions.

First, when all firms or one of them are facing very high linkage costs, the firms that cannot afford those costs will leave the market. So the crucial element here is to understand the reason for high linkage costs. They may arise as a result of high transaction costs in networking. For example, if establishing a collaborative R&D network, all the firms involved must invest resources to maintain the network. When this network does not have effective communication among agents, then some firms will definitively leave the network, and in turn will not be able to contribute to the collaborative projects. So linkage cost will be determinative for creating innovation, which is same as in the coordination situation.

Second, when the linkage costs, say, are high but are affordable for both sides, firms will choose B and the game becomes a dilemma, because all firms want to maximize their own payoffs. We assume that $n \in N$ connected agents on network g are investing in one collaborative project and deciding which strategies to play.

At the initial stage, k agents are playing A and $n - k - 1$ are playing B. If agent i is playing A, the payoff is:

$$\pi_{i,A} = ka + (n - k - 1)c$$

Because the linkage cost is small, for simplicity, we remove it from the payoff function. Then, if agent i wants to change their strategy to B, the number of spontaneous adjusting connections (l_{ε}^{AB}) will be relevant. We then have:

$$\pi_{i,B} = \left(k - l_{\varepsilon}^{AB} - 1\right)d + \left(n - k + l_{\epsilon}^{AB}\right)b$$

As long as $\pi_{i,B} > \pi_{i,A}$, agent i will move to a new equilibrium. It requires:

$$l_{\varepsilon}^{AB} > \frac{k(a + b - c - d) + n(c - b) - c + d}{b + d}$$

Because there is no difference in the profile of Nash equilibria, the solution is that agents only change their strategies when it becomes profitable to do so and there are enough connections to adjust their strategies simultaneously, because once they coordinate using different strategies no one can improve the payoff. But in a coordination situation, this is not the case. In collaborative R&D, if different firms are able to make their own specific advantages and contribute to the whole project, then we can expect an innovative product. Nevertheless, if some firms are good at producing B, then they will get d, and then some firms should leave from the network or switch to produce A.

Towards an interactive system for innovation policies

We suggest a comprehensive framework for innovation policies should comprise policies: (a) which aim at specific science and technology activities; (b) which provide surrounding facilities and resources for the real innovation activities; and (c) which help innovators to have several shared tags (see below) of policies (a) and (b), and coordinate and generate innovative actions. In addition, the suggested policy (c) partly reflects the model of the emergence of innovation in last section.

Policies should be rooted in the specific interactive process (Elsner, 2001, 2015). First, a good policy should, in an explicit way, impose effects on the incentive structure (payoffs to the strategic actions) of the production process. For example, the agents involved in innovations will have a concept of the real benefits from a successful attempt, as the policies have guaranteed. Second, a policy should, in an implicit way, convey the information to the interacting agents of the future. That is to say, a policy for innovations should deliberately offer the conditions for the individual agents to cooperate in projects, rather to defect from and exploit others. Such policies therefore include, for example, those that can maintain the reputations and protect the intellectual property rights of innovators, as well as those that can help to establish an efficient interactive environment and to enlarge the significance of the future for innovators.

Here we give an innovation policy framework, which is more comprehensive and inclusive compared to those proposed in the OECD reports and derived from the Freeman-Alborg approach. We propose that policies should be designed from three dimensions. The core of an innovation policy framework is Policy I, because it immediately affects the investment level and efforts made to innovate by an entity. That is why we normally evaluate an entity's innovation activities from the R&D investment level. But given the investment level, the performance of innovation activities are mainly determined by the quality of Policy II, which provides surrounding institutional support for Policy I. In fact, Policies I and II are easily comparable and easier to transplant in different countries, so if we try to understand the distinctive trajectories of national innovation systems, Policy III should in turn be the subject of focus.

Policy I: The science and technology policies

"Policy I" refers to the institutions and actors which structure the knowledge flows in the production systems where technological innovation takes place. Policies that immediately target the activities of science and technology in regulations, taxes, financing, competition and intellectual property are typically found (OECD, 1997). In general, government policies in this sense aim at correcting market failures, or encourage and help enterprises to invest in technology development through, for example, R&D tax credits and subsidies, in order to maximize the general public interest.

At the national level, of course, the favorable science and education policies are fundamental, and determine a country's innovation profile and direction in future. The most common policies aimed at science and technology comprise, for example, investment in and subsidies for R&D, public science laboratories, public procurement, and establishing laws and regulation which serve science.

The investment in R&D can not only generate new technologies and innovation in a broad sense, but also develop a firm's learning or absorptive capabilities (Cohen and Levinthal, 1989). Enhancing the innovation capacity of firms is another focus of "Policy I" (OECD, 1997). This perspective provides an angle from which to think about the innovation sustainability of innovation of firms, even of a country. Without doubt, technological innovation and performance is vital for firms, as we can observe from the outcomes of R&D spending within a given period. Nevertheless, to engage in long-run innovation investment is sometimes a struggle for managers and firms, but it is indispensable. In words, the "Policy I" is a set of immediate policies for science and technology.

Policy II: The surrounding institutional setups

"Policy II" aims at providing surrounding institutional support for "Policy I," because the real effects of "Policy I" depend greatly on how the "free market" works (Dodgson *et al.*, 2011). Viewed from this angle, innovation policies should take at least the following three orientations into account (Lundvall and Borras, 1998). The first is policies that provide economic incentives for any changes, for example competition policy. Shapiro (2002) states that competition policy plays a modest role in basic research which is not the interest of for-profit firms and, indeed, is similar to the intellectual property rights policies and has more pronounced effects on commercializing and diffusing new science and technology throughout the economy in the long run.

Second are policies that help agents to be innovative and absorb changes, for example human resource policy and labor market institutions. Developing the ability of individuals – including organizations – to be innovative is the major concern of this group of policies. A proper human resource system, for instance, may definitely help to shape and influence the skills, behaviors, and attitudes of individuals. Moreover, a labor market favorable to innovation will be more fundamental, because it matters how labor integrates with technological progress to be effective.

Third, policies that deal with innovation failures, i.e. the majority, are kinds of public policies. For instance, with regard to the potential risks of imitation, public policy should make efforts to stimulate the development of complementary assets which will be specialized or co-specialized for the targeted innovation (Teece, 1986). In other words, "Policy II" can persuade innovators to break the barriers and share innovation resources voluntarily, and in turn technological progress, infrastructure, information, and knowledge can flow at low cost within the firm's networks.

Policy III: Leading the ideology of innovation

"Policy III" refers to a set of policies to deal with the interaction between the innovation process and innovation-related agent behavior and cognition. So the basic principle of "Policy III" is to help and coordinate the cognitive processes of the related agents, and most importantly to lead all agents to have as many shared tags of innovation policies as possible, which is embedded in an interaction process of policy learning and innovation (Mytelka and Smith, 2002) and in a process of innovation diffusion (Young, 2009). And only those policies can really reflect the specific features of national innovation policies, which highly depend on its social environment where the innovations are created. Sometimes we never thought about those policies as relevant to innovations, but indeed they are more important than "Policies I and II" in terms of long-run national sustainable innovation capacity building. Those policies aim to form a national value of innovation, to coordinate cognition of innovative actions, to generalize an innovative environment. And, policy-makers should care for connecting the "Policy III" with the conventional "Policies I and II" in an appropriate way.

A systemic understanding of policies provides us with a perspective of how to design and implement them. The distinctive national (area, sectoral) innovation policies compromise a series of problem-solving interaction processes, for example negotiations, bargaining, lobbying, etc., and also reflect the mental attributes of policy-makers and other relevant agents. So as people are trying to design or implement innovation policies that are identical for everyone, they will integrate their own personal mental model into the whole process. This is termed the formation process of tags of (innovation) policies (Dai, 2015).

Tags of policies reflect the attributes of policies within certain underlying problem settings under subjective exploration. (For a detailed explanation of the term "tags" see Dai (2015: chapter 4).) Following on from this discussion of innovation policies, some tags will be obvious and are common for most, for example "Science and Technology," "Education," "R&D," "Novelty," etc. However, taking the cognitive ability of people into account, the tags may have a variety of meanings – some may understand innovation as "changes," "improvements," "evolutionary invention," or "imitation," while others may go further, using terms such as "open innovation", "patent duration", "complexity," and so on. The same innovation policies therefore will become subjectively heterogeneous and individually based. As different tags emerge, the shared tags policies have will be the connectors among them. Thus the connection structure will be diversified which will lead to the distinctive effects of these policies. The upcoming question accordingly is what will shape the connection structure. The answer is, "Policy III."

The individual capacity to understand, learn, and adopt innovation policies and in turn the new technologies and products will lead to different effects from innovation policies. In an emerging innovation system, individuals including firms, governments, universities, and research institutes have a limited capacity to understand the system systemically, and cannot establish a common understanding about the system. In contrast, in a mature system, all individuals involved can interact smoothly through market or non-market ways, since they already have had a common understanding about the system and can coordinate without too much formal communication. In between of these stages, policies promoting the establishment of linkages between the above mentioned organizations are crucial.

Hence, policy-makers must take this highly individually based feature into account in the policy-making process, and should know for whom and how they should intervene in the system (Chaminade *et al.*, 2010). At different development stages, for example, in parallel to the difference in developed and developing countries, government policies will have a specific focus, but generally speaking, governments are supposed to solve the systemic problems within the national innovation systems. The national systems are specific for countries, and need a specific context which is based on the individual interactions among firms, research institutes, and other immediate organizations. As this mechanism is to be formally identified, how to coordinate individual mental models which reflect the interactions among individual cognitive systems, external environment, and policies (Denzau and North, 1994) also becomes a crucial policy issue. In a country without strict patent protection, individuals will take "imitation" as the norm, any investment in innovation and cooperation will eventually of course finally fail to obtain desirable economic returns, and its national innovation prospects will also be dim in the long run.

Coordinating innovation policies across different platforms also specifically needs the third type of policy (or, technically, coordination mechanism – see, for example, Magro and Wilson (2013)). These coordination polices aim to solve such systemic failures in the vertical and horizontal dimensions (Brickman, 1979; OECD, 2010), external and internal units (Braun, 2008), and negative and positive interdependence (Scharpf, 2000), and are required to coordinate the policies in multiple platforms, levels, sectors, regions, etc. Taking the Basque innovation system as an example, Magro and Wilson (2013) identify several coordination mechanisms for managing the complexity of policies. The formal official councils and associations are the most common coordination settings to design and implement policies, for example how to distribute the budget, in different local regions and sectors. Their representatives, such as local governments, firms, industrial associations, universities, and science and technology committees, must be effective in policy design and implementation. The biggest challenge is "how to re-design both policies and the mechanisms for delivering them that account for the uncertain and unpredictable nature of innovation and structural change" (Dodgson *et al.*, 2011).

Conclusion

In this chapter, we investigated the emergence of innovation from the perspective of interactive agents. In different scenarios, agents will be innovative in different ways. If the abilities and resources agents had were homogenous, they could behave in the same way and take risks to be innovative, but sometimes they would be locked into a conservative situation where risk was relatively low. Of course, if it was costly to establish cooperation, they would have to be innovative to cover the cost. If they were facing small costs to cooperate, the only way to be innovative would be by having enough agents who cherish the same value of innovation moved into a risky position. And if agents want to extend the scope of interaction and try to maintain the same technology in a large group, it will result in a non-innovative situation. Of course, innovation does not mean that every innovator makes efforts with the same technology and in the same way; they can also depart from different positions and aim at the same innovation projects and finally share the market, rather than not compete with each other.

From an interactive policy angle, we proposed that besides the conventional innovation policies, we should also pay more attention to connecting those policies in an appropriate way through the agents involved. In fact, when it comes to policy design, a well-functioning NIS requires an understanding of the needs and properties of the interacting agents. Hence, besides the emergence of innovation, the interactive process between agents and policies was another focus here. However, we have not covered some indispensable phenomena of policy design, e.g. path dependence and lock-in, which are also important in understanding the linkage between innovators and the innovation process. This constitutes a future direction of research.

References

Arthur, W. B. (1989) "Competing technologies, increasing returns, and lock-in by historical events," *Economic Journal*, 99 (394): 116–31.

Braun, D. (2008) "Organising the political coordination of knowledge and innovation policies," *Science and Public Policy*, 35 (4): 227–39.

Brickman, R. (1979) "Comparative approaches to R&D policy coordination," *Policy Sciences*, 11 (1): 73–91.

Chaminade, C., Lundvall, B. Å., and Vang-lauridsen, J. (2010) *Innovation Policies for Development: Towards a Systemic Experimentation Based Approach*. Online: http://wp.circle.lu.se/upload/CIRCLE/workingpapers/201001_Chaminade_et_al.pdf.

Cohen, W. M. and Levinthal, D. A. (1989) "Innovation and learning: the two faces of R&D," *Economic Journal*, 99 (397): 569–96.

Cooper, R. W. and John, A. (1988) "Coordinating coordination failures in Keynesian models," *Quarterly Journal of Economics*, 103 (3): 441–63.

Dai, S. (2015) *Networks of Institutions: Institutional Emergence, Social Structure and National Systems of Policies*. Oxford and New York: Routledge.

Denzau, A. T. and North, D. C. (1994) "Shared mental models: ideologies and institutions," *Kyklos*, 47 (1): 3–31.

Dodgson, M., Hughes, A., Foster, J., and Metcalfe, S. J. (2011) "Systems thinking, market failure, and the development of innovation policy: the case of Australia," *Research Policy*, 40 (9): 1145–56.

Edquist, C. (2002) "Innovation policy – a systemic approach," in D. Archibugi and B.-Å. Lundvall (eds), *The Globalizing Learning Economy*. Oxford: Oxford University Press, pp. 219–38.

Ellison, G. (1993) "Learning, local interacion, and coordination," *Econometrica*, 61 (5): 1047–71.

Ellison, G. (2000) "Basins of attraction, long-run stochastic stability and the speed of step-by-step evolution," *Review of Economic Studies*, 67 (1): 17–45.

Elsner, W. (2001) "Interactive economic policy: toward a cooperative policy approach for a negotiated economy," *Journal of Economics Issues*, 35 (1): 61–83.

Elsner, W. (2015) *Policy Implications of Economic Complexity and Complexity Economics: Towards a Systemic, Long-Run, Adaptive, and Interactive Policy Conception*. Online: http://mpra.ub.uni-muenchen.de/63252/.

Elsner, W., Heinrich, T., and Schwardt, H. (2015) *The Microeconomics of Complex Economies: Evolutionary, Institutional, Neoclassical, and Complexity Perspectives*. Oxford and Amsterdam: Elsevier.

Foster, A. D. and Rosenzweig, M. R. (1995) "Learning by doing and learning from others: human capital and technical change in agriculture," *Journal of Political Economy*, 103 (6): 1176–209.

Harsanyi, J. C. and Selten, R. (1988) *A General Theory of Equilibrium Selection in Games*. Cambridge, MA: MIT Press.

Kandori, M., Mailath, G. J., and Rob, R. (1993) "Learning, mutation, and long run equilibria in games," *Econometrica*, 61 (1): 29–56.

Khalil, E. L. (2013) "Lock-in institutions and efficiency," *Journal of Economic Behavior and Organization*, 88 (1): 27–36.

Lundvall, B.-Å. and Borras, S. (1998) *The Globalising Learning Economy: Implications for Innovation Policy*. Brussels: EU Commission.

Lundvall, B.-Å., Gregersen, B., Johnson, B., and Lorenz, E. (2011) *Innovation Systems and Economic Development*. Aalborg: Aalborg University.

Magro, E. and Wilson, J. R. (2013) "Complex innovation policy systems: towards an evaluation mix," *Research Policy*, 42 (9): 1647–56.

Mytelka, L. K. and Smith, K. (2002) "Policy learning and innovation theory: an interactive and co-evolving process," *Research Policy*, 31 (8–9): 1467–79.

Nooteboom, B. (1999) "Innovation and inter-firm linkages: new implications for policy," *Research Policy*, 28 (8): 793–805.

OECD (1997) *National Sytems of Innovation*. Paris: OECD Publishing. Online at: http://www.oecd.org/science/inno/2101733.pdf.

OECD (2010) *The OECD Innovation Strategy: Getting a Head Start on Tomorrow*. Paris: OECD Publishing.

Scharpf, F. (2000) "Institutions in comparative policy research," *Comparative Political Studies*, 33 (6–7): 762–90.

Schumpeter, J. A. (1942) *Capitalism, Socialism and Democracy*. New York: McGraw-Hill.

Shapiro, C. (2002) *Competition Policy and Innovation*, OECD Science, Techonology and Industry Working Papers. Paris: OECD Publishing. Online at: http://dx.doi.org/10.1787/037574528284.

Shi, F. (2014) "Long-run technology choice with endogenous local capacity," *Economic Theory*, 59 (2): 377–99.

Stieglitz, N. and Klause, H. (2007) "Innovations and the role of complementarities in a strategic theory of the firm," *Strategic Management Journal*, 28 (1): 1–25.

Teece, D. J. (1986) "Profiting from technological innovation: implications for integration, collaboration, licensing and public policy," *Research Policy*, 15 (6): 285–305.

Young, H. P. (1993) "The evolution of conventions," *Econometrica*, 61 (1): 57–84.

Young, H. P. (2009) "Innovation diffusion in heterogeneous populations: contagion, social influence, and social learning," *American Economic Review*, 99 (5): 1899–924.

Young, H. P. (2011) "The dynamics of social innovation," *Proceedings of the National Academy of Sciences of the United States of America*, 108 (Supplement 4): 21285–91.

Index